Concepts and Categories

The Middle Range
Edited by Peter S. Bearman and Shamus R. Khan

The Middle Range, coined and represented by Columbia sociologist Robert Merton, is a style of work that treats theory and observation as a single endeavor. This approach has yielded the most significant advances in the social sciences over the last half century; it is a defining feature of Columbia's department. This book series seeks to capitalize on the impact of approaches of the middle range and to solidify the association between Columbia University and its Press.

Working for Respect: Community and Conflict at Walmart, Adam Reich and Peter Bearman
The Conversational Firm: Rethinking Bureaucracy in the Age of Social Media,
    Catherine J. Turco
Judge Thy Neighbor: Denunciations in the Spanish Inquisition, Romanov Russia, and Nazi
    Germany, Patrick Bergemann

Concepts

and

Categories

FOUNDATIONS FOR SOCIOLOGICAL AND
CULTURAL ANALYSIS

Michael T. Hannan
Gaël Le Mens
Greta Hsu
Balázs Kovács
Giacomo Negro
László Pólos
Elizabeth G. Pontikes
Amanda J. Sharkey

Columbia University Press   *New York*

Columbia University Press
Publishers Since 1893
New York   Chichester, West Sussex
Copyright © 2019 Columbia University Press
All rights reserved

Library of Congress Cataloging-in-Publication Data

Names: Hannan, Michael T., author.
Title: Concepts and categories : foundations for sociological and cultural
analysis / Michael T. Hannan [and seven others].
Description: New York : Columbia University Press, [2019] |
Includes bibliographical references and index.
Identifiers: LCCN 2018061321 (print) | LCCN 2019003474 (e-book) |
ISBN 9780231549936 | ISBN 9780231192729 (cloth : alk. paper)
Subjects: LCSH: Categorization (Psychology) | Concepts. | Social psychology.
Classification: LCC BF445 (e-book) | LCC BF445 .H365 2019 (print) |
DDC 121/.4—dc23
LC record available at https://lccn.loc.gov/2018061321

Columbia University Press books are printed on permanent
and durable acid-free paper.

Printed in the United States of America

COVER DESIGN:
Lisa Hamm

Contents

Preface

FOR MORE THAN A DECADE NOW, this group of coauthors has been studying how categorization affects economic activity. We have sought to understand the role of categories in markets by examining a diverse set of empirical phenomena, such as movie ratings, the entry of software firms into new lines of business, and investor reactions to accounting irregularities. Our research has consistently shown that categorization matters for important outcomes, such as the performance of products and the survival of firms. As a result of this line of work, as well as influential studies by researchers outside this group of coauthors, recognition of the fundamental role of categorization in market exchange has increased dramatically.

This extant work points to cognitive processes in explaining observed social behavior and market outcomes, but it does not delve deeply into the details of cognition. Rather, sociologists have tended to loosely invoke an understanding of categorization that scholars in fields such as cognitive psychology, anthropology, and linguistics have developed with greater clarity and precision. This loose approach was reasonable as a starting point for establishing that cognitive processes involving categorization influence market exchange. However, this research strategy has some drawbacks.

First, sociological work has avoided clearly defining what is meant by *concept* and *category*, often conflating the two. Concepts are mental representations by which people classify the entities that they encounter. A category is a set of objects that have been recognized as fitting a concept. How an object is categorized is the realization of a probabilistic process that depends on the set of concepts that the person holds. But this process also likely depends on social and environmental factors; as a result, people often have stable concepts that nonetheless yield varying categorizations of the same object in different situations. Analytically distinguishing between concepts and categories allows us, in our sociological analysis, to apply and extend the rich literatures from other fields. We develop a theory of social categories based on an explicit model of how humans use concepts.

Second, some sociological research on markets gives the impression that individuals, in roles such as consumer, critic, or investor, *choose* whether to rely on concepts to make sense of the entities that they encounter. These treatments suggest that they use concepts only when they lack more direct information on which to make inferences. This view runs at odds with research on cognition, which makes clear that people cannot avoid relying on concepts. Indeed, humans are hardwired for concept formation, as can be seen clearly in the research on the development of concepts in infancy. So we need to dispel the notion that reliance on concepts is somehow a second-best alternative to collecting and analyzing more detailed information. Concepts are foundational to human cognition and interaction, and relying on them represents a rational use of limited attention and working memory.[1]

Finally, although sociological analysis has prioritized the consequences of categorization, it also needs to examine the genesis and evolution of concepts and categories. We believe that answers to questions about emergence and change require taking the effects of social interaction into account and, in particular, obtaining a better understanding of how the concepts held by one individual evolve as a result of observing the everyday categorization behaviors of other individuals. The lack of a precise model of how categorization occurs at the individual level presents a barrier to understanding the dynamics of concepts. Although we do not treat such dynamics in this book, we think that the foundation we have built will support such important extensions.

With these issues as background, we began writing this book in an effort to better understand and clarify the cognitive foundations of our work on categorization in markets. Our goal is to build a model that formally specifies what concepts and categories are, stipulates how they are used, and draws out the implications for processes of sociological interest. We have learned from sociological applications that it is hard for readers to pin down many germane theoretical constructs, dealing as they do with inherently fuzzy interpretations. This motivated us to strive for clarity, and we devoted considerable attention to building a formal language with the right expressive power.

In undertaking this task, we turned to work in other relevant fields. We relied on three main strands of work for inspiration and specific arguments. The first is the psychology of concepts, beginning with the work of Eleanor Rosch (1973, 1975). We are fortunate that Gregory Murphy (2002) produced a nuanced overview of the field fifteen years ago. This book allowed us outsiders to grasp the contours of the sprawling field. We also found the stream of research by James Hampton (1979, 1997) on typicality and conceptual combination to be extremely helpful.

The second source is work on the geometry of concepts. This comes mainly from computational linguistics. We relied on book-length treatments by Dominic Widdows (2004) and Peter Gärdenfors (2004, 2014). Although our approach differs in significant ways from theirs, this work has helped guide our approach to representing the universe of concepts in a way that is amenable to empirical analyses of the types of data to which sociologists typically have access.

The third—perhaps most important—source of inspiration is Bayesian work on categorization as optimal statistical inference (Anderson, 1991; Ashby and Alfonso-Reese, 1995; Tenenbaum and Griffiths, 2002; Feldman, Griffiths, and Morgan, 2009; Sanborn, Griffiths, and Shiffrin, 2010). Following the Bayesian turn in cognitive science has allowed us to build a unified treatment of a variety of topics that have been developed in more or less separate silos in much previous research on concepts and categorization.

We were struck by the seeming isolation of these three strands of work. We hope that this book illustrates some of the potential gain from integrating aspects of the research streams, as well as investigating concepts and categories non-experimentally with the methods developed by sociologists.

Guide to Reading This Book

We focused this book on issues that arise in sociological research and social science research more broadly. For readers from these fields, we offer two suggestions about how to approach the book.

As one progresses through the chapters, the treatment becomes more formal, especially in its reliance on probability theory. Because the theoretical notions are elusive, we do not see any way around such technical exposition. Nonetheless, we have included substantial textual expositions of the key ideas. We think that these will suffice for those who prefer not to decode the formulas.[2]

Readers will find that the early chapters focus heavily on cognitive science. We think that it would be a mistake to think that this material is irrelevant to sociological concerns. In an effort to make the relevance to sociology clear throughout, we have included introductions to each part of the book that deal explicitly with the connections with sociological theory and research. We also illustrate the basic relations with original experiments tuned to social science applications and with analyses of observational data taken from cultural domains.

By the same token, researchers in cognitive science might find our focus on contextual factors and processes unfamiliar. Cognitive science is interested in studying the mind, and psychological work in this area often develops context-free hypotheses and uses controlled laboratory experiments. We share some features and methods of this approach, but we also follow the general idea that cognition occurs in the context of other people, social relationships, and social group memberships. In cognitive science, when the relation between the mind and the social and cultural context is taken into account, as in the situated cognition approach, the physical body is involved in intensive moment-to-moment interaction with its immediate environment. Our attention to context is distinctive and sociological. The processes of conceptualization and categorization studied here depend on abstractions such as roles that individuals play in social settings or the social acceptance (legitimacy) that concepts have gained within a group. Although this approach might be uncommon for them, cognitive scientists might find in it some new connections to their work.

Acknowledgments

Amir Goldberg made many contributions to this project as a member of the research group that conceived the book. We are also grateful to Jerker Denrell for encouraging us to base our analysis on Bayesian models of categorization and to Jerker, Glenn Carroll, Özgeçan Koçak, Min Liu, Bob Lord, Susan Olzak, Michele Piazzai, and Olav Sorenson for providing valuable critical reactions to earlier versions of the manuscript. We are also grateful to Klaus Fiedler, Florian Kutzner, Ulrike Hahn, Adam Sanborn, participants in course 15.S10 Modeling Organizational Adaptation at the MIT Sloan School of Management (particularly professors Hazhir Rahmandad, Ray Reagans, and Ezra Zuckerman), and in OB653 Categories in Markets at the Stanford GSB, Micro-Organizational Behavior at ESADE, for discussions of key aspects of the theoretical framework delineated in the book. Joint work of GLM with Elizaveta Konovalova provided inspiration for several models described in the book. Anjali Bhatt, Solène Delecourt, and V. Govind Manian designed and ran the Earring Experiment (chapter 9) under the supervision of MTH and GLM.

We would like to thank Peter Hedström, Klaus Fiedler, Florian Kutzner, and Nuffield College for providing a meeting space for some of our work meetings at inspiring locations (Stockholm, Heidelberg, and Oxford).

MTH received financial support from the Stanford Graduate School of Business and Durham University Business School.

GLM received financial support from Universitat Pompeu Fabra, the Barcelona School of Management, the University of Southern Denmark, the Stanford Graduate School of Business, the Spanish Ministerio de Economia (Grants PSI2013-41909-P, AEI/FEDER UE-PSI2016-75353, and Fellowship RYC-2014-15035), the BBVA Foundation (Grant IN[15]_EFG_ECO_2281) and the Barcelona Graduate School of Economics

(Seed Grant). Parts of the book were developed while GLM was on sabbatical at New York University, with support of grant CAS15/00225 from the Spanish Ministerio de Educacion, Cultura y Deporte. The most recent updates to the manuscript were completed while GLM's research was supported by ERC Consolidator Grant #772268.

GH received financial support from the University of California, Davis.

BK received financial support from the Università Svizzera Italiana and Yale University.

GN received financial support from Emory University.

LP received financial support from the Durham University Business School.

EGP received financial support from the William S. Fishman Faculty Research Fund at the University of Chicago Booth School of Business.

AJS received financial support from the William S. Fishman Faculty Research Fund at the University of Chicago Booth School of Business.

CHAPTER ONE

Concepts in Sociological Analysis

CONCEPTS PLAY A FUNDAMENTAL ROLE in social life. We identify and give meaning to the individuals, objects, and situations we encounter by categorizing them—assessing them in terms of their concepts, or abstract mental representations of the world. Subsequent behavior and communication typically proceed on the basis of understandings formed through this process.

Three general characteristics of the concepts that structure individual perception have special relevance for sociologists and others interested in the study of social processes. First, although some concepts might be innate or biologically driven, most get socially constructed. For example, while common biological characteristics dictate that many of us would apply the concept sweet to a red apple, our understanding of red apples also includes knowledge that does not come from the interaction of the apple with our taste buds, or any other physical response per se. The Americans among the group of authors believe that apples serve as an appropriate breakfast, lunch, snack, or dessert food, while they are eaten less frequently at dinner. Many people think of apples as an appropriate gift for a teacher, and it is not apparent why, for example, pears are not thought of in a similar manner in American culture. As this example illustrates, socially constructed concepts nonetheless take on both constitutive and normative roles. They provide the social ontology by telling what things are, and they also often entail sets of rules, rights, and expectations (D'Andrade, 1984).

Second, having recognized that concepts generally get socially constructed, it becomes important to consider the extent to which meanings diverge or coalesce across individuals and groups. Shared concepts enable communication and coordination between people; in that sense, conceptual agreement is fundamental for creating and maintaining a social order.

But most concepts are neither universally agreed upon nor entirely unique to each individual. Rather, there tends to be more consensus on concepts within communities and more divergence across communities. Some would say that such clumping of concepts marks what it means for knowledge to be cultural. This aspect of conceptual knowledge leads scholars to attend to questions of how and when consensus will arise and, likewise, when divergent meanings will persist, as well as to the consequences of either consensus or divergence (DiMaggio, 1987).

Finally, many of the concepts that are most interesting from a sociological standpoint are laden with value (Douglas, 2008 [1966]). That is, a particularly consequential facet of concepts is that they often become infused with a moralistic or evaluative dimension, as Selznick (1957) claimed applies to the elements of formal organization. When concepts have positive or negative valence, these valuations extend to persons, situations, and objects through the process of categorization. This means that categorization can generate affective reactions and potentially profound social consequences. Consider, for example, the use of the concept developing countries to refer to nations with lower- and middle-income levels. The World Bank recently banned the use of this term in its flagship data publication, in part because it was increasingly interpreted as implying that such countries were inferior to so-called developed nations (Kenny, 2016).

1.1   Toward a Sociology of Concepts and Categories

Within sociology, foundational work by Goffman (1963) and Berger and Luckmann (1966) drew early attention to the importance of concepts and categorization in enabling everyday social interaction. Today several core subfields within sociology are defined by their focus on particular concepts— gender, race, social class, occupation. But much less attention has been paid to how concepts operate more *generally*, involving common properties and processes. This is surprising given the centrality of concepts and categorization to virtually all social interaction.

Initial Steps: Concepts in the Study of Organizations and Markets

The most sustained progress toward building a Sociology of Concepts and Categories (SCC) has taken place in the study of organizations and the economy. This work has uncovered empirical regularities in how concepts operate and has exposed new empirical and theoretical puzzles. Our group of coauthors has been especially active in this area of research and over the past fifteen years has developed a research stream that examines a variety of questions involving the role of concepts and categorization in organizational and market settings.

Our research is grounded in a tradition referred to as organizational ecology, which aims to explain change in the organizational world. This perspective centers on organizational population dynamics, including change in the composition of organizations within a given population as well as among sets of populations (Hannan and Freeman, 1989; Carroll and Hannan, 2000). A key proposition of this line of work is that organizational populations are meaningful social units around which competitive dynamics, resource allocations, and other key processes shaping the composition of the organizational world flow (Hsu and Hannan, 2005). Given this focus, the correct identification of population boundaries is critical. In early work, researchers often specified populations by identifying "core" features and delineating population members based on whether they possessed those features. Under this approach, the researcher's judgment played a decisive role. As organizational ecology flourished, researchers began to question this approach and increasingly considered what it means for a set of populations to constitute a meaningful social unit (Romanelli, 1991). Specifying the appropriate way to define populations emerged as a central issue to be resolved.

A few studies pointed to the utility of developing a new approach to defining populations—one that emphasized how organizations are perceived by relevant audiences, such as customers or investors, rather than what their core features were. These studies highlighted that audiences' behaviors toward particular producers/products are driven by their expectations and beliefs about them and that these specific beliefs are in turn grounded in broader understandings of the concepts that structure the market. For example, beer drinkers had a certain set of beliefs about mass producers of beer, and the microbrewery movement arose as consumers began to recognize a group of breweries operating according to a set of practices that diverged sharply from what they had come to expect (Carroll and Swaminathan, 2000). In an opposite example, production of disk-drive arrays never became a distinct form because a number of early entrants were generalist firms who derived their primary identities from other markets, and thus consumers failed to recognize disk-drive array producers as a separate population (McKendrick and Carroll, 2001).

Eventually, a consensus began to emerge that populations should be thought of as sets of organizations that share a common collective identity in the eyes of the agents making decisions and allocating resources (Pólos,

Hannan, and Carroll, 2002; Hannan, 2005). In essence, a population consists of organizations that relevant agents regard as members of a common category at a given point in time (Hsu and Hannan, 2005). As such, the conceptual understandings of relevant agents upon whom organizations rely for resources, such as investors, employees, or customers, play a key role.

The specification of populations in terms of categories opened up a rich set of questions for organizational researchers interested in explaining market-based dynamics. A line of inquiry initiated by economic sociologists considers how the concepts that market audiences (such as investors, financial analysts, and consumers) use to interpret and evaluate market offerings discipline organizations to conform to category-based expectations (Zuckerman, 2000). Clear membership in an established category increases a producer's chances of being considered a relevant market player by key audiences (Zuckerman, 1999; Phillips and Zuckerman, 2001).

Our research shows that a clear position in one category tends to increase an offering's appeal, an effect found in a variety of contexts. Producers and/or offerings that span multiple categories are often viewed as both less appealing (Hsu, 2006; Hsu, Hannan, and Koçak, 2009) and less authentic (Kovács, Carroll, and Lehman, 2014) by relevant audiences. While producers who specialize in established categories might differ from generalists in terms of their accumulation of skills (Hsu et al., 2009; Roberts, Negro, and Swaminathan, 2013; Olzak, 2016), carefully constructed studies have found that this category-spanning discount occurs even in the absence of underlying quality differences (Negro and Leung, 2013; Leung and Sharkey, 2014).

More recent studies have refined our understanding of this so-called *category-spanning discount* by showing that the degree to which audience members penalize producers for spanning categories depends on the types of categories spanned. When the categories spanned are more established, more distant in cognitive space from one another, or high in contrast vis-à-vis other categories, the penalties associated with category spanning are higher (Ruef and Patterson, 2009; Kovács and Hannan, 2010; Negro, Hannan, and Rao, 2010; Kovács and Hannan, 2015). Studies by members of our author group have also aimed to formally specify how the appeal of an offering to an audience member depends on its distance in cognitive space from the audience member's schema for the focal category (Le Mens, Hannan, and Pólos, 2014). Finally, research under the broad topic of organizational valuation has highlighted that categories themselves are valenced, and membership in particular categories can impact how organizations are evaluated. For example, audience valuation of an organization is shaped by whether it is perceived to be a member of a higher- or lower-status category (Sharkey, 2014) or an instance of a category where membership operates as a collective market signal for quality (Negro, Hannan, and Fassiotto, 2015).

Another line of inquiry considers the role that relevant audience members' categorical understandings play in the emergence and growth of organizational populations. Organizational categories emerge when audience members perceive and label a group of organizations as members of a common set (Pólos et al., 2002; Hannan, Pólos, and Carroll, 2007). The identity of organizations influences the development of the emerging category. Emergence is facilitated when the identities of organizations in this group are highly focused or similar (McKendrick, Jaffee, Carroll, and Khessina, 2003; Hsu, Hannan, and Pólos, 2011; McKendrick and Hannan, 2014) or when the set occupies a position in identity space that the audience finds familiar (Ruef, 2000).

Research that we conducted also suggests that the legitimation of an organizational concept depends on consensus among relevant audiences about its corresponding schema–what it means to be an instance of the concept (Cattani, Ferriani, Negro, and Perretti, 2008; Pólos, Hannan, and Hsu, 2010). On the one hand, social movements can help to define and make salient particular schemas, increasing audience consensus on what it means to be a member of a population (Carroll and Swaminathan, 2000; McKendrick and Hannan, 2014). On the other hand, organizations that straddle concepts undermine the development of consensus over a concept by introducing disagreement about which features define membership (Negro, Hannan, and Rao, 2011).

Another general line of inquiry considers how the relative properties of categories, such as the degree to which a category stands out from its cohort or is close to many other categories in conceptual space, shape the producers' category-related decisions. Producers are both more likely to enter and to exit categories whose schemas are close to many others in cognitive space (Pontikes and Barnett, 2015) and span ambiguous categories (Hsu, Negro, and Perretti, 2012). Research has also found that the relationship between a producer's underlying technological ambiguity and its propensity to create a new category label depends on the extent to which the relevant categories are close to others in conceptual space (Pontikes, 2008). For example, newly formed producers are more likely to enter categories that stand out from the rest of their cohort, while producers already operating in other categories are more likely to enter categories lower in contrast (Carnabuci, Operti, and Kovács, 2015).

Finally, a recent line of research has investigated how categorization dynamics become more complicated when one considers producers' strategic interests as well as audience motivations. Firms strategically claim membership in categories based on their desires to both gain legitimacy and to differentiate themselves from rivals (Pontikes and Kim, 2017). Firms might also be prone to entering "hot" market categories, for example, those that have recently received investment or are otherwise attractive to consumers, regardless of category fit (Hsu and Grodal, 2015; Pontikes and Barnett, 2017). These claimed memberships then impact the coherence of a category and its collective identity. Differences among types of audience members also complicate category-based dynamics. For example, whether producers are penalized for failure to conform to categorical expectations can depend on the audience evaluating the organization. Some audience members seek novelty or have a preference for cultural practices that defy conventional categorical boundaries and thus are less prone to devaluing producers that span multiple categories (Pontikes, 2012; Goldberg, Hannan, and Kovács, 2016).

Overall, these studies have shown the importance of concepts and categorization in shaping significant economic outcomes ranging from stock valuations, venture capital funding, product ratings and sales, and ultimately organizational survival. Moreover, this body of work has uncovered properties of concepts and categorization that seem to operate similarly regardless of empirical context. Finally, these studies have identified new empirical and theoretical puzzles that call for further examination.

Expanding the Scope

We believe a similar approach to building sociological understanding of concepts and categories could benefit other areas of study. Consider research within the sociology of culture, which studies mental representations that encode knowledge about the world. For example, Ann Swidler's (1986) influential article "Culture in Action" explores how people use culture in their everyday lives. Swidler observed that people know much more culture than they use and that cultural knowledge varies to a surprising degree across individuals even within the same society. Building on these observations, Swidler proposed an image of culture as a "toolkit" containing a wide range of symbols, stories, styles, and habits that people draw upon selectively to create more-or-less coherent strategies of action.

In accordance with this new view, scholars adopted notions such as scripts, frames, and schemas—instead of shared values—to understand phenomena ranging from stratification to social movements. Yet, in some sense, the shift to scripts and frames as drivers of action skips over an important step. Before a person can know what to deploy from her toolkit in a given situation, she must be able to make sense of the situation. This means recognizing or understanding the people and objects in the situation as instances of available concepts. Such recognition (called categorization) provides the basis for forming expectations for the situation. Put differently, devising a strategy of action depends on how concepts mediate experience and shape perceived social reality. Indeed, as we discuss at length in chapter 10, experimental research demonstrates that the structure of a person's conceptual knowledge shapes— and warps—what they perceive. So the mediating effect is very fundamental.

Agreement that concepts—mental representations—constitute a foundational element of culture has grown in the decades since Goffman's and Berger–Luckmann's early work and Swidler's introduction of the toolkit metaphor. Moreover, the link between culture and cognition has been increasingly recognized as important for understanding how culture operates. Paul DiMaggio (1997), for example, argued that "sociologists who write about the ways that culture enters into everyday life necessarily make assumptions about cognitive processes" [p. 266]. He therefore urged scholars to shift their attention to the cognitive underpinnings of culture, "to treat the schema as the basic unit of analysis for the study of culture, and to focus on social patterns of schema acquisition, diffusion and modification." More recently, in his review piece on the sociology of culture, Orlando Patterson (2014) drew numerous connections between work in sociology and in cognitive psychology, asserting that "the basis of all cultural knowledge is our capacity to categorize" [p. 8].

While there have been some efforts to better understand the connections between culture and cognition (Vaisey, 2009), work in this area has been fragmented. Although empirical studies draw upon the toolkit metaphor, as well as associated notions such as scripts and frames, which clearly involve mental representations, they generally do not specify these terms and their relationships with any precision. This research has generated important insights about specific empirical phenomena, and yet it is less clear whether (or precisely how) such insights relate to one another and cumulate.[1] Given widespread agreement on the importance of conceptual knowledge, we believe a systematic, general approach to specifying concepts and categories can help advance understanding of the shared mental structures that are central to meaning-making and therefore foundational to culture.

1.2   Our Goals and Approach

Building a theory of concepts and categories that can be applied across different substantive areas within sociology demands more clarity about its foundational elements: concepts and categorization. Developing a formal representation will aid this process; it will also allow us to delve deeper into aspects of concepts and categorization which we have until now only touched upon.

Our central aim in this book is to provide a systematic and unified model of concepts and categorization—one that captures their universal aspects but also is flexible enough to serve as a foundation for the sociological analysis across a wide range of empirical settings. We begin by building a sociologically grounded understanding of concepts, which embody much of our knowledge of the world, telling us what kinds of things there are and what properties they have or should have (Murphy, 2002).

We specify how people use concepts in everyday life, namely, to identify and give meaning to the objects, people, situations, and actions that they encounter. Assignment of objects to concepts is called categorization—a process to which we give considerable attention. We draw out the implications of categorization for perception, inference, and valuation. We extend our model to consider concepts at the group level, developing measures of conceptual agreement within a group, and we begin to address the question of how concepts operate in social interaction, including how the categorization of an object by one individual is related to the inferences others make about it.

Several distinctive aspects of our approach to representing concepts and modeling categorization support the overarching goal of the book. Our model draws from research in cognitive psychology, work on the geometry of concepts, and Bayesian work on categorization as optimal statistical inference, as we mentioned in the Preface. At the same time, we build on and highlight important sociological characteristics of concepts and aspects of categorization. We provide an overview of the key elements of our model and a flavor for our theoretical arguments below.

Our work locates concepts in what Gärdenfors (2004) calls a conceptual space: a space defined by a set of relevant features. We refer to this as semantic space in order to show that it is a space in which meanings are located. Many treatments define concepts as subsets of this space. For example, if individuals have concepts denoting various types of food dishes (e.g., lasagna, hamburger, quiche), those concepts might be thought of as pointing to subsets of a space defined by ingredients or style of preparation. Likewise, if people have concepts delineating different types of protest activities (e.g., boycott, march, sit-in), such concepts could be arrayed in a space defined by a set of goals and actions undertaken.

Unlike previous geometric analyses of concepts, we adopt a probabilistic approach. We represent concepts as probability densities defined over the semantic space. Positions within the space that have maximal probabilities correspond to highly typical instances of a concept, whereas positions with lower probabilities capture less typical instantiations. This representation reflects the fact that individuals can and do identify and differentiate between more or less typical instances of concepts. It also allows for concepts to be fuzzy and overlapping.

Objects can analogously be represented as positions in multidimensional feature space. Having represented concepts and objects in this space, we then take a Bayesian approach to modeling categorization, treating it as a process that occurs as a function of subjective probabilities involving the candidate concept(s) and prior beliefs. We also specify how categorization depends on distances in semantic space: the probability of assigning an entity to a particular concept decreases with the distance between the center of that concept (i.e., the position with highest typicality) and a person's mental representation of the object as a position in the semantic space (the space of the relevant features).

We also consider what it means for multiple concepts to be related to one another, with a particular focus on local hierarchical arrangement of sets of related concepts (which we call domains). For example, the concept of film encompasses subconcepts such as drama, sci-fi, and comedy and so on. We model subconcepts as inheriting properties of their parents to varying degrees, depending on how typical they are. We can then characterize concepts in terms of their informativeness by measuring how much information they contain relative to the parent concept from which they descend, and their distinctiveness by assessing how much they differ from the cohort of concepts at the same level in a domain.

While our model draws from and builds upon insights from cognitive psychology, as well as the important lines of works mentioned above, we incorporate and emphasize distinctly sociological aspects of concepts and their use. In particular, the social environment plays a key role in our model. We posit the role of the social environment in determining which concepts are available to an individual in a given situation. We do so formally by specifying concepts as existing within domains (hierarchies of concepts) and noting that the social environment both primes the domain and provides situational knowledge. Such background and situational knowledge, in turn, affect categorization. As a result, categorization behaviors by the same individual can vary across situations, even when a person holds a stable concept. This accords well with the notion that culture—including the concepts that an individual might draw upon and deploy via categorization—does not necessarily manifest as a coherent set of behaviors but rather varies across time and place.

We also examine the process and implications of multiple categorization, such as when, for example, someone describes a restaurant as serving Japanese and Thai food or when a job candidate's previous work history indicates the person is both an accountant and a doctor. Such situations occur commonly in everyday life and carry important implications for inference and evaluation, yet they have not received a great deal of scholarly attention outside of sociology.

We devote considerable attention to group-level constructs and processes. Issues such as the group level of agreement with respect to the meaning of a concept have important implications for how a concept gets used in social interaction. However, such issues also have not drawn much attention from researchers studying concepts from other disciplinary vantage points. Our approach to representing concepts as probability clouds in semantic space lends itself to the development of measures of the conceptual distance between individuals and/or groups, which we use to capture the extent to which individuals and/or groups agree with respect to particular concepts.

We recognize that individuals typically do not have direct access to others' concepts (rarely does someone explain to another person exactly what they mean by a specific concept). Rather, individuals most commonly learn about others' concepts by observing their categorization behaviors. This provides a basis from which they can then gauge whether the conceptualizations of others resemble their own. Thus, we also create measures of agreement that are based on such observables.

We then begin to move into a more explicitly social realm as we consider what happens when individuals interact, bringing their respective concepts and categorizations into contact with one another. As a first step toward understanding the social dynamics of concepts and categories, we build a dyadic model of social influence in which an individual can update her or his beliefs about an object as a function of having observed another person's categorization of it. We refer to this process as social inference because it entails making inferences about an object based on the categorization behaviors of others. Within our framework, the strength of social inference is driven by the weight that one puts on another person's categorizations, or how much one trusts that the other's categorization behaviors would correspond to their own (meaning that their concepts are highly similar).

We argue that an individual will be particularly likely to put faith in another person's categorization when it involves a concept that is taken for granted. That is, people are most likely to update their beliefs about a specific object as a function of the categorization behaviors of another individual when they believe that everyone in the group shares a common understanding of a concept. Drawing on this reasoning, we can provide a clear definition of the somewhat elusive sociological notion of taken-for-grantedness. While in this book we focus on explicating how a person's beliefs about an object might change as a result of another's categorization of it, we believe that formalizing how a person's concepts themselves might change as a result of social interaction is a natural and exciting next step in this line of work.

Throughout the book, we use real-world examples to ground the abstract theoretical constructs that are the focus of our arguments. We also offer original experimental evidence in support of our main arguments and seek to relate the theoretical approach to research practice in sociology.

1.3 Implications and Contributions

In specifying formal models of categorization and categorization-related processes, we revisited our own work as well as that of other scholars active in this area. Our examination of the body of categories-related sociological research as a whole made apparent areas of ambiguity and/or underspecification. We therefore devoted considerable effort to clarifying ambiguous constructs, and we introduced new ones as necessary to capture more precisely the operation of concepts in everyday life. As such, readers familiar with our previous sociological work in this area will note some changes in terminology and constructs. We briefly outline the most noteworthy of these developments.

First, we previously employed the notion of grade of membership to capture the idea that an object's membership in a category lies on a continuum from nonmembership to partial membership to full membership (Hannan, 2010). Much previous work captured this type of variation by using simple ratios, such as the number of times an object was categorized as an instance of the focal concept relative to the total number of times it was categorized. Because a foundational aspect of our new approach is to delineate concepts and categories, we reformulate the notion of grade of membership to have an explicit basis in concepts rather than categorizations. We now employ the notion of *typicality* to capture the extent to which the object is perceived as being similar to the center of a concept—the extent to which it is a full-fledged member of the concept.

Another construct that gets refined is that of categorical niche width, which we previously used to refer to an object's profile of category memberships (e.g., a food that spans the categories of Thai, Asian, and French). We reformulate this idea as *conceptual ambiguity*, which captures the extent to which an object's position in conceptual space is associated with many concepts. A maximally ambiguous position is one where an object could be in some small sense an instance of all concepts in a domain. Cognitive research suggests that ambiguous objects generate an experience of disfluency or difficulty in processing (Winkielman, Halberstadt, Fazendeiro, and Catty, 2006)—a relationship we demonstrate through new experiments on categorization. We then employ the notion of ambiguity in specifying that the valuation penalty often observed for entities that span categories stems partly from an emotional reaction that spanning engenders. We provide evidence of such emotions using text-based data capturing evaluations of restaurants. In doing so, we clarify mechanisms for the often-observed multiple-category discount (Zuckerman, 1999; Hsu et al., 2009; Negro and Leung, 2013; Leung and Sharkey, 2014).

Third, our previous work highlighted the role of contrast, the extent to which a concept stands out from the background. While research found contrast to be an important property of concepts (Negro et al., 2010; Kovács and Hannan, 2015), this idea of "standing out from the background" lacked precision. By specifying more explicitly the relation of concepts to one another—in particular, the notion of subconcept relations within a domain—we can clarify what it means for a concept to stand out. We thus introduce the term *informativeness* to capture the idea of a subconcept that provides a great deal of unique information relative to its parent. At the same time, we note that concepts at the same level can overlap more or less, a notion we capture by introducing the construct of "distinctiveness." Both informativeness and distinctiveness are measures that rely on comparisons of concepts—probability density functions—in our specification. We retain the notion of contrast to refer to the inverse of average ambiguity among categorized objects.

Finally, we sought to eliminate lack of clarity in the notion of taken-for-grantedness. In previous work, we had defined this notion in terms of the amount of information an audience member requires about an object before automatically inferring its fit with the rest of a concept's schema (Hannan et al., 2007; Pólos et al., 2010). At high levels of taken-for-grantedness, the audience member needs a very small amount of information (e.g., a mere claim to the label) to infer schema-conforming features by default. Yet, this definition missed a key social aspect of taken-for-grantedness—that it is a group-level phenomenon that arises when audience members believe a concept to be widely shared. This belief is what enables taken-for-granted concepts to achieve the status of "objective fact." Our revised formulation accordingly specifies taken-for-grantedness in terms of an audience member's propensity to accept another individual's categorizations and highlights the role social interactions play in shaping taken-for-grantedness.

These new and updated constructs feature prominently in our models of general social processes such as categorization, valuation, and social inference. We envision these models as providing a foundation for analyzing a wide variety of empirical phenomena. We highlight a few of these processes in chapter 15, but we are optimistic that creative and energetic scholars will envision many unforeseen applications. Overall, we believe the payoff of our attention to concepts and categorization, as well as our approach to modeling them, is substantial.

PART ONE

Concepts and Spaces

THIS PART OF THE BOOK builds the groundwork for our approach. We begin in chapter 2 with a selective overview of standard characterizations of concepts from cognitive psychology and cognitive science. Our goal here is to provide a rough map of the terrain within which to situate our approach. More importantly, this sketch motivates our delineation of four desiderata for a model of concepts that can provide a useful foundation for sociological analysis.

In chapters 3 and 4, we argue that concepts can be regarded as expectations of what kind of properties an arbitrary object that we encounter will have. In classical approaches, these expectations consist of a set of allowable features. In contemporary work, the meaning of a concept is not sharp. Accordingly, we model a concept as a probability distribution over a space of features. Such a distribution tells the likelihood of each set of relevant features. We call the space of features a *semantic space* because its dimensions are used in expressing the meaning of a focal concept. We make this abstract notion concrete with examples of how sociologists use empirical materials to create semantic spaces.

The second part of the construction is a probability function. This function, called a *concept likelihood*, gives the distribution of feature values (positions in a semantic space) for instances of a concept. We tie these ideas to traditional views about the structure of concepts, especially Eleanor Rosch's demonstration that concepts have a structure of graded typicality. We use the results of a simple experiment and observational data from sociological research to illustrate the approach.

Chapters 5 and 6 deal with what we call *conceptual spaces*, which are spaces that allow explicit comparisons of multiple concepts. We focus on the subconcept relation as a motivation for considering such spaces. And we pay special attention to defining domains, sets of concepts related by a direct subconcept relation. Domains have important implications because subconcepts generally inherit properties from "parent" concepts. But the strength of this tendency varies with the similarity of the subconcept to the parent—its typicality as a subconcept.

Relating concepts to one another requires expressing related sets of concepts in a common space, which in turn requires adjusting concept likelihoods. We propose a way of doing so. Once this is done, we can express distances between concepts, which will be crucial in many sociological applications.

Chapter 7 uses this kind of distance measure to define the informativeness of a concept as the information gain arising from supplementing the background knowledge of the domain with the concept. While informativeness depends on the distance of a concept from its parent, the distinctiveness of a concept (a subject in much recent sociological research) can be defined in terms of the distances among the subconcepts in a domain. So the rather abstract idea of a conceptual space has direct implications for sociological analysis.

CHAPTER TWO

Preliminaries

CONCEPTS are the mental representations through which we identify and give meaning to our experiences. They are the building blocks of our model. We turn first to characterizing them in this chapter and the next. Our sketch of the intellectual background of concepts is selective; we discuss what we see as the central themes. This will help make clear in later chapters how we depart from the mainstream approaches. In this overview, we also introduce notions that play a central role throughout the book: distance, similarity, and typicality.

We use the concept of family as an illustration. Imagine someone tells you that a new family has moved into the house down the street. In the United States, you likely interpret this statement to refer to two married persons and their children. But a number of other possibilities might strike you as quite plausible, depending on what family means to you. Perhaps the new residents are an older, retired couple with no children, or a mother and her daughter, or two unmarried individuals. Some configurations might strike you as less probable than others: perhaps you would be less likely to assume the family consists of same-sex parents and children than different-sex parents and children.

The various configurations evoked by the concept of family give some sense of what the concept means. If asked directly, some might define family in terms of persons being tied to one another by blood or law (e.g., marriage). Yet, if pressed, the same person might consider two unmarried individuals who are not romantically involved to be family, provided they have lived together for a sufficient period of time. This might suggest that the presence of a long-term relationship involving caring and cohabitation fits the concept well. The most important implication of this example is the absence of a set of necessary and sufficient conditions that define the concept.

Of course, the meaning of family also differs cross-nationally and has changed over time. A key aim of our work in later chapters is to build foundations for modeling the social process by which meanings evolve both across communities and temporally. Yet, whatever those meanings might be for a given person at a certain time, the configurations evoked by family would likely come to mind automatically, with little conscious effort.

Research in cognitive psychology shows that our concepts profoundly shape how we perceive, recall, and act on information. For example, a number of studies find what Kuhl (1991) calls a perceptual-magnet effect: concepts distort how individuals process stimuli. Concepts mediate our experiences, which means that culture shapes our reality.

Concept representations have several aspects. First, concepts have "centers," combinations of characteristics that a person considers to be the most central or emblematic. In the example described above, a person's image of the family with husband, wife, and two children might qualify.

Second, characterizing a concept entails more than simply recognizing and understanding which properties (feature values) are most central. An important additional aspect of concept representations involves the distinctions between better and worse instances of the concept. Here, better and worse simply refer to the degree to which the instances fit the concept. In the example discussed above, for example, a person can point to various instances of family as more or less typical. Typicality does not necessarily refer to relative frequency, but instead points to the extent to which an instance is a "good" representation of the concept.

Finally, concepts often, but not always, have reflections in language. Berger and Luckmann (1966), for example, propose that language plays a key role in the process of typification. People who interact repeatedly show specific patterns of conduct and can come to predict each other's actions. Through social interaction, meaning becomes embedded in sign systems such as language. Language is used to communicate among people who interact regularly.[1] Language also gets used in new encounters. With language, meanings become abstracted and are shared more broadly. Overall, language fills the gap between one's experience and the experience of others.

2.1   From Crisp to Blurred Concepts

Concepts are the foundation of our model. In this chapter draw on widely agreed-upon understandings of how concepts are cognitively stored to build a model tuned to sociological applications. We first review mainstream approaches to representing the structure of concepts before providing our formal specification.

Historically, in an approach now called the *classical view*, concepts were treated as sharply bounded. It was assumed that there existed necessary and sufficient conditions that determine whether something is an instance of a concept. This standard is still assumed in mathematics and most of science. For instance, the concept of prime number divides the natural numbers into those that are primes (natural numbers greater than one divisible only by themselves and one) and the rest. Such a classical concept lacks *internal structure*: no prime number is more "prime" than any other. In the classical view, objects (or more generally the position they occupy as a mental representation) are either fully in or fully out of the concept.

Virtually all modern work on concepts rejects the classical view because it is inconsistent with empirical evidence.[2] The first important move away from the classical view was Ludwig Wittgenstein's proposal that concepts capture family resemblances.

Wittgenstein's influential analysis of the social use of natural language concluded that it is unrealistic to model ordinary concepts as sets of objects that satisfy necessary and sufficient conditions. Take, for example, family and game—there are not definitive feature values that demarcate these concepts. Wittgenstein argued that the borders of these (and presumably other) concepts are blurred (*verschwommener*), but this does not make them useless. Blurred concepts are used successfully in communication (language games). People normally do not even recognize (or bother about) their blurred nature. Furthermore, he argues that sometimes a vague concept is exactly what is appropriate for communication. For example, when we describe an evening out with friends as "nice," we mean many things at once and not precisely so. Yet, this description is normally enough for communication with others.

Wittgenstein attributes the blurriness of concepts to two sources. First, concepts are not based on necessary and sufficient features, but on similarities among objects. Second, similarity judgments depend on context, and the features considered tend to shift as one considers different pairs of objects.[3]

We can get the flavor of his argument by quoting his famous analysis of the concept of game.

> Consider for example the proceedings that we call games. I mean board-games, card-games, ball-games, Olympic games, and so on. What is common to them all?—Don't say: "There *must* be something common, or they would not be called games"—but *look and see* whether there is anything

common to all.—For if you look at them you will not see something that is common to *all,* but similarities, relationships, and a whole series of them at that.... And we can go through the many, many other groups of games in the same way; can see how similarities crop up and disappear....

And the result of this examination is: we see a complicated network of similarities overlapping and criss-crossing: sometimes overall similarities, sometimes similarities of detail.

I can think of no better expression to characterize these similarities than "family resemblances"; for the various resemblances between members of a family: build, features, colour of eyes, gait, temperament, etc. etc. overlap and criss-cross in the same way.—And I shall say: games form a family. ...

And the strength of the thread does not reside in the fact that one fibre runs through its whole length, but in the overlapping of many fibers. ...

One might say that the concept game is a concept with blurred edges.— "But is a blurred concept a concept at all?"—Is an indistinct photograph a picture of a person at all? Is it even always an advantage to replace an indistinct picture by a sharp one? Isn't the indistinct one often exactly what we need? (Wittgenstein, 1953, Aphorisms 66, 67, and 71)

Wittgenstein's central notion of family resemblance gives an informal rendering of similarity. Indeed, similarity plays a key role in theories of concepts. We turn next to this topic.

2.2   Similarity and Distance

Psychologist Roger Shepard motivated his masterful paper on similarity and distance by remarking that "recognition that similarity is fundamental to mental processes can be traced back over two thousand years to Aristotle's principle of association by resemblance" (Shepard, 1987, p. 1317). It makes intuitive sense that similar things are associated with one another. Unsurprisingly, similarity continues to occupy center stage in cognitive science.

Yet philosopher Norman Goodman famously argued: "Similarity, I submit, is insidious, ...is a pretender, an imposter, a quack" (Goodman, 1972, p. 437). His influential critique questions whether similarity is a dependable notion on which to build theories of concepts. The foundation of his argument is that no constraint to the comparisons is allowed when similarity gets invoked. The problem arises because any object has an unbounded number of features. Consider, for example, taking two books at random from a library shelf. How similar are they? Presumably, the answer to this question relates to the ratio of the number of feature values they share relative to the number they do not share.

But where do we start to identify the features of the books? It immediately becomes apparent that we face an overwhelming task. We might start with the title, author, date of publication, publisher, and language. Next we might consider subject matter and the many details with which the book addresses its subject. Then we might consider details of the typesetting and production, including font, type size, page size, properties of the paper, location of notes, and format of references. Then there are physical properties such as weight, physical dimensions, and color(s) of the cover. And the list can go on indefinitely (word-frequency counts, etc.). Here we see Goodman's problem: any arbitrary pair of books is similar on at least one dimension and dissimilar on most. An assessment of similarity depends on how far we go in explicating the features and which ones we include. For this reason, Goodman argues that "similarity is relative, variable, culture dependent" (p. 438).

This critique has force if we assume that similarity does not have some timeless external existence. Cognitive psychologists in response have argued that similarity for them pertains to pairs of mental representations, which, given limits on working memory, invariably have low dimensionality. Indeed, the key strategic move in Shepard's formulation of a "universal law of generalization" was to recognize and articulate the need to characterize the psychological space within which representations are formed.

Shepard's (1987) universal law of generalization proposes that the similarity of a pair of objects is a negative exponential function of the distance separating them in a psychological space. Chater and Vitányi (2003) have generalized Shepard's law in terms of transformation distance: similarity is a negative exponential function of the length of the shortest program that transforms one mental representation into another. The geometric approach to similarity requires a distance metric but applies equally well to situations in which the semantic space is real-valued and it is Boolean (each feature is binary).

Much of the work on similarity used in characterizing concepts focuses on Boolean spaces. In the so-called feature-based approach which we discuss in more detail below, mental representations are modeled as lists of positive features.[4] A natural distance metric here is Jaccard distance, a symmetric measure defined as the ratio of the count of feature values that match for the pair of representations to the count of those that do not match. Then similarity has a negative relation with distance in the trivial sense that Jaccard distance is defined as one minus Jaccard similarity.

Psychologist Amos Tversky (1977) argued that symmetric representations of similarity, such as Jaccard, do not fit well with reality. In particular, he proposed that many similarity judgments are directional (asymmetric) as for metaphors: "We say that Turks fight like tigers but not that tigers fight like Turks." Similarly, Tversky's experimental subjects judged portraits as more similar to their subjects than the reverse. He also reported that subjects judged North Korea as more similar to Red China than the reverse. In general, he claimed that an asymmetry in the knowledge of the features of two objects generates an asymmetry in similarity judgments such that the one with the sparser feature description is seen as more similar to the one with the richer description than is the reverse. The subjects presumably knew more features for China than for North Korea, and this accounts for the asymmetry.

More recent work by Ulrike Hahn and colleagues has also found evidence that similarity often shows asymmetry. This work has focused on transformation distance, or the number of mental steps people take to shift from the mental representation of an object to the representation of another object (Hahn, Chater, and Richardson, 2003; Hahn, Close, and Graf, 2009). This distance, like other measures of psychological distance, is essentially the inverse of similarity and is asymmetric.[5] In the context of computational linguistics, Widdows (2004, p. 111) posits that variants (exemplars) are more similar to prototypes than prototypes are similar to variants.

Given this evidence, in what follows, we build models that allow the possibility that both similarity and psychological distance are asymmetric.

2.3   Handling Blurred Boundaries: Alternative Approaches

There are two main approaches in psychological research on concepts: those based on prototypes and those based on exemplars. Similarity judgments are fundamental to both. But the specifics of how similarity judgments drive categorization differ markedly.

The Prototype Approach

The modern research tradition surrounding the psychology of concepts began with cognitive psychologist Eleanor Rosch's (1973, 1975) landmark studies. She asked subjects to tell, for instance, how typical were certain types of fruits (e.g., apples, pineapples, olives). Subjects generally report great differences in typicality, supporting the view that concepts have blurred boundaries. Moreover, they generally agree strongly about the degrees of typicality: apples and oranges are very typical; pineapples are only moderately typical; and olives and coconuts are very atypical. Rosch and Mervis (1975) claimed that these replicable patterns of *graded typicality* reveal that concepts involve Wittgensteinian family resemblances. Typicality is a special case of similarity in which a concept serves as the point of reference. The prototypes of a concept are those with maximum typicality, or the "best examples."

Numerous strands of prototype theory and measurements of typicality have emerged. What ties them together is aptly summarized by James Hampton's (1991) formal characterization of a concept prototype:

> A: a prototype concept is constituted by a set of attributes, each with a particular weight corresponding to its "definingness" or contribution to the concept's definition. The instantiation of the full set of attributes in an individual instance would therefore produce a prototype example of the concept....
>
> B: a similarity scale is defined for the domain of possible instances based on the set of weighted attributes....
>
> C: ratings made by subjects of item "representativeness" or "typicality" are monotonically related to the similarity scale. (Below a certain level, items will be seen as merely related to the concept, rather than being representative or unrepresentative of it.)
>
> D: a criterion is placed on the similarity scale such that membership in the category is positive for items with similarity above the criterion, and negative for items below the criterion.
>
> (Hampton, 1991, p. 93)

Rosch and collaborators proposed that typicality be considered a *grade of membership*, a degree to which an object belongs to a set. Other studies, including those by some of the authors (Hannan et al. (2007) and Hannan (2010)), have followed this approach. However, the grade-of-membership approach presents a problem for our model because it does not admit a clear probabilistic interpretation. We find this to be a substantial limitation when addressing some important questions. For example, we will want to formulate the probability that an object will be categorized as an instance of a specific concept. In chapter 4, we introduce a characterization of concepts rooted in probability theory. This retains the "fuzziness" of the grade of membership perspective while serving as an internally consistent modeling perspective.

Feature Matching. Much of the research built on the prototype view obtains people's views of typicality without reference to the attributes (feature values) on which the typicality judgment is made. For example, usually subjects are asked about a subconcept as an instance of a concept—"how typical is a rug as furniture?" Nonetheless, from the early days of this research tradition, some investigators have sought to build a feature-based description of prototypes. Rosch and Mervis (1975) proposed a way to measure the similarity of an instance to a prototype when the relevant features are binary. Their "family resemblance score" was inspired by Wittgenstein's view that relevant features need not be shared by all highly typical instances but that a concept reflects the overlap of the generally shared ones. This measure begins by eliciting from respondents the lists of features that they associate with the concept and then calculates a weight for each feature mentioned equal to the number of respondents who listed the feature. Then each instance is assigned a score that equals the number of features on which it matches the prototype (possibly with weights that reflect the importance of a feature to the meaning of the concept). Rosch and Mervis (1975) find a strong correlation between this scale and a global assessment of typicality of the instance. Hampton (1995) has refined this measure and shown similar patterns. In Hampton's model of feature matching, the weights on features play the important role of distinguishing the most core-like features.

These measures can be interpreted as weighted distances in a Boolean space. But this aspect was not highlighted in the standard analyses of feature matching. As an exception, Rips, Shoben, and Smith (1973) developed an explicitly spatial representation of prototypes and typicality structures. They proposed that the prototype be regarded as a point in a space defined by the set of relevant features. Typicality of an instance was equated with the inverse of the distance from the prototype in the space. Although this paper has been widely cited, its proposal to build models of prototypes in a semantic space seems not to have affected subsequent developments. In some respects, the model we present in subsequent chapters can be regarded as a recasting of the Rips–Schoben–Smith model in probabilistic form.

The Exemplar Approach

Another approach often discussed in parallel to prototype structures centers on what cognitive psychologists call exemplars. Whereas prototypes are abstract mental representations of sets or classes, exemplars are stored representations of individual *objects* (Medin and Schaffer, 1978). Newly encountered stimuli are categorized on the basis of similarity to the available exemplars. Crucially, exemplars get stored in memory with tags that mark collections of like-objects. As far as we can ascertain, this aspect of the approach is implicit, in that exemplar theorists do not discuss the conditions for the decision to create a tag for a set of exemplars.

A main claim made by proponents of the exemplar approach is that concepts do not provide an overall, unified view. Instead, people rely on mental representations of the instances of a concept encoded in a common way (Medin and Schaffer, 1978).

Exemplar representations have been used successfully in studies of classification and recognition judgments. For example, Nosofsky (1988) developed an exemplar-based model to illustrate how category learning can be determined by computations of the summed similarity of a stimulus to be classified (people, dot patterns, geometric forms) to individual exemplars rather than to the category prototype. As an application in which exemplar models are used, physicians are more likely to categorize skin diseases using superficial similarity to previous instances they have observed than whether or not the items are members of the same category (Brooks, Norman, and Allen, 1991).

Gregory Murphy (2016), whose earlier text (Murphy, 2002) treated the exemplar approach as a theoretical competitor to prototype and schema theories, has revised that view sharply. His 2016 paper argues that the exemplar approach does not satisfy the basic requirements of a theory of concepts. We sketch his argument here because it resonates strongly with the view that we have developed. Murphy's core claim is that exemplar models perform well when explaining how people learn categories that are small, poorly structured, or very difficult to learn, but there is no theory of concepts based on exemplars.

A first challenge for an exemplar-based theory of concepts concerns the structure of the concepts in what we will call a domain. An enduring impact of Rosch's research is the wide acceptance of the view that concept structures have a "basic" level. This is the level at which concept learning is fastest, recall of categorizations is highest and concept use is most frequent. Murphy (2002) surveys the evidence. The standard analysis considers three levels: superordinate (e.g., furniture), basic (table), and subordinate (desk). Prototype theorists represent such structures in terms of links between concepts (desks are tables, and tables are furniture). People learn basic-level concepts faster, recall instances more quickly, and so forth. The difference between the basic level and others cannot be explained by the exemplar approach. If every remembered object is tagged with all applicable concepts, then using basic-level concepts would not provide any information advantage.

A second challenge for an exemplar theory of concepts concerns generalization. Prototypes and schemas define membership for whole classes of entities. Therefore, they can warrant generalizations about those entities. Exemplars only encode features of specific entities and not generalizations, but generalizations do indeed occur.

Category-based inference presents a third challenge for exemplar theory. How do people make predictions about new objects and situations? Features tend to be transferred more easily between concepts when they are more similar. Accordingly, inference arguments are stronger when the categories being linked are more similar. Typicality can be used in prototype-theory analyses to explain differences in inferential judgment. However, if only the features of exemplars get encoded, inference runs into problems. Some features of objects are not observed or encoded for all exemplars (whether robins or other birds have ulnar arteries). Also, some categories are very large, with thousands or even millions of objects. Inference in a similar situation becomes a very complicated process for exemplar models.

In sum, a theory of concepts based on exemplars would be ill equipped to explain some important cognitive processes such as hierarchical representation, generalization of knowledge, and induction. This does not mean that people do not remember exemplars or do not use exemplars in categorization. Rather, a theory of concepts needs something more.

Structured Representation: The Schema Approach

Prototype theory's notions of a concept prototype and graded typicality have been enormously influential in shaping the shift from the classical perspective on concepts. Yet, the consideration of concepts as mental structures remains underspecified. Prototype models do not indicate what it means for something to be a concept. We learn from empirical research that apple and orange are prototypical fruits. This is an extensional specification of the concept in the sense that the concept is specified as a *collection* of its prototypical members. But what does it *mean* for something to be a fruit?

The search for an answer to this question leads us to consider schema theory. As we shall see, this approach sought to exploit interdependencies or conditionalities among feature values in accounting for meanings.

The schema approach is compatible with prototype structures, and it expands on research on prototypes by emphasizing the structure of how information gets organized in our cognitive processes. Much research in the prototypes vein has tried to fill out the sparse meaning of "prototype-as-excellent-example" by specifying prototypes in terms of *lists* of feature values. An apple is a highly typical instance of a fruit, and table is a highly typical instance of furniture, respectively, because each matches the expected values of the features associated with the superordinate concept, as we sketched above. A considerable body of research sought to estimate typicalities by checking correspondence with lists of the values of features.

How valuable is the view of concepts as lists of feature values? Think of an object that consists of a wooden rectangular slab with legs attached to both sides of the larger surface. Is this a table? It does have the required flat surface and legs. So checking feature values might suggest that it fits the concept. But it clearly does not. Why? Because the object does not conform to a *relational* constraint, namely that the legs should be attached to the *same* side of the larger flat surface.

The apple examples also involve such a constraint, one of containment: the seeds and pulp should lie inside the skin. An object that resembles a standard apple in all respects except that the seeds are placed on the outer surface satisfies the list of appropriate feature values but does not satisfy the containment constraint.

These constraints are examples of the conditionalities that represent structure in general. A structural representation attends to parts and their interrelations. Such mental representations of structures are generally called schemas (Rumelhart, 1980). Schemas are found not only in "material" concepts such as fruit or furniture, but also in sociological notions such as cultural genres. For example, Dancyger and Rush (2002, p. 81) summarize the conventions of the Western film as follows:

- "The hero, a man alone, functions with a worldview that is both moral and decent.
- The hero has a distinct skill with guns and horses.
- The antagonist has mercantile goals—the accumulation of money, land, cattle—and will recognize no person or ethic that stands in his way.
- The land plays a pastoral but critical role. It not only represents freedom, but also primitivism.
- Civilization is represented by those forces that represent an organizing influence on life—the town, the army, married life, and children.

- The struggle between the forces of primitivism (such as the land and the Indians) and those of civilization (such as the army or the town) forms a particular dilemma for the Western hero. In which world will he reside? ...This is the classic conflict for the Western hero.
- The drama plays itself out in a ritualized form—gunfights, cattle drives— and individual conflicts are acted out rather than negotiated."

This schema has high dimensionality and complex connections among feature values—it is clearly relational. For instance, it builds on the conflicts between (1) the moral hero and the mercantilist villain and (2) between civilization and primitivism.

Nonetheless, this schema can still be described usefully in terms of a combination of the values of the relevant features. For example, one feature of the schema is the gender of the hero, and according to the definition above only one feature value belongs to the concept: *male*. Similarly, another feature is whether the worldview of the hero is moral or immoral, and the only acceptable value is: *moral*. As to the paired roles, the relevant feature is the form of the relation between the hero and villain: *the presence of moral conflict*.

More generally, a schema's structure can generally be represented as a set of *relations* over features. That is, a schema contains some kind of relation, such as implication, defined over sets of feature values. Then a good instance of the schema is a position in the semantic space (a set of feature values) that satisfies these relations. If we return to the simpler example of apple, then we might have a representation that includes the feature values: sweet, acid, seeds, sweet pulp, thin skin, and seeds-and-pulp-inside-skin. It might be helpful to consider the standard definition of material implication ("if A then B"). The implication relation is false if A is true and B is false, and it is true otherwise. The conditionality is expressed by the pairs of values of the truth conditions. Schemas generally contain such implications.

The center of a concept with a schema structure can sometimes be defined in terms of a single combination of related features (a position in the feature space); in this special case the concept has a single prototype. But this need not be so generally. For example, in an experimental study, Medin and Shoben (1988) found that subjects regarded both a metal spoon and a wooden spoon as prototypical spoons.

Given the possible multiplicity of prototypes, we define the center as a *set* of positions in the space. From this perspective, the conceptual center is a collection of positions in semantic space (prototypes) that have the same meaning. These positions are defined such that they can represent conditionalities among feature values. As we have already noted, research shows that apple and orange are both prototypical fruit and that table and chair are both prototypical furniture. So the concept centers of these higher-level concepts include at least two prototypes.

Consider again the example of spoon. The research we cited verifies the existence of two prototypes. So the schematic for the concept spoon can be represented as: schema(spoon) = {metal-spoon,wooden-spoon}. The conditional relation here relates the size of the spoon and the material used. If the material is metal, then the size should be small, and so forth. Consider the simple space defined over the common elements in the spoon concept, "shallow bowl on the end of a handle" (or sbh), size (small vs. large) and material (meal vs. wood). If the prototypical metal spoon is small and the prototypical wooden spoon is large, then we can express the spoon schema as: schema(spoon) = {⟨sbh, small, metal⟩, ⟨sbh, large, wooden⟩}.

From the schema perspective, typicality means closeness of fit to schema. To return to the Western film, audience members generally regard a film that matches this pattern exactly as being fully typical of the genre. For example, *Stagecoach* (1939), *My Darling Clementine* (1946), and *High Noon* (1952) are commonly cited prototypical examples of the genre. By contrast, some other well-known films blend this genre with elements of other genres. Examples include:

- musical/Western, e.g., *Annie get Your Gun* (1950), *Calamity Jane* (1953), and *Oklahoma!* (1955),
- comedy/Western, e.g., *Cat Ballou* (1965), *Blazing Saddles* (1974), and *City Slickers* (1991), and
- science fiction/Western, e.g., *Wild Wild West* (1999), *Firefly/Serenity* (2005), and *Cowboys and Aliens* (2011).

These hybrids display some features typical of the Western genre and some atypical of it based on the definition provided above. Thus, they would be considered less than fully typical of the genre. Of course, most films do not fit this genre at all and are not considered to be instances of the genre to any degree. One important aspect to note is that schemas need not be set in stone. New features might become relevant, or the set of values of features can be expanded. This is what we commonly intend when we say that a film genre has evolved, for example, when female Western heroes populate films such as *Calamity Jane* or in more recent decades filmmakers criticize the assumption of cultural superiority of civilization found in traditional Westerns.

Anthropologist Roy D'Andrade (1995) argues that the view that concepts are stored as prototypes and schemas fits well to a wide range of applications of work on culture—see also DiMaggio (1997). Schematic representations as mental structures used to perceive, process, and retrieve information feature in cultural sociology. For instance, sociologist Michèle Lamont (1992) explores what it means to be a worthy person in groups of white male professionals in the United States and France. She identifies three forms of boundaries, or what we refer to as features for the schema of worthy. Moral boundaries are drawn based on moral character, centered on qualities (concepts) such as honesty, work ethic, and integrity. Cultural boundaries center on education, intelligence, refinement, manners, curiosity, and aesthetic sophistication. Socioeconomic boundaries center on wealth, power, and professional success.

The interactions of the features in the schema of worthy person show specific connections and variation. Take the case of moral boundaries. This dimension of meaning is important in each country, but the concepts/feature values stressed differ by country. In the United States, the meaning of honest is opposed to phony, and a phony is someone who pretends to be someone he is not. Honest is also opposed to social climber, someone who is overambitious and overly aggressive. Honesty in France is primarily defined by intellectual integrity, consistency with one's self, taking responsibility for who he is, not adapting to circumstances, and not being a salaud, loosely translated as bastard and meaning someone ready to sacrifice the interests of others to his own by repressing them or being unfair to them. Meanings also vary by context. For example, in the French workplace, competence is defined by articulation, brilliance, and versatility, whereas in the American context it is defined primarily by expertise.

2.4   Appraisal and Proposal

A formal approach to concepts and categories that can animate sociological theory and research should build on the regularities found in research in cognitive research. The work sketched in this chapter provides key inspirations.

Sociological applicability imposes more constraint. Four properties are crucial for choosing fundamentals.

Desideratum 1. The big question is whether we need an abstract representation of concepts in addition to categories. Our answer is that we do need a model of concepts. This view decisively shapes our approach.

A key issue for us is the unstable nature of similarity when the dimensions (relevant features) are left open. Suppose someone recalls that she tagged a set of items as similar. She cannot know from just the composition of the set exactly how she made the categorizations, whether the dimensions used in the similarity judgments were the same for all pairs of items that ended up in the set. This is because what gets stored is the result of the judgments, not the process that led to them.[6]

This kind of fragility looms large in social contexts, such as those in which individuals can observe the results of each other's categorizations. As often happens in discussions, two individuals might learn that they disagree about how an object should be categorized. For instance, they might dispute the genre assignment of a film, say *Fury* (1936), which they have both seen. One individual thinks that the film is a melodrama and crime, and the other thinks it is a film noir. People seek to make sense of such disagreements. Efforts in this direction often start with questions like "So what do you mean by film noir?" If the response to such a question takes the form of producing a list of films that belong to this genre, this does not answer the question. The conversation proceeds more usefully once it turns to the question: what does it mean to be an instance of the genre? The answer to this question is an attempt to delineate the feature values that determine whether a film is or is not an instance of the genre in question. This is a move toward elucidating an abstract concept.

Generally, people cannot easily communicate and coordinate without reasonably stable concepts. Instability will erode consensus about meanings, causing people to constantly interrogate others about what they currently mean by the labels they use. We propose a formal way to characterize the desired stability of concepts, rendered in probabilistic form, in §8.5.

This means that our model requires high-level representations rather than detailed accounts of how the brain processes information. Research on cognition has been shaped by a three-level analytic scheme proposed by Marr and Poggio (1977) and Marr (1982). This proposal claims substantial analytic independence among three different levels of the cognitive system. At the highest level is the so-called *computational level*. Here the mind develops abstract identifications and specifications of the cognitive problems to be solved. The intermediate *algorithmic level* specifies the cognitive processes used to solve the problem given at the higher level. Finally, the *implementation level* deploys the basic hardware of the brain to implement the algorithm.

We have postponed discussion of a perspective, in some respects that is close to ours, that builds on a variant of the three-level framework. Harnad (1987b, p. 22) developed an approach called categorical perception (CP) that ties psychophysical perception (the lowest level) to semantic categories (the highest one).

CP is defined by the discrimination and identification function. Discrimination requires analog stimulus traces for making relative comparisons and for performing other analog operations. These representations need not—indeed cannot—be categorical. Identification requires a feature-detector that reliably picks out the features that distinguish the members of an all-or-none category from confusable nonmembers.... Categories always remain context-relative and approximate. Yet, when they are well-learned, most categories are nevertheless all-or-none, not graded or fuzzy....

Given Hanard's insistence that perception is analog and that concepts are discrete, the intermediate level must consist of an analog-to-digital conversion.

Peter Gärdenfors, logician turned cognitive scientist, has built on this approach by embedding Harnad's key insight in a spatial model in Gärdenfors (2004), and Gärdenfors (2014). The space contains combinations of the values of the features that are relevant for expressing the meaning of the concept. (Gärdenfors calls the space a conceptual space; we call it a semantic space.) The continuous space can represent perception in a Shepard-like way. Objects are perceived as positions in the space. Getting from this continuous representation to discrete concepts relies on the use of Roschian prototypes, which are also positions in the space. Gärdenfors proposes that sharply bounded concepts arise from a process in which each position in the space is mapped to the closest prototype. All of the points associated with a prototype are *fully* in that concept. In this kind of representation, concepts are classical—there are no partial memberships. Concepts represented in this way are formally Voronoi sets, partitions of the feature space.

We illustrate this kind of construction in figure 2.1. The figure portrays a space defined by two continuously valued features. Points in this space are what we call positions. The space contains representations of four concepts (with positions chosen at random from a uniform distribution). Each concept is a convex set of positions surrounding its prototype, which we denote as P_1, P_2, P_3, and P_4. The concepts are Voronoi cells, which means that they contain the positions that are closer to the focal prototype than they are to any other. By construction, the concepts are crisp subsets of the feature space: any position in the space is an instance of only one concept.

The crisp representations proposed by Harnad and Gärdenfors do not fit well with the body of empirical work on the internal structure of concepts begun by Rosch. Consider the representation in figure 2.1 and the three positions that we labeled y_1, y_2, and y_3. These points are very close in the space

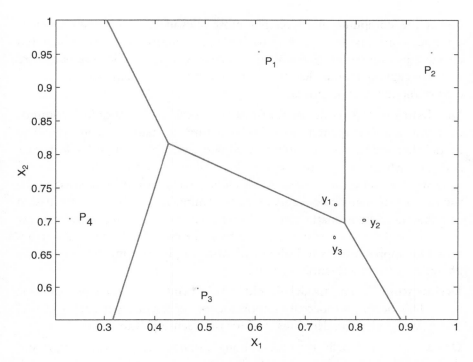

Figure 2.1 Illustration of a representation of four concepts as Voronoi cells in a two-dimensional feature space. See text

but on different sides of the divisions between concepts. Indeed, these points are much closer to each other than to any prototype. Nonetheless, the crisp construction casts each as a full member of one concept and as a nonmember of the others. We do not find this very plausible from a psychological perspective. In particular, this kind of representation is consistent with one piece of Rosch's formulation that concepts are organized by prototypes but inconsistent with the other piece that typicality as an instance of a concept is graded.

As we just sketched, Gärdenfors's model begins at the hardware level and works out implications at a higher computational level. Some of the differences between this approach and other strands of work arise because they operate at different levels in characterizing concepts. Prototype and schema models are purely computational (in Marr's terminology). Exemplar and connectionist approaches operate largely at the algorithmic level.

For sociologists and other social scientists who are interested in looking at "macro" implications of concepts and categories, research carried out at the computational level has most relevance.[7] Such research characterizes concepts as tools for making sense of situations for which full characterization would overwhelm processing capacity. The core issues are how concepts get built, learned, communicated, and deployed in diverse environmental circumstances.

Desideratum 2. A model useful for sociological analysis should accommodate the well-documented typicality structure of "natural" concepts. The model therefore should be able to deal with concepts such as bank, family, and jazz, which we use, in everyday life, where we find it hard to tell exactly what membership means. Such an approach would be less useful for the analysis of analytic concepts in formal languages, such as the discussion of prime numbers in mathematics. As we mentioned before, in the context of specialized scientific analysis, concepts can be crisp and lack internal structure. Our approach aims at dealing with how people use concepts in everyday life rather than in a scientific debate.

Desideratum 3. The model should have a firm and explicit probabilistic basis. This becomes especially important for representing concepts in use, that is, categorization decisions, and for representing ambiguity.

Desideratum 4. Finally, the model should provide a sound way to represent the interaction of multiple concepts. This means articulating a space in which concepts can be compared formally. In combination, the third and fourth desiderata call for a model of probability distributions over a common space of feature values.

The approaches to explicating concepts described in this chapter have been extremely productive. However, none, as currently constructed, satisfy the four desiderata. As we see it, the exemplar approach can deal well with typicality, categorization, and inference. However, it does not provide either an overarching representation or a spatial representation for multi-concept analyses. The approach proposed by Gärdenfors gives a mirror image: it provides the space but does not represent typicality and the properties of concepts in use.

The closely-related prototype and schema perspectives provide more of what we want, although they are not embedded in a probabilistic or a spatial perspective. But we find more on which to build in these perspectives.

Our effort here can be viewed as one of extending the prototype and schema perspectives in two ways: (1) tying concepts explicitly to a space of relevant features, which we call a semantic space; and (2) expressing concepts as probability measures over the space. We explain the two steps in the next two chapters (chapter 3 and chapter 4).

Following this, we build a model in line with the desiderata, in which we:

1. characterize the structure of subconcept relations (chapter 5) and spaces of concepts (chapter 6);
2. represent the effect of background knowledge from a conceptual space and the information context of a concept (chapter 7);
3. account for categorization decisions (chapters 8 and 9);
4. analyze implications of category membership for inference about unobserved features (chapter 10);
5. characterize the conceptual ambiguity of the mental representations of objects (chapter 11);
6. explain the effects of conceptual ambiguity on valuation of objects (chapter 12); and,
7. formulate a model of social inference and the emergence of taken-for-grantedness (chapter 14).

CHAPTER THREE

Semantic Space

IN CONCLUDING THE PREVIOUS CHAPTER, we proposed a suitable formal model for analyzing concepts and stated that categories should contain two key ingredients. The first is a specification of the space over which a concept's meaning is defined, and the second is a specification of a concept as probability measure over the space. This chapter takes up the first of the components.

All of our analyses build on the idea of a *semantic space*. This is the space (set of features) in which the meaning of a concept is expressed. We think of this space as one whose dimensions are the features that people use as the mental representations of the concept. When we turn to thinking about the categorization of objects with respect to a concept, then this is also the space for the mental representations of the objects. The positions in the space are particular combinations of feature values.

3.1 Representing Semantic Space

In building a formal model, we assume that the set of the psychologically and culturally relevant features for a concept is finite and can be given a fixed enumeration. We use $\mathbb{F}_c = F_1 \times F_2 \times \cdots \times F_C$ to refer to the space of relevant features for the concept c.

When viewed formally, our approach to specifying concepts can be seen as stating a simple semantic relation. The meaning of a concept, its mental representation, is given by a probability distribution over the semantic space associated with the concept. If we employ a standard notation for the semantic value of an expression, $[[\cdot]]$, then we propose that the meaning of the concept labeled c is given by:

$$[[c]] = P_{\mathbb{F}_c}(\cdot \mid c),$$

where $\mathbb{F}_c$ is a space of feature values and $P_{\mathbb{F}_c}$ is a suitably chosen probability measure defined over the space. In the next chapter, we will give a more precise specification. For now, this probability measure expresses how likely are the various positions in the semantic space—combination of values of the relevant features—for something that is a c.[1]

This definition of the meaning of the concept imposes a structure. The set of features over which $\mathbb{F}_c$ is defined are those that a focal person uses in constructing the meaning of that concept. This is the sense in which it is a *semantic* space.

This is straightforward in theory. But application in empirical research requires specification and measurement of semantic spaces. In sociological research, an excellent early attempt at capturing this type of space can be seen in Martin Ruef's (1999, 2000) examination of the ontological landscape in which U.S. health care organizations resided during 1966–1994. For that analysis, Ruef extracted text data from medical journals and applied the techniques of multidimensional scaling to identify the underlying features of the space and then to place relevant medical concepts (organizational forms and activities, in this case) within it.

In general, few other attempts have been made to characterize such spaces in previous sociological research. Therefore, instead of relying on published research, we illustrate what we regard as useful ways to approach the task in sociological research using materials from our ongoing research. We repeat this kind of demonstration in subsequent chapters.

The first step in building the model specifies the features (or properties) that are relevant for: (1) deciding questions about goodness of representation as instances of a concept and (2) providing an overall mental representation. Where do these ingredients come from in empirical research? This chapter provides empirical illustrations to show how sociological research can address these issues.

3.2   From Judgments by Audiences

In some contexts, there are persons or organizations that do much of the work of identifying the relevant semantic spaces, pointing to the relevant feature dimensions and feature values for concepts. For example, studies of the film industry have often relied on the data supplied by industry-focused organizations such as the American Film Institute (AFI) to identify relevant feature dimensions and feature values for concepts shared by a segment of the film audience. These organizations have amassed comprehensive catalogues of films that provide genre assignments for each film as well as each film's key subject matters. Media scholars observe that films within a genre often share similar topical features and structure, and in turn features are related to basic subject matter and thematic preoccupations (Altman, 1999). This relation allows a straightforward interpretation of the semantics: the objects are the films, the concepts are the genres, and the feature values are the major subject matters associated with each film. Armed with these essential pieces of information, we can place genres and individual films within a semantic space.

This setup directly translates to other settings as well. For hedge funds, organizations such as Tremont Advisors Statistics Services (TASS) build databases containing characteristics of the funds. The objects are the funds, and they are categorized as belonging to a primary investment style. The semantic space can be defined in terms of particular investment and strategic foci—all data that TASS has collected and organized (Smith, 2011).

Example: The Semantic Space for Impressionist Art

We can illustrate the use of expert judgments as a basis for constructing the space using the example of the visual artistic style called Impressionism that evolved in mid-nineteenth-century France from genre and landscape painting. Impressionist artists[2] capture a scene or object as reflected in a brief glimpse or "impression" (ArtMovements, 2016). Key identifiable techniques associated with this style include "short, broken brushstrokes that barely convey forms, pure unblended colors, and an emphasis on the effects of light. Rather than neutral white, grays, and blacks, Impressionists often rendered shadows and highlights in color." Landscapes and outdoor scenes were frequent subjects of Impressionists' work and were modernized through "innovative compositions, light effects, and use of color" (Samu, 2004).

This technical definition of Impressionism gives two types of information: a set of relevant feature dimensions—a semantic space—and a set of typical values on these feature dimensions. We provide a simplified rendition in table 3.1.

What does it mean for a painting to be Impressionist from the perspective of someone for whom Impressionism is well described by the illustrative

TABLE 3.1
Features defining semantic space and typical values for
Impressionist painting

Feature	Typical value
Length of brushstrokes	short
Continuity of brushstrokes	broken
Blending of the colors	no
Importance of light effects	very high
Rendering of shadows and highlight	color based, not black–white
Subject	landscapes and outdoor scenes
Detail of rendering	low
Composition	innovative

feature dimensions and typical values listed in table 3.1? It means that the feature values of the artwork correspond closely to the configuration described by the typical values. For example, the position that includes the most typical values of the relevant features for an Impressionist painting (according to table 3.1) is the feature-value vector (position in the space):

$$x \in \mathbb{F}_c = \langle short, broken, no, very\ high, color\ based, landscape, low, innovative \rangle.$$

Of course many other positions describe different patterns of feature values. Some of these are close to the concept of Impressionist art, and others are far from it.

3.3   From Analysis of Texts

In other contexts, the researcher must figure out for herself how to identify and extract the relevant features in a way that matches the semantic spaces of the people under study. Researchers can take advantage of availability of texts and apply computational methods (natural language processing, quantitative semantics, etc.) to extract the feature dimensions that agents use in particular domains (Pontikes, 2012; Hoberg and Phillips, 2016). Improvements in machine-learning algorithms provide opportunities to identify schemas empirically. Schemas for concepts are often described in text, in the past through paper "guides" issued by critics, and recently, online. These documents can be digitized by scanning old archives, scraping websites, or compiling media articles, press releases, and annual reports.

The Semantic Space for Rap *Styles*

When experts identify relevant features in a domain, categorization and feature values can be readily extracted. Here we consider how researchers might approach constructing a conceptual space when feature values are less directly supplied. In many cases, researchers have data on text descriptions of objects and can apply natural language processing algorithms to extract feature values. We use topic modeling, an automated, inductive method to identify themes in large corpora of text (DiMaggio, Nag, and Blei, 2013). Topic models extract meaning from text in a relational manner: they assume that meaning is embedded in relationships among words rather than within the words themselves (DiMaggio et al., 2013). This is a strength of topic modeling for research interested in studying categorization because this approach recognizes that words vary in meaning, depending on context.

Topic models assume that each document in a corpus contains a set of topics, which are treated as hidden variables. Topics are revealed by words within the document, which are observed. Models such as Latent Dirichlet Allocation (LDA) define a joint probability distribution over both hidden and observed random variables to extract the topics within the corpus and words that represent the topic (Blei, 2012; Blei, Ng, and Jordan, 2003). In our use, revealed topics are features of objects in the domain.

We apply topic modeling to a large corpus of rap music lyrics, 28,340 songs on from 3,481 albums released between 1978 and 2011, where albums are classified by style by a prominent music critic. We include albums for which we have lyrics for more than five tracks, which gives 2,039 albums and 24,884 songs. We use the texts of lyrics as documents and apply LDA to extract topics.

We use this kind of analysis to construct the semantic space for rap music where each meaningful topic is a feature dimension of the semantic space. LDA requires the number of topics to be input as a parameter. It is a stochastic method, so topics will vary over runs of the procedure. We experimented with different numbers of topics and ran a number of models to arrive at a set of consistent topics (DiMaggio et al., 2013). The model we chose uses ten topics, seven of which can be easily interpreted. Table 3.2 lists the interpretable topics and in order the fifteen most representative words for each topic. Note that a given word might appear in more than one topic, because the same words can be used in different ways to convey different themes in the corpus. Topic modeling allows us to reduce dimensionality in the corpus of lyrics to seven features that define the dimensions of the semantic space.

TABLE 3.2
Topics from a corpus of rap lyrics, 1978–2011

Topic	Name	Top words
0	*Swagger*	bitch, nigga, hoes, wit, ass, money, fuck, niggas, big, bout, lil, dick, club, hoe, game, baby
1	*Religion/history*	zu, speech, black, history, people, men, president, children, truth, forth, earth, world, tree, christ, water
2	*Party*	cos, yes, aiyo, party, killah, shawty, moe, rude, girls, yeahhh, oil, dance, american, tooth
3	*Rapping*	mic, rhymes, rap, music, rhyme, rappers, flow, style, mcs, hiphop, beats, raps, rock, priest
4	*Street violence*	niggas, nigga, die, streets, fuck, gun, dead, shit, kill, murder, fucking, block, ghetto, war, guns
5	*Romantic love*	love, life, would, away, could, things, ive, god, said, girl, heart, day, shes, id, world
6	*Pride*	9th, thoed, fantastic, hogg, man, booth, goons, swag, couldve, sto, kush, love, fly, feel, really

With the semantic space in hand, we turn to locating concepts (styles) in this space. We use the categorization of rap albums by styles as developed by the online music guide Allmusic.com, also described in chapter 9.[3] We identify the features that comprise the schema for a style based on the topics in albums classified as a particular style. We place styles in the semantic space by taking the mean of each topic in tracks on an album classified as a particular style. Figures 3.1–3.3 show the distribution of features based on topics for select styles.

The *swagger* topic is a prominent feature in every style, as it is the most prevalent style across all songs. This topic is a common identifier that ties each style to the genre. But some styles are more heavily characterized by this feature than others.

Geography represents one major division in rap music, especially in the time period covered by our data. A strong musical rivalry was constructed between rappers on the East Coast and West Coast in the 1990s, and Southern rappers emerged on the scene to stake out a unique musical position. Although this categorization reflects geography, it is a stylistic classification. A rapper who lives in New York could be classified as political and not East Coast.

The schema for East Coast rap focuses most heavily on *street violence* and *swagger*, but there are strong influences from *rapping* and *romantic love*, as well as some contribution from *religion/history*. This contrasts with the

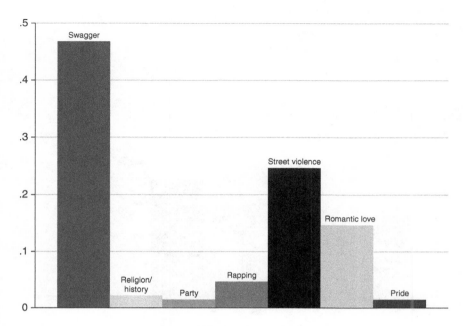

Figure 3.1 Schema for Southern rap based on lyrical topics

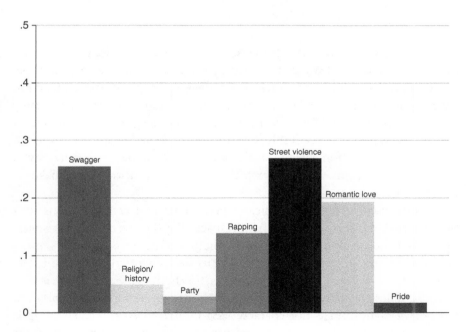

Figure 3.2 Schema for East Coast rap based on lyrical topics

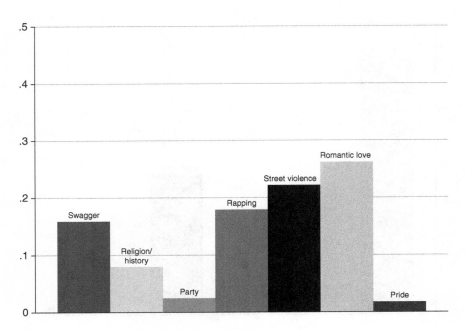

Figure 3.3 Schema for political rap based on lyrical topics

schema for Southern rap, which focuses on the *swagger* topic, with *street vi-olence* as a secondary feature, followed by *romantic love*. The *rapping* topic has low representation, as does *religion/history*. As expected, the political rap style is much more distant in feature space. This style focuses on *romantic love* and *street violence*, followed by *rapping*. The *swagger* topic has one of the lowest representations in this style. Interestingly, political rap has a much more even distribution across feature dimensions compared to other styles which heavily weight the *swagger* feature. This even distribution makes it distant in the semantic space.

We can also provide a graphical representation of style locations in a two-dimensional slice of the semantic space, for the twenty largest styles. Figure 3.4 shows an inverse relationship between the *swagger* and *romantic love* dimensions: in styles where lyrics focus on romantic love, there is less swagger and vice versa. As figure 3.5 shows, for the *swagger* and *street violence* features, styles are scattered across the semantic space. For example, party rap has *swagger* lyrics but is not characterized by *street violence*, gangsta rap is high on both *swagger* and *street violence* features, and jazz rap is low for both features.

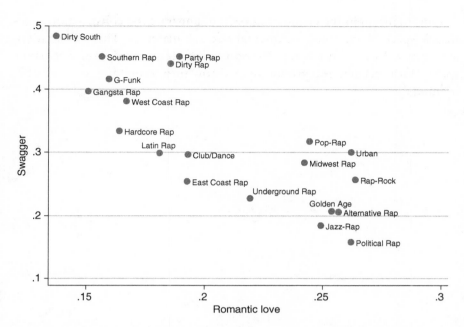

Figure 3.4 Semantic space locations of styles on the dimensions *swagger* and *romantic love*

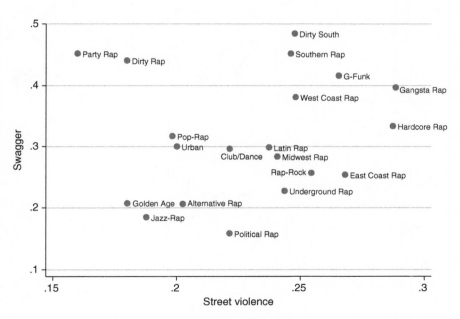

Figure 3.5 Semantic space locations of styles on the dimensions *swagger* and *street violence*

Our intention in the chapter has been to illustrate the construction of semantic spaces from non-experimental research materials. These illustrations are intended to make tangible the somewhat elusive notion of a semantic space. With this practical grounding, we now turn to building the probability model.

CHAPTER FOUR

Concepts as Probability Densities in Semantic Space

NOW WE TAKE UP the second component of the formal model: representing concepts as probability distributions over semantic space. In particular, we argue that embedding concepts in a formal Bayesian model allows for the desired unified approach.

In building this part of the framework, we take care to fine tune it to the needs of sociological research applications. This means tying the concept likelihood to typicality, a relation that has not been treated in the relevant work in cognitive psychology. We emphasize the link to typicality because, as we show by example, non-experimental research can better measure typicality than the concept likelihood. So we begin with a rendition of the standard construction of concepts as likelihoods, and we emphasize the space over which the likelihoods are defined, the semantic space as delineated in the previous chapter. Then we use a standard argument about distance in psychological space and similarity and a definition of typicality as similarity to the positions in the center of the concept to link distance of a position in semantic space from a concept center to concept likelihood and typicality. The resulting structure implies a positive monotonic relation between typicality and the concept likelihood, which allows researchers to use measured typicality to draw inferences about the structure of a concept.

4.1   Concept Likelihood

Concepts specify which positions in semantic space are more likely than others for objects that "belong" to a concept. As we discussed in the previous chapter, prototype theorists represented this aspect of concepts in terms of graded typicality. We prefer to do so with a subjective probabilistic construction that can be used for all of the analytical issues we address. Moreover, this framework allows us to build predictive models so that the accuracy of these predictions can be exposed to empirical tests.

Specifically, we express our arguments in terms of $\pi_{\mathbb{F}_c}(x \mid c)$, the subjective probability (or belief) that an object known to be an instance of the concept c has some particular combination of values of relevant features (is at position x in the semantic space, $\mathbb{F}_c$).[1] As the domain of the function $\pi_{\mathbb{F}_c}(\cdot \mid c)$ is the whole of the semantic space, $\mathbb{F}_c$, and the function maps into the real interval $[0, 1]$, this function tells the subjective probability distribution of positions in semantic space for cs. It identifies a blurred region that expresses the concept in a non-trivial way. We make this vague assertion more precise in chapter 7.

Formally, this function is a probability-density function (*pdf*) over positions in the semantic space. Positions at which this function yields high values are typical of the concept, whereas positions at which the function is low are very atypical. In that sense, it captures what Rosch calls the internal structure of a concept—its graded typicality. We will derive the relation between the concept likelihood and typicality from elementary considerations of distance and similarity below.

In later chapters, we will supplement this barebones representation with another component: the conceptual background knowledge that comes from knowing the location of the concept with respect to other concepts.

Note that concepts are tagged with indices. We refer to these tags as the *labels* associated with the concepts. Although labels might be idiosyncratic and private, this is not the main case (as Wittgenstein (1953) argued in his critique of the possibility of a private language). Generally, labels are public and get used in public discourse. Social life demands the use of explicit labels.

The Semantics of Labels Revisited

In the previous chapter, we introduced the idea that the meaning of a concept can usefully be represented as some probability measure over the semantic space of the concept. Now we pin this down to a specific measure: the concept likelihood:

$$[\![c]\!] \equiv \pi_{\mathbb{F}_c}(\cdot \mid c).$$

Of course, judgments about what-is-an-instance-of-what come with varying degrees of confidence. Degree of confidence in belief maps neatly to the idea of variable typicality as we show below. With this setup, it is natural to use the probability model designed to express subjective uncertainty: Bayesian probability. This approach has become the standard machinery for modeling judgment in cognitive psychology.

As we detail in chapter 8, Ashby and Alfonso-Reese (1995) show that this representation of concepts as probability density function can be used to formulate a Bayesian model that specifies what the mind computes when people categorize objects and make inferences about their features. They demonstrate that many of the leading categorization models in the prototype view and the exemplar view can be seen as mental algorithms that approximate Bayes' rule.[2] In other words, the Bayesian model specifies *what* computations the mind performs when people deal with concepts whereas prototype- and exemplar-based models specify *how* the mind performs the computations. Because our purpose here is not to investigate the details of the mental algorithms that people use, specifying a Bayesian model of categorization and inference allows us to operate at the desired level of analysis.

The use of Bayesian models has become very common in cognitive psychology, especially in the literature on categorization and inference. Such models fit in a research tradition that psychologists call rational analysis (Anderson, 1991; Marr, 1982). This approach focuses on the role of the environment and the individual's goals instead of on the details of the computations that happen within a person's mind—in that sense, it fits sociological analysis very well.

Readers familiar with the research program on heuristics and biases initiated by Tversky and Kahneman (1974), and recently summarized by Kahneman (2011), might be surprised by our choice to rely on Bayesian models. After all, the program of research on judgments and biases has demonstrated forcefully that the heuristics—mental shortcuts—that people use do not generally approximate the computations prescribed by Bayesian models. This research program on heuristics has been successful as it has identified *specific* conditions in which people make *systematic* mistakes. At the same time, there are many other less specific conditions under which people perform well—the computations their minds perform lead to judgments close to the prescriptions of the Bayesian model. In particular, there is overwhelming evidence that categorization is one such setting (Anderson, 1991; Feldman et al., 2009; Sanborn et al., 2010). Building our approach on Bayesian models of categorizations allows us to stand on firm theoretical and empirical grounding.

4.2   Distance and Typicality

We can connect the probabilistic formulation of a concept with the analytic constructions from other programs discussed in chapter 2 and with sociological empirical research by focusing on typicality. In this section, we explain how the probabilistic view can reflect the graded nature of concept membership captured by typicality. Consider first concepts with just one prototype. Prototypicality as rendered by Rosch means "excellent example." The prototype is thus the best example of a concept, whereas objects that are very different from the prototype are poor examples. But the concept likelihood over positions in feature space captures exactly this idea.

Suppose we have a one-dimensional real-valued feature space, that is, $\mathbb{F}_c = \mathbb{R}$ (the real line), and the concept likelihood is a normal density with mean of ten and standard deviation of one. The best example of this concept is at the mode of the distribution (where $\pi_{\mathbb{R}}(x \mid c)$ is maximal), at $x = 10$. How good examples of the concept are the other positions? $\pi_{\mathbb{R}}(x \mid c)$ corresponds to the probability that an object that is an instance of the concept finds itself at position x. If $\pi_{\mathbb{R}}(x \mid c)$ is low, the position is very unlikely; in other words, this position is not a good example of the concept—it is atypical. This discussion suggests that the concept likelihood captures the typicality of positions in the semantic space, the space of the relevant features.

Directed and Symmetric Elementary Distances in a Semantic Space
We start with elementary distances between positions in the space. To represent the relevant arguments, we need notations for both directed and symmetric distances. Consider two mental representations, m and m'. We denote the distance *from* m to m' in the semantic space $\mathbb{F}$ by $\vec{d}_{\mathbb{F}}(m, m')$ and the symmetric distance *between* m and m' by $d_{\mathbb{F}}(m, m')$. When the context makes clear what space is being considered, we write simply $\vec{d}(m, m')$ or $d(m, m')$. Note that we will use this notation for distances involving any pair of mental representations, such as an object–concept pair or a concept–concept pair. We use directed distances in building the model.

As delineated in chapter 2, we would like our representation of concepts to capture potentially complex schemas made of more than just one prototype. Despite the important differences between the prototype and schema perspectives, both give rise to the important notion that concepts have centers. This insight can be stated as holding that *the center of a concept is a subset of its semantic space.* It is easy to capture this notion of conceptual center in the probabilistic model. We define the center of a concept, in notation $\mathbf{cen}_c$, using the concept likelihood as follows.

Definition 4.1 *The center of a concept is the set of positions in semantic space for which the concept likelihood is a maximum.*

$$\mathbf{cen}_c \equiv \{x \mid \pi_{\mathbb{F}_c}(x \mid c) \text{ is a maximum}\}.$$

The distance between a position and a concept center can be expressed using the standard definition from set theory. This distance is the smallest of the distances from the object representation to the representations of the members of the set. Because we want to distinguish syntactically the difference between the distance between a pair of positions and between a position and a concept and we cannot simply do so by changing the designations of the terms in the "variable" slots in the distance function, we state the meaning of the distance of a point from a concept in the following meaning postulate.

Definition 4.2 *The distance from a position to a concept in semantic space is the point-to-set distance from the position to the concept's center.*

Let $[\![c]\!] = \pi_{\mathbb{F}_c}(x \mid c)$.

$$\vec{d}_{\mathbb{F}_c}(x, c) \equiv \min_{y \in \mathbf{cen}_c} \vec{d}_{\mathbb{F}_c}(x, y).$$

Typicality of a Position

We use $\tau_c(x)$ to denote the typicality of a position in concept c (for a focal individual). Typicality is a function that maps from pairs of concepts and positions to the non-negative real line. This function can be elicited empirically by showing a stimulus at position x and asking "how typical is the stimulus of concept c?" (as reported in the empirical illustration below). This standard empirical approach attempts to sidestep the issue of specifying the semantic space. As we discuss in detail in chapter 8, such work assumes that the dimensions that the experimenter designed into the stimuli set the space for the subjects (as in our arrowhead experiments discussed below). Suppose that this set of dimensions yield the space $\mathbb{F}$. Then a more complete notation for the typicality function would have a form like $\tau_{\mathbb{F}}(x, c)$, which makes clear that x is a point in some space and that typicality judgments depend on the choice of the space. We stick with the more conventional notation that avoids reference to the space; however, we pin down the dependence of

$\tau_c(c)$ on a semantic space below in meaning postulate 4.1. This construction requires that we pay explicit attention to distance and similarity.

Typicality is a special case of similarity: the typicality of a position in a concept corresponds to the similarity between the position and the concept. Because a concept is a distribution, it is not clear what is meant by the similarity of a position and a concept. We fill the gap by defining such similarity using the center of the concept, which is a set of positions. When the center contains more than one position, then we regard similarity of the position and the center as the maximum of the similarities of the position and the positions in the center.

We need a notation for similarity: let $\vec{s}_{\mathbb{F}_c}(x, y)$ denote the similarity of the mental representations of the positions x to another y in the semantic space, $\mathbb{F}_c$.[3] This real-valued function maps from pairs of positions to $[0, 1]$.

The following meaning postulate instantiates our notion of typicality formally. (We call the following claim a meaning postulate, rather than a definition, because it equates to terms that can be measured independently, allowing one to test whether our claimed relationship is true.)

Meaning Postulate 4.1 (Typicality of a position) *The typicality of a position in a semantic space for a concept is equivalent to the maximal similarity of the position and the positions in the center of the concept.*

Let $[\![c]\!] = \pi_{\mathbb{F}_c}(x \mid c)$.

$$\tau_c(x) \equiv \max_{y \in \text{cen}_c} \vec{s}_{\mathbb{F}_c}(x, y),$$

where $\vec{s}_{\mathbb{F}_c}(x, y)$ *denotes the similarity of* x *to* y *over the semantic space* $\mathbb{F}_c$*; the vector-like notation means that it is a directed similarity (we discuss this issue in detail below).*

4.3 Tying the Notions Together

We now tie together formally some of the central notions in standard theories, as sketched in chapter 3, by building connections among similarity, typicality, distance from a concept center, and concept likelihood, using the probabilistic formulation. It is important to keep in mind that all of these constructs pertain to representations of concepts and objects in the mind of an individual—they are psychological constructs that are individual specific and possibly depend on time and situation. To keep our notation simple, however, we do not indicate these possible dependencies in the variables we use to refer to these psychological constructs.

Concept likelihoods are probabilities, and, as such, they are constrained to fall in $[0, 1]$ and to sum to one over the space. But typicalities, as measured in previous research, are not so constrained. Let $\tau_c(x)$ denote the typicality of a position in concept c for an individual. This can be obtained by showing a stimulus at position x and asking, "how typical is the stimulus of concept c?" (as reported in the empirical illustration below). We make the obvious adjustment by rescaling typicalities so that they are bounded in $[0, 1]$ and sum to one over the space. Specifically, we define $\tau_c^*(x)$ as the ratio of $\tau_c(x)$ to the sum of the $\tau_c(x)$ over the space:

$$\tau_c^*(x) \equiv \frac{\tau_c(x)}{\sum_{x' \in \mathbb{F}_c} \tau_c(x')}. \tag{4.1}$$

The key step assumes that concept likelihoods are scaled typicalities and therefore depend on the structure of the concept, the location of its center.

Postulate 4.1 (Concept likelihood and typicality) *The concept likelihood of a position in semantic space associated with a concept equals its scaled typicality.*

$$\pi_{\mathbb{F}_c}(x \mid c) = \tau_c^*(x).$$

Empirical investigations have found that stimuli tend to be judged as less typical of a concept when they are also judged to be dissimilar to the prototypes (or, presumably, positions in the concept center (Hampton, 2007; Dry and Storms, 2010; Verheyen, Hampton, and Storms, 2010). This suggests that we can regard typicality as a form of similarity measure, similarity between an object and a concept that might be applied to it. But an awkwardness arises. What is the similarity of a point (a position) to a set (the center of a multi-prototype concept)? Is it the average similarity, the maximum, the minimum? To the best of our knowledge, such a similarity is not well defined. We can address the problem if we translate from similarity to distance.

Shepard's law, already discussed in chapter 2, gives a parametric translation between similarity and distance in a psychological space: a negative exponential function. This is more specific than we need for building a theory. Moreover, some research shows that similarity declines with distance with different functional forms, for example, with the square of distance (implying that the concept pdf is from the normal family). Hampton's (1987) threshold model posits the existence of a region around the concept center in which the typicality–distance relation is flat (see also Verheyen et al. (2010)). Because we want our argument to be insensitive to the exact form

of the relation of distance and similarity/typicality, we make a weaker quali-
tative claim: that more distant positions are less similar than closer positions
in semantic space.[4]

Postulate 4.2 (A weak version of Shepard's law) *There is a negative relationship between the similarity of two mental representations and the distance
between them in semantic space.*

Let x, x', and y be any three positions in the space $\mathbb{F}_c$.

$$\vec{d}_{\mathbb{F}_c}(x, y) > \vec{d}_{\mathbb{F}_c}(x', y) \leftrightarrow \vec{s}_{\mathbb{F}_c}(x, y) < \vec{s}_{\mathbb{F}_c}(x', y).$$

These forgoing considerations imply a relationship between typicality/
concept likelihood and distance from a concept in semantic space, $\vec{d}(x, c)$,
which definition 4.2 defines as the distance from x to the nearest point in
the center of the concept c.[5]

Proposition 4.1 *The concept likelihood of a position and its typicality decline
with distance from the concept.*

Let $[\![c]\!] = \pi_{\mathbb{F}_c}(x \mid c)$, *and let x and x' be any two positions in* $\mathbb{F}_c$. *We have*

$$\vec{d}_{\mathbb{F}_c}(x, c) > \vec{d}_{\mathbb{F}_c}(x', c) \rightarrow \pi_{\mathbb{F}_c}(x \mid c) < \pi_{\mathbb{F}_c}(x' \mid c) \wedge \tau_c(x) < \tau_c(x').$$

This relationship has received considerable empirical verification. Our experiment about the typicality of arrows in the Akka concept provides consistent
evidence. Details are presented in the next section.

4.4   Experimental Evidence

We can explore proposition 4.1 using data from an experiment that used a
particularly simple structure. Le Mens, Hannan, Bhatt, Delecourt, and Manian (2016) asked a group of adult subjects to evaluate the typicality of a
series of stimuli in two concepts.[6] The instructions began as follows:

```
You are an apprentice in an archaeological museum.
Your task is to classify the arrowheads in the
museum's collection by styles. In what follows, we
will be using simplified drawings of arrowheads.
First, you will be shown a representative set of
arrowheads from the collection. Then you will be
given information about two styles of arrowheads.
And finally, you will be asked to tell which styles
apply to a series of arrowheads.
```

The semantic space for the task was a one-dimensional space of arrowheads. The relevant feature of the space was the width of the arrowhead at its widest point. Consistent with this, all the stimuli participants were shown were arrowheads of the same length and color, but with different width. To ensure that participants knew the nature of the semantic space, they were shown a sequence of arrowheads. More precisely, they were shown one arrowhead for each possible position in the semantic space (twenty-five stimuli arrows with width from 0.02 to 0.98 in steps of 0.04). The program cycled quickly through the whole set of stimuli, showing each for 0.2 second.

> Next, you will see a representative set of
> arrowheads from the collection. You will see each
> arrowhead for about half a second. It will take
> about 30 seconds to go through the whole set of
> arrowheads. When you are ready to start, press
> "next."

The two styles were Akka and Boko. These are the two concepts of interest in the experiment. For simplicity, by design the centers of these concepts are singletons, unique positions in the semantic space. That is, there was one prototype for each style. The Akka prototype had an arrow width of 0.7, and the Boko prototype had an arrow width of 0.3. We present only the results for the Akka style because those for the other style are very similar and the discussion would be repetitive.

The participants read:

> There are different styles of arrowheads associated
> with two West African tribes. We will focus on two
> styles: the style of the Akka tribe and the style of
> the Boko tribe.

When the random draw picks the Akka style, the participant is told:

> Next we will focus on the Akka style. Here is an
> ideal example of the Akka style of arrowhead. Please
> take a moment to study it carefully.

Then each participant went through loops of questions (here we only report the results for typicality judgments, although participants were also asked to categorize stimuli into styles—see chapter 9). For each stimulus, the participant was asked "How typical is the sample arrowhead of the Akka

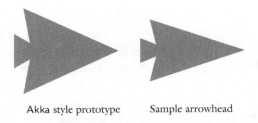

Akka style prototype   Sample arrowhead

Figure 4.1 Example of a comparison of a prototype and a stimulus from the experiment

style?". The participant responded by clicking on a slider with a range from 0 ("extremely atypical") to 100 ("extremely typical"). We refer to these responses as *typicality judgments.*

The scatterplot of figure 4.2a plots the typicality ratings given by the participants for all the stimuli (responses to the question "How typical is the sample arrowhead of the Akka style?").[7] On the horizontal axis, we have the position of the stimulus in the "objective" Euclidean space of arrow widths. Typicality ratings tend to be high for stimuli close to the prototype

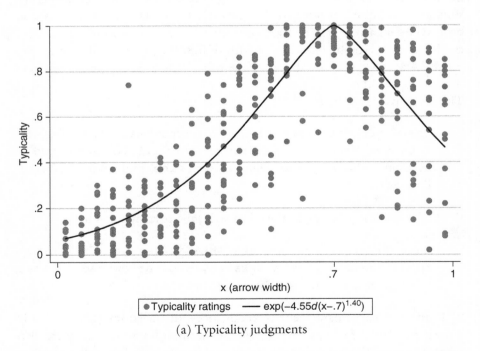

(a) Typicality judgments

Figure 4.2 The relationship between typicality judgments and estimates of concept likelihoods with distance from the Akka prototype (arrow width = 0.7)

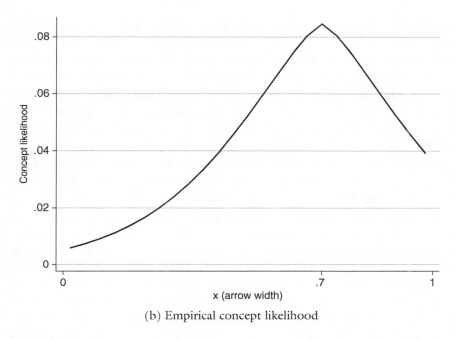

(b) Empirical concept likelihood

Figure 4.2   (*Continued*)

($x = 0.7$) and to become lower for stimuli further away from the prototype. Under the assumption that the Euclidean space of arrow width corresponds to the semantic space,[8] this pattern was to be expected. Prior research has shown that typicality functions are often of the exponential family (e.g., $\tau(\text{Akka}, x) = \exp(-\alpha |x - 0.7|^{\beta})$, with $\alpha > 0$ and $\beta \in [1,2]$). The graph also shows the best fitting function of this family.[9]

Figure 4.2b plots the concept likelihood implied by the rescaled typicality function for this concept. Unsurprisingly, it has exactly the same shape as the typicality function, but the y-axis is rescaled such that the sum of the concept likelihoods over the space equals one. Consistent with proposition 4.1, the concept likelihood decreases with the distance from the prototype, ($x = 0.7$).

4.5   Measuring Typicality with Observational Data

As we just illustrated, we can measure typicality directly based on respondents' ranking of particular objects vis-a-vis a given concept in experimental settings. This can also be done in surveys and interviews. For example, Keller and Loewenstein (2011) use a multi-method approach to study workers' categorizations for the concept of cooperation. They first conducted interviews to identify a set of workplace situations that subjects believed related to the construct. Then they asked a separate set of subjects to complete a questionnaire assessing whether each situation indicated cooperation. If the respondent said "yes," then he or she was asked to rank how strongly the situation indicated cooperative behavior. From each individual respondent's perspective, the "yes" or "no" response reveals whether the respondent believes the concept of cooperation applies to each situation. The ranking of how strongly the situation indicates cooperative behavior then reflects the extent to which the respondent views it as typical of cooperation.

Archival studies require a different approach. To measure an object's distance from its concept center, the researcher must first determine how to construct a representation of the concept's center. For example, when modeling the typicality of hedge funds, (Smith, 2011, p. 76) uses information compiled by a hedge-fund industry database and constructs a "hypothetical average, or central tendency vector for the fund's primary category." In these data the funds are assigned binary values corresponding to each of thirty-three investment approaches and strategic foci chosen by the managers of the database. The hypothetical central fund's vector is calculated as the proportion of the funds in the category that display each of the thirty-three features.

Once the concept center's position in semantic space is specified, each object's distance from the category/concept center or prototype can then be calculated with the distance between the relevant vector in the feature space of the object and the prototype/center. When there is more than one prototype/center, a point-to-set distance must be used. Given the above-described approach to calculate such distances, this is a straightforward step.

As this example shows, specification of an object's distance from its concept center requires data on both categorizations and feature values. This distance measure can then be used to calculate the typicality of an object as an instance of a concept.

Example: Rap Music. We will now provide a concrete example of calculating typicalities, returning to the example for rap music. In chapter 3, we applied topic modeling to a corpus of rap lyrics to create a semantic space based on seven meaningful feature dimensions (table 3.2). We use this space as the basis for calculating typicalities for rap albums, compared to style genres. For tractability in this exercise, we further reduce dimensionality to the three most prevalent features: *swagger*, *street violence*, and *romantic love*. Because

TABLE 4.1
Most typical albums for select rap styles

Album	Typicality
Southern rap	
B.G., *Livin' Legend*	1.0000
T.I., *Urban Legend*	0.9999
East Coast rap	
Afu-Ra, *State of the Arts*	0.9998
Puff Daddy, *Forever*	0.9997
Alternative rap	
Aceyalone, *Love & Hate*	0.9999
De La Soul, *The Grind Date*	0.9999

we will use this semantic space for several illustrations in subsequent chapters, we introduce a notation for it: $\mathbb{G}_{rap3}$.

We conduct our analysis on the twenty largest styles in the corpus, and we include albums for which we have lyrics for at least ten tracks. We use the positions of album in the semantic space $\mathbb{G}_{rap3}$ to compute album typicality in styles.

The location of an album in the semantic space is set to the average of the values along each of the three features for the album's songs.[10] The center of the style is the average of the respective positions of all albums in the style. Figures 3.4 and 3.5 plot these positions for two-dimensional slices of this space.

To compute the typicality of an album in a style, we construct an album matrix of the location of each album along each dimension in semantic space A and a similar matrix for styles S.[11] Specifically, we set an album's typicality in a style to its feature-space similarity to the center of the style. Albums and styles are placed in this three-dimensional semantic space according to the results of the topic model. We compute typicalities within this space using cosine similarity between the album's position and the center of the style:

$$T_S(A) = \frac{A \cdot S}{\|A\| \cdot \|S\|}. \tag{4.2}$$

The most typical albums for select styles are listed in table 4.1. Albums and styles are placed in feature space based on lyrical content along the top three features identified in the topic model. As a result, it is possible that an album that is very typical of a style based on lyrics will not be assigned to the style, presumably based on other features that are unmeasured. In most cases, the albums that are most typical of a style in semantic space are also assigned to the style.

Discussion

The model we propose treats concepts as mental representations that can be regarded as probability clouds in semantic space, more precisely as probability distributions in the space. It has the following properties:

1. Concepts are modeled as probability distributions (likelihoods) over a semantic space, the space of features that get invoked in their meanings.
2. Concepts have centers that might be represented in a variety of ways (prototypes, central tendencies, schemas). In all cases the center can be defined as a subset of the semantic space for which the concept likelihood is a maximum.
3. Scaled typicality is assumed to be equal to the concept likelihood.
4. Regarding the typicality of a position in semantic space as a similarity judgment and using Shepard's law, we find that the typicality and concept likelihood of a position in semantic space is a decreasing function of its distance from the center of the concept.

Much of this chapter illustrates how the components of the model can be measured/estimated in experimental and non-experimental sociological research. This discussion shows that measurements of typicality judgments play a key role.

CHAPTER FIVE

Conceptual Spaces: Domains and Cohorts

IN THE PREVIOUS CHAPTERS, we have treated concepts in isolation. However, it is abundantly clear that concepts interrelate. Concepts can be related in a vertical sense, such as when one concept is a subconcept of another (e.g., comedy is a type of film), or in a horizontal sense, when two concepts at the same level partially overlap (e.g., some media companies are also tech companies and vice versa).

In this chapter, we focus on vertical relations between concepts, deferring the issue of horizontal relations until chapter 7. The observation that concepts relate in a hierarchical sense stems from at least the work of in Durkheim and Mauss (1969 [1903]), who expounded on the issue of hierarchical relatedness at length as they compared "primitive" classification systems to more modern forms. They argued that the relatedness of concepts within classification systems characterizes both "primitive" and "modern" systems:

> Like all sophisticated classifications, they are systems of hierarchized notions. Things are not simply arranged by them in the form of isolated groups, but these groups stand in fixed relationships to each other and together form a single whole.... Their object is...to advance understanding, to make intelligible the relations which exist between things. Given certain concepts which are considered to be fundamental, the mind feels the need to connect to them the ideas which it forms about other things. [p. 81]

Some system of relationships among concepts is necessary to accommodate the limitations of human cognitive processing powers. Because humans are cognitively constrained, it is likely that a person can focus only on a small subset of available concepts at any given time. We wish to incorporate this constraint as we model processes such as categorization and valuation in later chapters. We will do so by localizing comparisons within branches of the "tree" of an individual's concepts. Think, for instance, of science which (for many) includes physics, biology, sociology, and so forth.

We initially set out to construct a model to represent broad swaths of a person's knowledge, complete conceptual inventories. Much work in cognitive science builds on the notion that the macrostructure of such an inventory is a tree or set of trees, that conceptual knowledge is organized hierarchically. This focus follows a long tradition beginning at least with Aristotle and developing in full-blown form with the *Philosophia Botanica* (1735) by Carl Linnaeus, "the father of taxonomy." (Ethnobotanists have established that non-literate societies generally developed botanical hierarchies of their own.) Linnaeus proposed a seven-level tree to organize all known plant forms. The Linnean system has only recently been supplanted by hierarchies based on genetic information. Similar formal systems of classification abound for the social world, including the U.S. Census Department's *Dictionary of Occupational Titles* which organizes roughly 13,000 named jobs in a five-level tree. As we discuss in later chapters, scholars of genres in various art worlds create such hierarchies as well. All such systems of classification serve to simplify the structure of knowledge by allowing people to focus narrowly on one branch at a time, as needed.

A considerable literature on concept hierarchies has developed in cognitive psychology and computational linguistics. Murphy (2002, Chapter 7) reviews the psychology, and Widdows (2004, Chapters 3 and 8) reviews the linguistics. For decades cognitive psychologists have debated the issue of how hierarchical structures get stored in semantic memory. The original proposal by Quillian (1966) (see also Collins and Quillian (1969)) held that the sets of hierarchical links are stored and are used in inference. The alternative proposal maintains that hierarchies get stored implicitly as the sets of feature values consistent with membership in the concepts at different level are stored and that inference simply compares similarities of the feature sets without reference to the hierarchical links (Smith, Rips, and Shoben, 1974); (see also Murphy, Hampton, and Milovanovic (2012b)).

We set out to build on this work but eventually realized that strict hierarchy might offer a poor description of the macrostructure of concepts for two reasons. The first is that social concepts sometimes violate the hierarchical constraint of "inheritance" down a single branch of the tree. Hybrid forms are generally seen as tied to two or more roots (different branches). For instance, according to conventional understandings of brewpub, this concept is a subconcept of brewery and restaurant. For sociological applications, ruling out hybrids would be unreasonably limiting.

The second reason for doubting the value of hierarchy as a model for the macrostructure is that it relies on the assumption of *transitivity*. If the structure is a tree (or even a semi-lattice, which allows hybrids), then knowing that an object satisfies the conditions for membership in a concept at one level means that it satisfies the conditions for membership in all the concepts at higher levels on its branch. (We discuss this property formally below.) Transitivity is a strong constraint, akin to one of the core axioms of rational choice. It says that if someone believes that a mental representation m_2 is an instance of another m_1 and also that m_3 is an instance of m_2, then she necessarily believes that m_3 is an instance of m_1. This might turn out not to hold in some cases. Indeed, if the relations are probabilistic, then this would not be surprising. Hampton (1982) found, for instance, that his subjects generally think that chairs are furniture and that car seats are chairs. But almost none of them thinks that car seats are furniture. Overall, while the transitivity might be satisfied for some concepts, we do not wish to stipulate that this is generally the case.

We take these two doubts seriously. To sidestep these issues, we limit our analysis of categorization and valuation in subsequent chapters to incorporating only localized sets of concepts at the "same level." This restriction has been used informally in previous sociological research (e.g., Hsu et al. (2009).) Now we want to develop more formally what it means for a person to have a set of concepts at the "same level." Doing so requires that we develop a space within which to compare concepts and then characterize the local structures formed by concept relations. We begin with the space.

5.1   Conceptual Space

In the previous chapters, we used the term "semantic space" to refer to a feature space in which the meaning of the concept is represented. Now we consider sets of concepts together. By our construction each concept comes with its own semantic space. We want to build an imagery of the set of concepts taken together in a space. To keep the distinction clear, we refer to the latter type of space as a *conceptual space*.

A main goal of this chapter is to begin building a formal model of conceptual spaces that allows us to make appropriate localizations of sets of concepts. We start by introducing a terminology that isolates related sets of concepts in the structure so that we can represent localized cognitions.

In line with our overall approach and as a sharp departure from existing accounts, we propose that judgments about subconcept relations are *subjective and graded*. Indeed, all of our examples of Roschean typicality structures pertain to concepts and subconcepts, not just objects and concepts. The notion that apple is a typical fruit and that olive is an atypical one states that those giving these judgments regard the subconcept relation as stronger, more certain, in one case than in another. If asked whether an olive is a fruit, a respondent might answer "yes" on some occasions and "no" on others. Therefore, we cast the subconcept relation as a judgment that is inherently probabilistic. In this chapter we focus on the relation and its consequences.

An important reason for articulating the relations among concepts for sociological analysis is that relatedness has implications for inference. For example, on encountering an unfamiliar type of food dish that is said to be a form of Thai food, the person likely infers that it has a certain set of features, such as the use of particular ingredients and styles of preparation. This is because concepts likely inherit some minimal set of properties associated with a concept that sits directly above. This idea plays an important role in our effort to define the informativeness of concepts in chapter 7.

5.2   The IS-A Judgment

Membership judgments serve as the foundational building block that links one concept to others. For example, a person might judge that orange and pineapple are types of fruit and that physician and lawyer are types of professional worker. All of the approaches to modeling concepts (including relationships between concepts) address this relation in one way or another. However, the role of the relation is left largely implicit. The lack of explicit treatment hampers efforts to address the full range of tasks we undertake.

We can build models that represent this kind of relationship more generally using one simple notion: the *instance-of relation*. In a cognitive context, this relation tells whether a focal person believes that one mental representation (of a person, situation, or even concept) is or is not an instance of a concept. We emphasize that the relation is a judgment because we want to accommodate the possibility that a person might judge that such a relation holds at one particular time and place but not at another, as we mentioned earlier. In other words, the *instance-of relation* can be thought of as the realization of an underlying probabilistic process by which a person relates mental representations to one another. In this chapter, we temporarily set aside complicated considerations involving the probabilistic nature of relations between concepts in the interest of being able to first introduce the general structure of relations. We bring probabilities back into the picture in the next chapter.

We introduce a predicate that expresses belief in the instance-of relation for any pair of mental representations (which in our analyses is either a position in a semantic space, a concrete object, or a concept). This predicate has the formal representation IS-A(m, m'), with the intended reading "the focal person believes that the mental representation m' is an instance of the mental representation m."[1] The representations can be of object–concept pairs (as in chapters 8 and 9 on categorization) or concept–concept pairs (as in this and the next chapter).

In formal treatments of issues under discussion, many analysts find it natural to assume that the subconcept relation satisfies the properties of a preordering, for example, Piazzai (2018). These properties are as follows:

1. reflexivity: IS-A(m, m) is a property regularly assumed for mathematical convenience;
2. antisymmetry: IS-A(m, m') $\wedge$ IS-A(m', m) $\to$ $m = m'$; and
3. transitivity: $\forall m, m', m''$[IS-A(m, m') $\wedge$ IS-A(m', m'') $\to$ IS-A(m, m'')].

This approach is attractive because it yields an algebraic structure with interesting properties and implications (Piazzai, 2018). In the simplest case, the algebraic structure is a tree. In a tree, each concept sits on only one branch (as we noted above).

But does this picture provide a cognitively sound view? Reflexivity and antisymmetry are non-problematic in our view. Antisymmetry is a sensible constraint on the IS-A relation. Reflexivity does not cause a problem in the sense that people would not have any trouble agreeing that, say, a cow is a cow. On the other hand, it does not appear to be a natural constraint. The problem arises with transitivity. We doubt that the transitivity property *generally* holds for mental representations, as we explained above.

One reason for exploring the structures of subconcepts is to build representations of the intuition that people can reason about concepts using the information stored in sets of subconcept relations. The power of the subconcept relation for inference comes from what psychologists call *property inheritance*, properties of concepts are properties of their subconcepts too. Such inheritance depends on the IS-A relation's satisfying transitivity. Given our doubts that transitivity holds generally, we do not try to exploit arguments based on global characterizations of entire conceptual inventories (based on preorders). Instead we concentrate on localized sets of concepts, which we call domains. We turn now to defining such local structure.

5.3   Local Structure: Roots and Domains

We want to consider localized sets of concepts among a person's concepts. Given that we have fixed the mental representations of interest to be concepts, we will refer to the IS-A relation as a *subconcept relation*.

Because ranging in cognition over a large number of concepts likely exceeds human cognitive capacities, people naturally "chunk" concepts into related bundles. We can identify each bundle with a *root* in a person's conceptual inventory, which we denote as L. In informal terms, a root sits at the "highest" level among the set of nodes that constitute the bundle.

Definition 5.1 (Root) *A concept r is a root in a subset Λ of conceptual inventory L, in notation* ROOT(r, Λ), *if and only if the concept satisfies two conditions:*

1. *There is at least one concept in Λ, say c, such that $c \neq r$ but c is a subconcept of r, and*
2. *r is not a subconcept of any other concept in Λ.*

Considering only a root and its subconcepts will yield only two-level hierarchies. However, we know that many subjective hierarchies are deeper than that. This affects our decision about how to localize sets of concepts that sit at the same level. For instance, suppose we consider the domain whose root is profession and its subconcepts. A person might believe that medicine, internal medicine, and law (among others) are professions. Now if take simply the satisfaction of the subconcept relation as the set of concepts that sit below profession, then we are mixing levels because the agent likely believes that internal medicine is a subconcept of medicine. To get the sets of comparable subconcepts right we need a way to distinguish first-level subconcepts and lower-level ones.

So we introduce a terminology that allows separation of the first-level subconcepts from the subconcepts of subconcepts within a domain. Informally we will call a concept a *first-level* subconcept of another concept if no other concept "sits between them."

Definition 5.2 (First-level subconcept relation) *One concept c' is a first-level subconcept of another c for an individual at a moment in time if she judges* *that c' is a subconcept of c and the subconcept relation between them is first level in the sense that the individual does not judge that some other concept c'' is subconcept of c and that c' is a subconcept of c''.*

FIRST-LEVEL SUBCONCEPT(c, c') *is true for an individual at a moment in time if and only if*

1. *c' and c are different concepts;*
2. *c' is judged to be a subconcept of c; and*
3. *there is no other subconcept of c of which c' is a subconcept at that time.*

The formal construction does not rule out that a concept is tied from above by two or more branches (roots). Indeed we think of hybrids as concepts that are subconcepts of different roots. Table 5.1 provides an illustration of a possible set of judgments about the IS-A(c, c') relation for a set of eight concepts ($\Lambda = \{c_1, c_2, ..., c_8\}$). Referring to the example above, such a table records a person's answers at a given point and time to a series of questions such as "is medicine a profession?" and "is internal medicine a profession?". (We allow that the person's answers to such questions might vary over time, in accordance with the idea of probabilistic relations between concepts, but here we focus on a single set of responses in order to represent the structure of relations between concepts at that particular time.) The concepts listed on the rows are the concepts (c) in this relation, and the concepts in the columns are the subconcepts in the relation (c'). An entry of one in a cell in the table indicates that the focal person judges that the subconcept relation holds between the concept in the column of the table and the concept in the row. An entry of zero indicates that she does not.

TABLE 5.1
Example of a set of judgments about the IS-A (subconcept) relation for a collection of concepts: see the text for an explanation.

	IS-A(row,col)							
	c_1	c_2	c_3	c_4	c_5	c_6	c_7	c_8
c_1	1	1	1	1	0	0	0	0
c_2	0	1	0	1	0	0	0	0
c_3	0	0	1	1	0	0	0	0
c_4	0	0	0	1	0	0	0	0
c_5	0	0	0	0	1	1	1	0
c_6	0	0	0	0	0	1	1	0
c_7	0	0	0	0	0	0	1	0
c_8	0	0	0	0	0	0	0	1

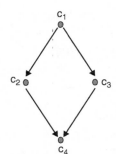

Figure 5.1 Graphical display of one domain ($\mathfrak{D}_1$) derived from table 5.1

Notice that c_1 and c_5 are roots in Λ: each has subconcepts but is not itself a subconcept of another. And c_8 has no connection with the other concepts; it is an isolated concept. So the conceptual space can be characterized as being occupied by two structures that are not degenerate.

It is perhaps easier to see the pattern if we represent one substructure in the table in terms of a directed graph as in figure 5.1. We have structured this graph to represent the first-level subconcept relations. Notice that c_4 is a subconcept of c_1. However, c_4 is not a first-order subconcept of c_1 because c_2 and c_3 sit between c_1 and c_4.

Note that while we have used solid lines here to represent a person's judgment of the relationship between these concepts at a given time and place, the issue is actually more complicated for two reasons. First, we are used to thinking of the nodes in graphs as concrete objects; here they are mental representations (which take the form of probability densities). Second, because judgments about relationships between concepts are probabilistic in nature, the directed graph would vary over time and place for a given person. We will turn to that issue in the next chapters.

Each root can be considered as a maximal concept in a subset of a person's full set of concepts. That is, each root carves out bundle, a separate domain in the full conceptual space.

Definition 5.3 (Domain) *A domain consists of a root in a conceptual inventory and all of its subconcepts.*

$\mathfrak{D}_r = \mathbf{c}$ *if and only if*

1. $\forall c [(c \in \mathbf{c}) \rightarrow \text{IS-A}(r, c)]$*; and*
2. $\forall c, \mathbf{c}' [[(c \in \mathbf{c}') \rightarrow \text{IS-A}(r, c)] \rightarrow \mathbf{c}' \subseteq \mathbf{c}]$*.*

Because we do not impose transitivity, this definition limits a domain to the subconcepts of a root, those for which the focal person judges the subconcept relation to the root to be true. Notice that we index a domain by its root. The root plays a special role in specifying the domain because it determines the minimal set of features over which the concepts in the domain can be compared. This is because the subconcept relation requires that subconcepts satisfy the IS-A relation with the higher-level concept.

Consider an example. Suppose we have the concept film and subconcepts of film including drama, comedy, adventure, and romance, as well as sub-concepts of comedy such as slapstick, black comedy, romantic comedy, and parody. Then film is a domain for this set, and the domain consists of the root and all of its subconcepts and sub-subconcepts. In this example, the domain of film contains drama, comedy, adventure, romance, slapstick, black comedy, romantic-comedy, parody, and so forth.

And, as we indicated in the preceding paragraph, the specification of each genre includes values of features of the root of the domain: film. So, for example, when a person is told about an unfamiliar type of film, he or she would be very likely to infer from the film designation that the genre conforms to certain features, such as a series of moving images displayed on a screen.

Presuppositions Entailed by the Structure of a Conceptual Space

Linguists use the term "presupposition" to refer to implicit assumptions about the world (background knowledge) entailed by a statement as well as its negation. For instance, both "it has stopped raining" and "it has not stopped raining" imply that it had been raining previously. The structure of a conceptual space warrants a strong set of presuppositional inferences. Treating as true that IS-A(c, c') carries the presupposition that the things that are true of a c will also be true of a c'.

This understanding of this presuppositional structure is generally coded in linguistic usage. Speakers seldom mention a superconcept when they refer to a concept. Consider some examples that run against this tendency: hammer tool, ballet dance, chemistry science, chardonnay wine. All sound awkward, presumably because adding the superconcept states the obvious.[2]

Considerable knowledge gets stored as background knowledge, coded in the structure of domains. Knowledge that a concept lies in a domain tells that some features play a role in its meaning. All of the features that figure in a schema for a concept are inherited by the schemas of all of its subconcepts. In other words, a domain constrains the relevance of features. Schemas need not be constructed *ab initio*; the structure of a domain supplies a basic set of ingredients. What needs to be specified at lower levels in a domain are only those features or constraints that distinguish a concept from the higher-level concepts in that domain.

5.4　Cohorts of Concepts

The set of concepts at the same level in a domain plays an important role in our analysis. We will argue in subsequent chapters that the context orients one's focus to such sets when categorizing and interpreting object representations.[3]

Because we will refer to sets of concepts at the same level in a domain repeatedly, we introduce an explicit terminology, using the term "cohort" in its taxonomic sense. We introduce the function *cohort*(r, Λ) that maps from a root (r) of a conceptual inventory (Λ) to a set of concepts, the cohort of that root.

Definition 5.4 (Cohort of concepts) *The cohort of concepts associated with a root consists of the set of all of its first-level subconcepts.*

cohort$(r, \Lambda) = \kappa$ *if and only if*

1. $\kappa \subset \mathfrak{D}_r$, *and*
2. κ *consists of all of the first-level subconcepts of* r.

To illustrate the construction of cohorts, we return to figure 5.1. The domain $\mathfrak{D}_{c_1}$ has the cohort $\kappa_{c_1} = \{c_2, c_3\}$. Of course, the first-level subconcepts in this domain are roots in more restricted domains. There we have $\kappa_{c_2} = \{c_4\}$ and $\kappa_{c_3} = \{c_4\}$.

5.5　Inheritance of Feature-Dimension Relevance

At every step in building our framework we have seen that context shapes cognition and judgment. One way it does so is by focusing attention on a domain and a particular cohort of concepts. This narrowing shapes the comparisons made and the alternatives considered. It also makes relevant certain background knowledge. The structure of a conceptual space plays a role in inference due to property inheritance. As we see it, inheritance of feature values can entail two types of transfers from a concept to a subconcept. First, we propose that subconcepts inherit the set of features that is relevant for defining their semantic spaces. Second, subconcepts will also tend to take on the feature values of the root. In our probabilistic treatment, it is important to emphasize that feature-value inheritance entails only a *tendency* toward taking on feature values rather than certain inheritance. The extent of inheritance of feature values relates to the typicality of a concept with respect to the root concept. Highly typical subconcepts tend to share many feature values with the root, whereas atypical subconcepts share fewer.

Consider the example of medical doctor and various subconcepts, such as family practitioner, surgeon, psychiatrist, radiologist, and pathologist. For most people, the concept medical doctor might bring to mind a person who has completed a medical degree and who interacts with patients to diagnose and treat illnesses of the body. These attributes (completion of a medical degree, interaction with patients, diagnosis and treatment of bodily illness) can be thought of as the relevant features that subconcepts would inherit. However, inheritance of particular *values* of these features is probabilistic, with subconcepts sharing many but perhaps not all feature values. In other words, some subconcepts can lie away from the root concept in its semantic space. For example, pathologists are medical doctors who specialize in examining lab samples of body tissues for diagnostic or forensic purposes, and sometimes their work occurs postmortem. They inherit from medical doctors some feature values, such as a level of medical education, but they differ from the root concept in that they do not treat living patients.

We now treat the first of the two aspects of inheritance—the inheritance of relevance of features. We deal with the second aspect, the inheritance of the likely positions on these features, in chapter 7.

To believe that entity is an instance of a subconcept requires the belief with some level of certainty that this entity is an instance of the root concept, and also satisfies some specific further conditions that was not required by the root concept. Satisfying the conditions that define the root requires that the feature dimension that are relevant for thinking about the root are also relevant for thinking about its first-level subconcepts. In other words, the features (dimensions)—and possibly, but not necessarily, the values of the features—that define a semantic space for a concept are inherited by the semantic spaces of any of its subconcepts. Suppose we denote the semantic space for a root concept as $\mathbb{F}_r$ and that of one its first-level subconcepts as $\mathbb{F}_c$. Then we argue as follows:

Postulate 5.1 *The semantic space over which a subconcept is defined includes the features that define the semantic space of the root concept. Specifically if a feature f is a dimension of the root concept of the semantic space, $\mathbb{F}_r$, then it is also a dimension of the subconcept semantic space, $\mathbb{F}_c$.*

Consider the concept of professional (worker) and two of its (likely) subconcepts, medical doctor and lawyer. The dimensions that define the concept of professional worker (such as levels of formal education, codification of knowledge, standards of practice, and degree of self-regulation by professional associations) also serve as defining dimensions for these subconcepts. Each subconcept further contains dimensions that are not likely to be salient for the broader concept of professional. In the case of medical doctor, for example, specialization in a branch of medical practice and clinical training (such as through a residency program) are defining dimensions.

An interesting issue is whether people generally use larger semantic spaces (those containing features not used in the semantic space of the concept) when judging the subconcept relation. Abundant evidence shows that people use both strategies.

In one case, subconcepts are probability distributions at some remove in the space over which the concept likelihood of the concept is defined. The extensive body of research on color perception and conceptualization provides an example *par excellence* (Gärdenfors, 2004). No new features are needed to get from red to pink or scarlet. In the social world, concepts that have a size dimension (e.g., shop with likely subconcepts boutique, supermarket, hypermarket) or a frequency dimension (e.g., newspaper with subconcepts daily and weekly) have broader ranges for their size or frequency dimensions than their respective subconcepts.

In the second case, each subconcept has added features. Consider, for example, the concept tool which is generally defined as "a device or implement, especially one held in the hand, used to carry out a particular function." If a person has something like this in mind, she uses her semantic space for "device" and adds the condition "usually hand held," and leaves open the function slot in the schema. Subconcepts such as awl, hammer, and shovel fill in the function. But they also bring other features into the picture. For instance, a hammer has properties that support its general use to break things or drive nails: "a heavy metal head at a right angle at the end of a handle." It is hard to imagine someone including all of this information in the semantic space for tool. The first case is easily dealt with because little attention needs be paid to the space. However, we think that concepts used in social life generally have the form of the second case. The second case creates analytical problems, which have not yet been addressed in the literature on concepts. We will turn to these issues in the next chapter.

5.6   Stored Hierarchy versus Feature Comparisons

At the beginning of the chapter, we sketched a debate about whether conceptual hierarchies are stored in semantic memory. The standard way to evaluate the claim uses a particular relationship between distance in the hierarchy and response time (RT) for evaluating statements that involve inference over a hierarchy. One way to do this is to teach subjects a hierarchy of concepts and sets of feature values that exemplify prototypes at the different levels. It is easier to describe the alternative that uses hierarchies of concepts that subjects presumably already have learned. In this case, the researcher asks experimental subjects to consider a lower-order concept and a higher-order one in the same branch (e.g., house mouse and mammal) and notes the graph distance between them. Do this again for another pair with smaller distance, say rodent and mammal. Then tell the subjects that some fact that is true for all mammals, such as "has a four-chambered heart." Finally, calculate RT of subjects to evaluate the truth of statements such as "a house mouse has a four-chambered heart" and "a rodent has a four-chambered heart."

The standard interpretation of inference using a hierarchy stored directly in semantic memory is that a person must traverse. So in making the inference that the property that is true of all mammals is true of house mice, the mind has to move one or more extra steps as compared with making the inference for rodents. If each step involves some cognitive effort, then it will on average take longer to evaluate the "longer-distance" inference.[4] Evidence in favor of a positive relationship between distance and RT is mixed at best. For instance, Murphy et al. (2012b) did not find such a relationship in three of four studies. Instead they found evidence consistent with the interpretation that the experimental subjects made inferences based on similarity of feature values. In terms of our example, one would conclude that the similarity of the features of house mouse and those of mammal is as high as for the closer comparison. In other words, if the hierarchy is only implicit and people make similarity judgments prior to making inferences, then similarity can override distance, as long as the similarities do not decline too sharply with distance.

In our view, the semantic space is free-floating in both of these lines of research. The opposition between the two interpretations seems to vanish if people are making the judgments in a single conceptual space. Then the inheritance of feature relevance changes the picture. One does not have to move to high levels to make hierarchical inferences because the relevant features are replicated down the chains. Suppose for simplicity that the concept c_1 at highest level in the branch of a tree has a very high likelihood for possessing the property (a value of a binary feature) A; that its first-level descendant c_2 adds a high likelihood for the property B and therefore has high likelihoods for the properties $\{A, B\}$; and that a still-lower level concept c_3 adds high likelihood for the property C, which means that it has high likelihood for the properties $\{A, B, C\}$. Now suppose that (for some reason) we have not been able to observe for instances of c_3 whether or not they possess the property A. How do we make the inference that they do? The distance hypothesis says that we have to work up to the level of c_1. But clearly this is not generally the case. We could have observed all of the properties of (prototypical) instances of c_2 and learned that they possess A (as is highly likely in this example). The inference can stop there; there is no need to go higher.

Discussion

This chapter developed the notion of conceptual spaces, which will figure prominently in sociological applications. These spaces are algebraic structures populated by concepts and structured by the IS-A relation (short for "is an instance of") without any reference to feature values, positions in the semantic space.

This notion allows for some reflection on the age-old issue of hierarchical classification systems. The history of these systems goes back to Aristotle's *Organon* where substantive definitions are offered in terms of *genos* and *diaphora*. Throughout the centuries-long history of scholastic thought, the prescription for the appropriate definition evolved into one given in terms of the *genus proximum* and the *differentia specifica*. This prescription requires not only a family (*genus*) but also a notion of distance by the term *proximum*. The assumption of the existence of the closest family led to the often implicit image that the classification schemata are trees.

Unfortunately, we cannot rely on the simple tree structure for thinking about conceptual spaces. The common presence of hybrid concepts, such as romantic comedy and brewpub, undermines the relevance of tree structures. Whenever such hybrids are in the picture, the structure of the conceptual space cannot be a tree.

It still might be the case that the space, while not a tree, has a simple algebraic form: a lattice. As we discussed, a lattice depends on the IS-A relation satisfying the properties of a partial order. We see no difficulty with accepting two properties: reflexivity and asymmetry. It is the third property—transitivity—that causes doubts. We read the psychological research as providing strong counterexamples to transitivity. And we think that such violations are likely common outside the laboratory. For instance, many scholars accept that IS-A(social science, cultural anthropology) and IS-A(science, social science). Yet, many cultural anthropologists now disavow the claim that IS-A(science, cultural anthropology).

Nonetheless sociological application of concepts requires some local structure, parts of the space that constitute trees. We think that previous empirical research on concepts in markets has implicitly relied on such local structure. We identify this structure as a root and a cohorts of its first-level subconcepts. Cohorts will play an important role in the analyses presented in the chapters that follow.

CHAPTER SIX

Expanding Spaces to Compare Concepts

THIS CHAPTER TAKES UP an important issue that we believe has not been explored in research on concepts. Comparing concepts by, say, measuring their similarity or the distance between them requires that they be represented in a common space. But different concepts can come with different semantic spaces, as we discussed in chapter 5. How then do we make this comparison?

6.1 Uniform Expansion of a Probability Function

In general, we want to contrast two subjective probability distributions. For instance, the next chapter compares a concept with its parent (the root of the domain). This involves comparing a concept likelihood, $\pi_{\mathbb{F}_c}(\cdot \mid c)$, which reveals the likely locations of things that are cs, with the likelihood given by the background knowledge of the domain.

Here we run into a problem: the two subjective probabilities refer to different spaces, $\mathbb{F}_r$ and $\mathbb{F}_c$, respectively. To make the problem tractable, we must express the probabilities in a common space. One possibility would be to reduce $\mathbb{F}_c$ to $\mathbb{F}_r$. But this would not help because it loses important information. So we must go in the other direction, representing the background knowledge distribution in the semantic space of the concept. We now sketch a simple way of doing so that is consistent with Bayesian reasoning.

The same problem arises when we seek to measure the distance between two concepts. For such measurement to make sense, the concepts must be represented in a common semantic space.

To develop an intuition about the nature of an appropriate expansion, consider a simple example: the concept of an athlete. This concept is the root of domain $\mathfrak{D}_{\text{athlete}}$. The cohort of concepts in this domain includes various types of athletes such as swimmer, runner, jumper, and cyclist. Here we focus on the root concept, athlete; one of its subconcepts, swimmer; and how they relate to each other.

First, we define the meaning of athlete. For simplicity, we assume that this concept is defined along just one binary feature dimension: *practices sports daily* (denoted by x). This feature can take two values: yes (denoted by 1) and no (denoted by 0). The feature space for athlete is thus a one-dimensional space, $\mathbb{F}_{\text{athlete}} = \{0, 1\}$.

Suppose that the concept likelihood tells us that most but not all athletes practice sports daily. More precisely, suppose that the likelihood that an athlete practices sports daily ($x = 1$) is 0.8. The likelihood that an athlete does not practice ($x = 0$) is 0.2:

$$[\![\text{athlete}]\!] = \pi_{\mathbb{F}_{\text{athlete}}}(x \,|\, \text{athlete}) = \begin{cases} 0.8 \text{ for } x = 1 \\ 0.2 \text{ for } x = 0. \end{cases} \tag{6.1}$$

Now take the concept of swimmer. This label points to a subconcept of athlete—swimmers are indeed athletes. We argued earlier that subconcepts generally have at least one feature dimension that is not entailed in the meaning of the higher level concept. Suppose in the case of this example that this additional feature is a binary feature dimension: *trains in an aquatic center*. It can take two values: yes (denoted by 1) and no (denoted by 0). The feature space for swimmer is thus two-dimensional: $\mathbb{F}_{\text{swimmer}} = \{0, 1\} \times \{0, 1\}$. We will write positions of objects in this space as $x = \langle x_1, x_2 \rangle$, with the first element, x_1, to be understood as the value of the first feature (*practices sports daily*) and the second element, x_2, to be understood as the value of the second feature (*trains in an aquatic center*). Note that the feature space of the root is contained *within* the feature space of the subconcept: $\mathbb{F}_{\text{athlete}} \subseteq \mathbb{F}_{\text{swimmer}}$.

Suppose that the concept likelihood of swimmer tells us that most but not all swimmers practice some sports daily and that most of them, but not all, train in an aquatic center (some train in clear water, lakes, or rivers). More precisely,

$$[\![\text{swimmer}]\!] = \pi_{\mathbb{F}_{\text{swimmer}}}(x \,|\, \text{swimmer}) = \begin{cases} 0.7 \text{ for } x = \langle 1, 1 \rangle \\ 0.2 \text{ for } x = \langle 1, 0 \rangle \\ 0.05 \text{ for } x = \langle 0, 1 \rangle \\ 0.05 \text{ for } x = \langle 0, 0 \rangle. \end{cases} \tag{6.2}$$

This likelihood function states that a swimmer has a likelihood of 0.7 to both train daily and train in an aquatic center, and so on.

Now we want to compare these two concepts. How can we do it? There is an obvious problem in that the semantic space of the root concept athlete is one-dimensional, whereas that of the subconcept swimmer is two-dimensional in our example. We have to represent the two concepts in a common space to allow formal comparison, as we noted earlier. We propose comparing the two concepts in the larger space, the semantic space of the subconcept $\mathbb{F}_{\text{swimmer}}$. To do so, we have to "extend" the concept likelihood of the root concept to this larger space. We have to transform $\pi_{\mathbb{F}_{\text{athlete}}}(\cdot \mid \text{athlete})$, a probability-density function over a one-dimensional space, $\mathbb{F}_{\text{athlete}}$, into a probability function over a two-dimensional space, $\mathbb{F}_{\text{swimmer}}$. We denote the result of this transformation by $\pi_{\mathbb{F}_{\text{swimmer}}}(\cdot \mid \text{athlete})$. (Note the change of index from the feature space of the root concept $\mathbb{F}_{\text{athlete}}$ to the feature space of the subconcept $\mathbb{F}_{\text{swimmer}}$.)

What would the concept likelihood of the root concept athlete look like in the larger space? Because the meaning of athlete does not specify anything about the second feature's dimension (*trains in an aquatic center*), we assume what probability theorists call an uninformative prior. That is, we assume that the concept likelihood in the larger space, $\pi_{\mathbb{F}_{\text{swimmer}}}(\cdot \mid \text{athlete})$, is such that the distribution on the second feature is *uniform* at all levels of the first feature (and then, as a consequence, constant in the marginal distribution). We also assume that the concept preserves its meaning on the first feature dimension (*practices sports daily*). The marginal distribution on the first feature remains unchanged.

The unique distribution that satisfies these two constraints is the following:

$$\pi_{\mathbb{F}_{\text{swimmer}}}(\cdot \mid \text{athlete}) = \begin{cases} 0.4 \text{ for } x = \langle 1,1 \rangle \\ 0.4 \text{ for } x = \langle 1,0 \rangle \\ 0.1 \text{ for } x = \langle 0,1 \rangle \\ 0.1 \text{ for } x = \langle 0,0 \rangle. \end{cases} \qquad (6.3)$$

This concept likelihood states that 40% of the athletes practice some sports daily and train in an aquatic center; another 40% practice some sports daily and do not train in an aquatic center; and so on.

Building on this example, we introduce what we call a uniform expansion of a concept likelihood to a space larger than the semantic space of the concept. Just as in the example, we start from the concept likelihood of the focal concept $\pi_{\mathbb{F}_c}(\cdot \mid c)$, defined over $\mathbb{F}_c$. Then we consider a broader space, $\mathbb{G}$, such that $\mathbb{F}_c \subseteq \mathbb{G}$. We transform the original concept likelihood into a concept likelihood defined over $\mathbb{G}$: $\pi_{\mathbb{G}}(\cdot \mid c)$. This transformation is not arbitrary:

- It preserves the marginal distribution over the feature dimensions of the larger semantic $\mathbb{G}$ that are also in the original semantic space $\mathbb{F}_c$.
- The distribution over the feature dimensions that are in $\mathbb{G}$ but not in $\mathbb{F}_c$ is uniform at all levels of the "added" variables.

These two choices align with our intent not to alter the meaning of the concept when we represent it on the larger space $\mathbb{G}$.

We introduce a predicate to make clear what we mean by a uniform expansion for use in later chapters. Because we will use this kind of uniform expansion not only for concept likelihoods but also for other probability-density functions, the predicate is defined in terms of generic spaces and probability-density functions.

Definition 6.1 (Uniform expansion of a probability distribution over semantic spaces) *Let $P_{\mathbb{F}}$ denote a probability function over the space $\mathbb{F}$ and $P_{\mathbb{G}}$ denote a probability function over the space $\mathbb{G}$. We call $P_{\mathbb{G}}$ a uniform expansion of $P_{\mathbb{F}}$ to $\mathbb{G}$, in notation $P_{\mathbb{G}} = uni(P_{\mathbb{F}}, \mathbb{G})$, if and only if*

> $\mathbb{F} \subseteq \mathbb{G}$, *and the distribution of $P_{\mathbb{G}}$ is uniform over the values of the features in $\mathbb{G}$ not contained in $\mathbb{F}$.*

To illustrate how the uniform expansion of the PDF looks, let us focus on a simple scenario, one in which we start with a one-dimensional case. Suppose the only random variable whose distribution is considered is X. Suppose furthermore that X can have eight different values $x_1, x_2, ..., x_8$. These values appear with an illustrative concept likelihood (the subjective probabilities) in table 6.1.

TABLE 6.1

An illustrative concept likelihood in a one-dimensional semantic space

	Concept likelihood							
	x_1	x_2	x_3	x_4	x_5	x_6	x_7	x_8
$P_x(X)$	1/8	1/8	0	2/8	3/8	0	0	1/8

TABLE 6.2
Uniform expansion of the concept likelihood (in figure 6.1) to two dimensions

	Uniform expansion of the concept likelihood								
	x_1	x_2	x_3	x_4	x_5	x_6	x_7	x_8	$P_y(Y)$
y_1	1/16	1/16	0	2/16	3/16	0	0	1/16	1/8
y_2	1/16	1/16	0	2/16	3/16	0	0	1/16	1/8
$P_x(X)$	1/8	1/8	0	2/8	3/8	0	0	1/8	8/8

Now we add a second dimension, Y, which takes on the values y_1 and y_2, and we want to expand the concept likelihood over the two-dimensional (X, Y) space. Table 6.2 illustrates the uniform expansion.

6.2   Distance Between Concepts

Our measures of informativeness and distinctiveness depend on distances between pairs of concepts. If concepts are represented as probability distributions, then a measure of distance must apply to distances between probability distributions.

Notation We denote the directed distance from one concept to another with a "vector arrow" atop the distance, for example $\vec{D}(c_1, c_2)$.

We begin with the Kullback-Leibler divergence. Then we use this directed distance to build a symmetric distance between concepts. Let P_1 and P_2 denote two discrete probability measures defined over a common space, $\mathbb{G}$. The Kullback-Leibler (KL) divergence of P_1 from P_2 is

$$D_{KL}(P_1 \parallel P_2) \equiv \sum_{x \in \mathbb{G}} P_1(x) \ln \frac{P_1(x)}{P_2(x)}.$$

We define the distance from one concept to another as the KL divergence (expressed in terms of concept likelihoods).

Definition 6.2 (Distance from one concept to another) *The directed distance from the one concept, c_1, to another, c_2, is*

$$\vec{D}(c_1, c_2) \equiv D_{KL}(c_1 \| c_2) = \sum_{x \in \mathbb{G}} \pi_{\mathbb{G}}(x \mid c_1) \ln \frac{\pi_{\mathbb{G}}(x \mid c_1)}{\pi_{\mathbb{G}}(x \mid c_2)}, \qquad (6.4)$$

where $\mathbb{G} = \mathbb{F}_{c_1} \cup \mathbb{F}_{c_2}$ and the concept likelihoods are distributed over this expanded space in the non-informative (uniform) way we have sketched above.

This measure does not satisfy the metric properties of symmetry and the triangle inequality. This does not cause any difficulty when the direction of comparison is given by the analytic purpose, as in the case of computing the informativeness and distinctiveness of a concept.

CHAPTER SEVEN

Informativeness and Distinctiveness

CONCEPTS EMBODY MEANINGS; in doing so, they encapsulate and convey information. In this chapter, we develop the notions of concept *informativeness* and *distinctiveness* to capture variation in the amount of information that concepts convey. Consistent with our strategy of representing concepts as existing within multi-concept domains, we argue that the amount of information a concept conveys should be thought of as relative to a domain. We identify and define two aspects that differentiate a concept from a domain. The first, which we call informativeness, tells how much information a concept adds to what is already presumed or known by virtue of its domain. The second, which we call distinctiveness, tells how much the information in a concept differs from that conveyed by the other concepts in its cohort of concepts, the other concepts in its domain.

Previous research on the issues we treat did not specify what was meant by the "conceptual background." We can sharpen the old arguments by using the structure of conceptual space to define more precisely what this means and in turn capture more precisely how much information gets activated when a concept is used.

The approach we now put forth specifies how much a concept stands out from the background in terms of the amount of distinctive information conveyed by the signal that an object (represented as a position in conceptual space) is an instance of a concept. In this case, the signal is the application of the concept label. When a concept stands out sharply from the background, categorization by one person is highly informative for those who accept her categorization, in the sense of offering a great deal of novel information about the object's properties and expected performance, compared to what the person would infer from background knowledge. In contrast, concepts that do not stand out much from the background provide little information relative to what was previously known.

One way of thinking of a concept's informativeness links it to atypicality. Informative concepts are atypical in that they diverge from what can be expected based on background knowledge provided by the domain. In our formal representation, this means that the probability distribution of an informative concept differs greatly from the probability distribution of the root concept in the domain.

We also model a second way in which concepts can embody distinct information: the degree to which a concept differs from the other concepts in its cohort. We refer to this dimension of information as distinctiveness.

7.1   Informativeness

We rely on the uniform expansion "tool" to propose a formal definition of the background conceptual knowledge.

Meaning Postulate 7.1 *The background conceptual knowledge of the domain with root r is given by $P_{\mathbb{G}}(\cdot \mid r)$, where $\mathbb{G}$ is the union of the semantic space of the cohort κ of subconcepts of r in the domain $\mathfrak{D}_r$:*

$$\mathbb{G} = \cup_{c \in \kappa} \mathbb{F}_c; \qquad\qquad (7.1)$$

and $P_{\mathbb{G}}$ is the uniform conceptual expansion of $P_{\mathbb{F}_r}$ to $\mathbb{G}$.[1]

One might ask whether $\mathbb{G}$ is the relevant semantic space for the root r. We do not think so in general. In our view, r refers to a concept in its own right (e.g., science) and has its own semantic space. This space should not depend on any additional relevant features that might be used in representing the subconcepts (e.g., astronomy, biology, chemistry, physics, and so forth).

It is crucial in the construction of meaning postulate 7.1 that $P_{\mathbb{G}}(\cdot)$ be defined over the expanded semantic space $\mathbb{G}$ for the comparison to make sense. If the concept is represented in the same space as the root (as in the example of color), then this condition is automatically satisfied. Otherwise, the space over which the conceptual background information is defined must be expanded to include any new features introduced by the concept c and the likelihood that expresses the conceptual background knowledge must be allocated over the expanded space.

In information theory, the idea of informativeness is captured by the *information gain* from switching from one distribution to another. The standard measure of such a gain is the Kullback–Leibler divergence. This formalism turns out to be very helpful for our purposes. So we adapt the standard definition of information gain to apply to the comparison of a concept and background knowledge from the domain.

Consider a function, $I_{\mathbb{G}}(c, \mathfrak{D}_r)$, that gives the informativeness of the concept c relative to background knowledge that comes from the domain $\mathfrak{D}_r$. We define the informativeness of a concept as the Kullback–Leibler divergence of the concept from the background. Because we want to define the informativeness of a concept as the information it provides relative to background knowledge, we calculate the information gain relative to the information contained in the domain's root concept.

Definition 7.1 (Informativeness) *The informativeness of the concept c in the domain $\mathfrak{D}_r$, with root r and cohort κ, is the information that it provides relative to background knowledge.*

$$I_{\mathbb{G}}(c, \mathfrak{D}_r) = \vec{D}(c, r) = D_{KL}(c \parallel r) = \sum_{x \in \mathbb{G}} \pi_{\mathbb{G}}(x \mid c) \ln \frac{\pi_{\mathbb{G}}(x \mid c)}{P_{\mathbb{G}}(x \mid r)}.$$

We can illustrate this with reference to the numerical example of the previous section. Using the values of the two likelihood functions given by equations 6.2 and 6.3, we get

$$D_{KL}(c, r) = .7 \ln \frac{.7}{.4} + .2 \ln \frac{.2}{.4} + .05 \ln \frac{.05}{.1} + .05 \ln \frac{.05}{.1} = 0.18.$$

This is the measure of the informativeness of concept c in the domain with root r.

Let us return to our example of the domain with medical doctor as a root from the previous chapter. We would expect that the divergence from the root would be greater for pathologist than for surgeon. As such, the information content in learning that a medical doctor is a pathologist is greater than learning that he is a surgeon. This is because a surgeon inherits more of the characteristics of a medical doctor than a pathologist does and because the pathologist also has some feature dimensions that are not part of the semantic space of medical doctor.

COMPUTING INFORMATIVENESS USING OBSERVATIONAL DATA: We illustrate the calculation of informativeness using archival data through the example of rap music. As in §4.5, we consider a semantic space, $\mathbb{G}_{rap3}$, made of three continuous features. Each album receives a score between 0 and 1 on each of the following three features: *swagger*, *street violence*, and *romantic love*. In this analysis, the rap styles are the concepts. In formulas, we refer to a generic style using the letter s. We include in our analysis the twenty largest styles and albums with at least ten tracks.

To measure informativeness empirically, we construct concept likelihoods on the positions over the semantic space for each style and the background conceptual knowledge (see definition 7.1). We begin with concept likelihoods.

The concept likelihood of a style is the probability that an album of a given style finds itself at a position in semantic space. To compute empirical estimates of these (and other) probabilities, we divide the space, $\mathbb{G}_{rap3}$, into discrete chunks. Each dimension in this space ranges over $[0,1]$. We divide each dimension into five chunks: $[0,0.2), [0.2,0.4), [0.4,0.6), [0.6,0.8)$, and $[0.8,1.0]$. This gives 125 positions in this three-dimensional space.

The analysis is complicated by the fact that albums are assigned more than one style. To deal with this complication in applying the theory to data, we use the album-style pair as the basic count unit. With this assumption, we define the following counts:

- N: total number of album-style pairs.
- N_x: number of album-style pairs at position x (note that albums assigned to multiple styles are contributing as many times as the number of styles assigned to them).
- N_s: number of album-style pairs that have s as a style.
- N_{xs}: number of album-style pairs at position x that have s as a style.

The concept likelihood of a style s at position x is the probability that an album of style s finds itself at x. We estimate it with the following ratio:

$$\widehat{\pi}_{\mathbb{G}_{rap3}}(x \mid s) = \frac{N_{xs}}{N_s}. \tag{7.2}$$

The background conceptual knowledge (denoted $P_{\mathbb{G}}(x \mid r)$ in definition 7.1) is the probability that an album whose style is unknown finds itself at position x. We estimate it with the following ratio:

$$\widehat{P}_{\mathbb{G}_{rap3}}(x) = \frac{N_x}{N}. \tag{7.3}$$

With $\widehat{P}_{\mathbb{G}_{rap3}}(x \mid s)$ and $\widehat{P}_{\mathbb{G}_{rap3}}(x)$ computed, it is straightforward to calculate style informativeness using definition 7.1. Table 7.1 lists informativeness for the twelve largest styles. Political rap is the most informative style, which is consistent with its albums being the lowest on the *swagger* feature, a characteristic feature of most styles in this genre. Hardcore rap, to which almost a third of the albums are assigned, is unsurprisingly an uninformative style.

TABLE 7.1
Informativeness of the twelve largest styles
in rap music

Style	Informativeness	No. tracks
Alternative rap	.52	2743
Dirty south	.67	2496
East Coast rap	.20	6729
G-Funk	.45	924
Gangsta rap	.23	5819
Golden age	.70	1194
Hardcore rap	.08	9863
Political rap	.86	750
Pop-rap	.37	1858
Southern rap	.40	3358
Underground rap	.31	3254
West Coast rap	.14	3106

7.2   Informativeness and Belief about Property Inheritance

With the notion of informativeness of a concept in a domain, we can return to the issue of typicality of a concept and inheritance of feature values from the root. The three key insights are that concepts differ in their typicalities as instances of the root of the domain; that inheritance from the root grows stronger with concept typicality; and that concept typicality declines with informativeness.

We will consider two cases, which we will call *refinement* and *divergence*. Refinement means that the concept is close to the root but adds some additional features. An example might be microbrewery, a subconcept of brewery. It matches brewery on most of its features but can be distinguished by its small size and use of artisanal production.

Divergence means the concept is far from the root on the feature values that distinguish the root. For example, penguin and ostrich lack the bird value "flies" on the feature *mode of movement*. We propose that feature inheritance is strong for refinements and weak for divergences.

Although it has not generally been described as such, the bulk of the empirical work on typicality measures the typicality of subconcepts as instances of a concept—or to stick to the language we use in the formal definitions, typicality of a concept as an instance of the root of its domain. Recall that Rosch began this research tradition by asking subjects to rate the typicality of apples, watermelons, olives and so forth as fruit and the typicality of tables, chairs, mirrors, rugs and so forth as furniture. We want to distinguish this kind of typicality from the typicality of object representations, discussed in the previous chapter.

One way to think about atypicality is in terms of distance defined within the semantic space of root of the domain in parallel to the typicality of a position as instance of a concept. Postulate 5.1 imposes the natural constraint that concepts inherit feature dimensions of the root. This means that the distance between a concept and the root can be evaluated in the expanded semantic space. This approach accords well with the notation that subconcepts differ on features that define the root of the domain. For instance, penguins are atypical birds because they differ on a key defining feature of birds, that they fly.

Instead, we use informativeness to propose an alternative way of thinking about the atypicality of a concept with respect to the root of the domain. A concept that is very typical of its root yields similar expectations, but an atypical subconcept yields different ones. So it is a natural expansion of the information approach to define atypicality within a domain $\mathfrak{D}_r$ in terms of how much information is gained from knowing that an object is an instance of a concept as compared to knowing it is an instance of the root concept, r. Knowing that a fruit is a pomegranate yields more information than knowing that it is an orange. So pomegranate is the more atypical—more informative—of the two (sub)concepts. Consider a pair of scenarios that differ in the concept mentioned:

- Peter was asked to bring fruit to the picnic. When Mary saw that he had brought a basket of apples, she remarked "Good."
- Peter was asked to bring fruit to the picnic. When Mary saw that he had brought a basket of pomegranates, she remarked "What?"

Knowing that he brought fruit, apples are unsurprising because of their very high typicality. However, pomegranates are highly atypical, so there is some surprise in the second scenario.

Remark 7.1 *The atypicality of a concept in a domain is equivalent to its informativeness, and the atypicality of a concept relative to another concept in its cohort is the ratio of the informativeness of the former to the latter.*

The central intuition here is that knowledge that something is a c yields expectations about the values of the features over which c is defined. The experimental evidence shows that subjects who are told that birds have a property that is hard to observe (e.g., possessing a four-chamber heart) express more confidence that typical subspecies (e.g., robins) share that property than they do for atypical subspecies (e.g., penguins).

When translated into our Bayesian model, strong inheritance with respect to feature values means that the concept likelihood for a focal concept does not differ much from that of the parent concept. If the two likelihoods are very similar, then the subconcept inherits the probabilistic structure of the parent concept: things that are likely to be the case for the parent concept are likely to be the case for the subconcept.

We can represent this idea well with our information-based notion of concept typicality. Suppose that one concept in a cohort is more typical of the parent concept than is another sibling concept. Then the modeling framework suggests that we believe more strongly for the more typical subconcept that the things that are likely true for the parent are also likely for the subconcept. The strength of inheritance increases with typicality (the inverse of informativeness). Inheritance is thus weak for highly informative concepts.

Remark 7.2 *The strength of (probabilistic) inheritance from a root to a concept in its cohort declines with the informativeness of the (sub)concept.*

7.3 Distinctiveness

Now we turn to the second way of characterizing the information content of a concept: the degree to which it stands out from its cohort.

It is evident that some concepts stand out from their cohorts. Aiming to capture and theorize about this important type of distinction, Hannan et al. (2007) argued that concepts that stand out sharply from the background have more social power and that association with such a concept conveys more benefits (provided that the concept has a positive valence, as we discuss in Chapter 12). They proposed that the sharpness of the boundary, what they called *contrast*, is what matters. They defined contrast as the average typicality of the objects categorized as instances of the concept. In other words, a high-contrast concept is one in which only very typical members (i.e., objects very similar to the center of the concept) belong; object representations with low typicality are generally excluded from such a concept.

Although the notion of contrast was intended to capture how much information was conveyed by a concept, it did so in a way that relied on categorizations. While this is valuable, it would also be useful to have a measure that does not depend on the set of objects encountered.

Moreover, what matters is not just that a concept stands out from the background knowledge (its informativeness, as defined above), but also how a concept differs from the other concepts in its cohort. In terms of our model, the natural way to represent this latter kind of difference uses distances between concepts in a common semantic space.

Defining Distinctiveness

We also use the Kullback-Leibler divergence to express the degree to which a concept stands out from its cohort. A concept has high distinctiveness if its concept likelihood diverges from the others. We propose that distinctiveness be measured as the average distance from concepts of its cohort (where the distance is the Kullback-Leibler divergence, definition 6.2).

Definition 7.2 *The distinctiveness of a concept with respect to its cohort is its average distance from the members of the cohort:*

$$\Delta_\kappa(c) \equiv \frac{\sum_{c' \in \kappa} \vec{D}(c, c')}{|\kappa| - 1}. \tag{7.4}$$

Two concepts can be equally informative (stand at equal distance from the root) but differ in distinctiveness if one is relatively isolated in the semantic space but the other has one or more near neighbors.

AN EMPIRICAL EXAMPLE: We return to our example of rap music to calculate distinctiveness, using equation 7.4. We first compute distances between styles using equation 6.4. This equation invokes the concept likelihood, $\widehat{\pi}_{\mathrm{G_{rap3}}}(\cdot \mid s)$, which we used to compute informativeness earlier in the chapter.

Following our previous design, we consider the semantic space defined by three features: *swagger*, *street violence*, and *romantic love*, and we divide each dimension into five chunks, resulting in 125 positions in the three dimensional space. We have already computed $\widehat{\pi}_{\mathrm{G_{rap3}}}(\cdot \mid s)$ in equation 7.2, which allows us to compute distances using equation 6.4. There is one additional consideration: in this example, there are chunks of the space in which there are no albums for particular styles, so the concept likelihood is zero. This poses a problem in equation 6.4 if the concept likelihood at an x for c_1 is nonzero but is zero for c_2, making the distance between the concepts at that x infinite. To address this issue, we add a small constant to N_{xs} and recompute the concept likelihood from equation 7.2. We chose to add $1/125 = 0.008$ to each cell, which adds a total of one count to the entire corpus.

TABLE 7.2
Distinctiveness of the twelve
largest styles in rap music

Style	Distinctiveness
Alternative rap	1.57
Dirty south	2.19
East Coast rap	1.11
G-Funk	1.71
Gangsta rap	1.45
Golden age	1.81
Hardcore rap	1.18
Political rap	1.92
Pop-rap	1.11
Southern rap	1.80
Underground rap	1.38
West Coast rap	1.32

We then compute distinctiveness according to equation 7.4, where the denominator is simply the number of styles minus one: 19. Table 7.2 reports distinctiveness for the twelve largest styles.

This example shows that informativeness and distinctiveness are related but contain independent information. Political rap is high in both informativeness and distinctiveness. Hardcore rap is lowest on informativeness but only moderately low on distinctiveness. Pop-rap ranks very low in distinctiveness, but it is in the middle in terms of informativeness.

Distinctiveness captures how close a concept is to other concepts in its cohort, whereas informativeness captures how much a concept stands out from the background. These can be different depending on how concepts cluster in the space and on the number of objects assigned to the concepts—the categories, as we define them in later chapters. Concepts with many members have a stronger influence on defining the background of the domain. As a result, smaller concepts that cluster together, but that are distant from highly populated concepts, will rank lower on distinctiveness relative to informativeness.

7.4   Basic-Level Concepts

We illustrate the advantage of our formal construction of conceptual spaces by reconsidering arguments about so-called basic-level concepts, as described briefly in chapter 2. Rosch explained the superiority of the basic level with reference to the levels above, which she called superordinate, and the level below, subordinate. The story has the familiar structure of the *Mother Goose* version of the classic folk tale *Goldilocks and the Three Bears* in which Papa Bear's bowl of porridge is too hot and his bed is too hard, Mamma Bear's porridge is too cold and her bed is too soft, and Baby Bear's porridge and bed are "just right." Classic examples of the basic level are apple and chair. Their superordinate concepts, fruit and furniture, are too inclusive and lack the specificity to be widely useful. Their subordinate concepts, such as McIntosh and sofa, are too specific, having an unfavorable trade-off of specificity and inclusiveness. Basic-level concepts are "just right."

An information-theoretic construction provides a way to make these notions more precise. Note that previous discussions of these issues focused on triplets of concepts at different levels and implicitly made the middle-level concept the focus of attention. But this seems to oversimplify if concepts are embedded in sets of subconcept relations. Instead, we propose to start with the root in a set of concepts and examine its direct subconcepts and sub-direct-subconcepts.

Suppose we have a three-level tree of concepts with root r. Let κ_r denote the cohort of the root concept and κ_r^2 denote the set of concepts at the next level down. The information gain from moving from the top level (the root) to the next level depends on the information gain with respect to each of the subconcepts. We think that the minimum information gain gives a reasonable way of thinking about how informative the root concept is relative to its subconcepts: $\min_{c \in \kappa_r} I_\mathbb{G}(c, \mathcal{D}_r)$. Then we can make the same calculation beginning with each subconcept as a root in its own right and take the minimum information gain of moving a level down in the tree. According to our reading of the research on the basic level, we can reformulate the key insight in terms of informativeness as follows. The level of the cohort κ_r is basic if (1) the least informative of the concepts in the cohort is highly informative relative to the root r, and (2) the minimal information gain in moving from the root to κ_r is larger than the minimum information gained from moving down to the level below κ_r.

An unsettling feature of the argument about the basic level is its reliance on three-level trees. What if there is a fourth or fifth level—for example, plant, flowering plant, tree, conifer, pine, pinyon or entertainment, films, comedy, slapstick? How do we decide a priori which level is basic? An easy answer is that it depends on the context. Sometimes the context focuses attention on a high level in the structure. Think of the variant of the "Twenty Questions" parlor game in which one person tells the other players (the questioners) which of animal, vegetable, or mineral describes the correct choice. Or consider the entertainment industry, which leads to a focus on games, movies, TV, sports, and so on. But a discussion of films focuses attention on its main genres. Which level is basic presumably changes across these contexts.[2] In other words, the context tells what root (domain) to choose. Then what is "basic" is the next level down. Of course, the context plays the decisive role in determining the domain and its root. Contextual focus is more a cultural matter than a psychological one.

Discussion

In this chapter, we formally specified two ways of characterizing the amount of information concepts convey. These measures, informativeness and distinctiveness, differ in terms of whether they pertain to the amount of information encapsulated in the concept relative to the root concept in a domain or relative to other concepts in the cohort, respectively. Calculating these measures requires comparing probability distributions within a common space. We proposed a way of doing so by relying on the uniform expansion introduced in the previous chapter to extend the root concept into the space of its descendants and by using the Kullback-Leibler divergence to compare the concept likelihoods. We view this approach as superior to attempts in earlier work to pin down the notion of how much concepts "stand out from the background."

How does considering variation along these lines inform research in sociology more broadly? As we will argue in more detail in the following chapters, concepts mediate people's everyday experiences by shaping what they perceive, and how people react to various objects depends on how they are categorized. Both of these processes depend on the set of concepts that people have—something we have formally defined in this chapter—and whether particular concepts that they have are invoked. This, of course, begs the question of when particular concepts will be more likely to be invoked; as Swidler (1986) famously noted, people have more cultural knowledge than they actually use.

Existing research does not provide a good general answer to the question of which concepts are most likely to influence perception and categorization. Yet DiMaggio (1997) proposed that the answer to this question likely has its roots in cognition and the process by which certain concepts are more readily recalled. Modeling the process of concept recall is beyond the scope of our analysis, but we speculate that properties such as informativeness and distinctiveness play a role. One possibility is that concepts that are more informative and/or more distinctive come to mind less easily and therefore affect perception and categorization less than others. On the other hand, in cases where objects are categorized with a concept that is relatively more informative or more distinctive, the objects might be more memorable precisely because such concepts are more atypical. Future work that tests these kinds of speculations could help clarify more systematically the way that culture enters into everyday life.

Understanding how informativeness and distinctiveness affect concept recall or activation, thereby shaping how individuals perceive the world, could also have implications for those who wish to use concepts more strategically. For example, social movements scholars have discussed the importance of framing grievances or demands in terms that resonate with people's existing conceptual understanding (Snow, Rochford, Worden, and Benford, 1986). In our terms, that might mean they should consider the level of informativeness as they choose among various concepts. Again, the prediction is not entirely clear. On the one hand, more informative concepts are more atypical and might therefore be more memorable. On the other hand, less informative concepts are more similar to the root concept in a domain and therefore are perhaps more deeply embedded in memory.

PART TWO

Applying Concepts

IN THIS PART OF THE BOOK, we apply and extend the foundational elements developed thus far to consider how concepts get used. This topic is crucial for sociological application of our theoretical approach. We build on the Bayesian approach to categorization and to inference about the properties of objects with uncertain properties.

We begin in chapter 8 with a Bayesian formulation of categorization. The model expresses the probability that an object with a particular position in semantic space gets categorized as an instance of a concept. In the Bayesian framework, such a categorization probability is interpreted as the person's belief that such an object is a member of the concept. The degree of belief depends upon the value of the concept likelihood for the position and on subjective beliefs about the likelihood that an arbitrary object would be found at the position and that such an object would be a member of the concept.

These beliefs depend on the context in which the categorizer finds herself. So we build context into the model explicitly. One kind of context is one in which only a single concept is considered. Another is one in which the person is constrained to pick one of a set of potentially applicable concepts (e.g., to answer the question "which of these concepts best fits the object?"). Chapter 8 treats both cases.

After treating the standard case, we make an important departure. In the interest of focusing on detailed mechanisms involving mental representations, research on concepts and categories in psychology and related fields often purposefully avoids some of the messy and fascinating realities of how people deploy concepts in everyday life. For example, outside of the lab a person might say that a music album sounds emo, indie, and punk, or that a software product provides business intelligence and management systems integration. Existing cognitive science has generally treated learning and deployment of concepts one at a time, as noted above. As a result we know little about how categorization works and what consequences it has when people are free to assign more than one concept to an object. While the complications of concept use outside the lab certainly raise challenges to the study of meaning-making processes, we believe it is important and sociologically interesting to tackle such issues.

Chapter 9 takes on this case, which we call "free categorization." This refers to situations in which the context makes it meaningful for a person to apply as many concepts as they like to an object. This is the case in which objects can be multiply categorized. We use examples from music, film, and software production to show that multiple categorization is common, often the dominant response. We adapt the Bayesian framework to this context and show that we generally lack some of the information needed to specify categorization probabilities for sets of concepts. Indeed this analysis shows what is confusing about multiple categorization: difficulty of interpreting what to expect of an object that bears multiple labels (from the same cohort of concepts). This theme will be considered extensively in later chapters.

Finally in the third chapter in this part (chapter 10), we introduce the very important notion that a person's concepts shape what they perceive. We concentrate on the ideas that concepts warp perceptual spaces, that concepts act as magnets. Sociologists likely find congenial the idea that concepts shape perception as in cases of racial and gender stereotyping. The precise notion of perceptual magnet provides a mechanism that can be used to sharpen the sociological intuitions.

CHAPTER EIGHT

Categories and Categorization

TO THIS POINT we have concentrated on developing the view that mental representations of concepts can be usefully viewed as probability distributions over positions in a semantic space and that concepts are generally embedded in domains. Now we bring into the picture what we call objects (or entities). This term serves as a placeholder for any of a wide variety of persons, products, artworks, collective actions, and so forth. We develop and share concepts to make sense of the world. When we encounter an object, we generally categorize it as an instance of a concept. Categories are *sets of objects* that someone categorizes as instances of particular concepts. Categorization means assigning objects to concepts.

Routine social interaction imposes demands for producing categories and categorizations. For instance, one might get asked what clubs are nearby?, where is the closest hospital?, which pub or wine bar would you recommend?, on which aisle can one find bakers yeast?, or who are the most distinguished linguists at your university? Engaging in such conversation requires constructing an extension of the concept—a list of positive categorizations—and then either sharing the list or choosing among the list. Indeed, such demands are so routine in social life that we take them completely for granted.

Market intermediaries, such as critics, curators, and regulators, also face demands to provide such extensions so that others will know how to search for an object, for example, which wing of an art museum to visit. For many intermediaries, constructing such lists is an important part of the value they provide. According to analysts at Gartner, for instance, identifying new market segments—and which companies participate in them—is one of the most important parts of their service (Pollock and Williams, 2009).

8.1   Category and Concept

The terms "concept" and "category" often get used interchangeably in cognitive science and sociology. We find it helpful to make and use a consistent distinction between the two notions. For us, a concept is an abstract object, what logicians call an *intensional* object. A category is concrete, an *extensional* object, one that demarcates a set of objects that are alike in that they have been associated with a concept. A probabilistic model of categorization, when applied to the objects in a domain, yields a category. In other words, a category is the set of objects that one associates with a concept. As Medin and Rips (2005, p. 37) put it, "concepts refer and what they refer to are categories."

How should we think about categories formally? We find it natural to assume that a category results from a set of categorization decisions. Of course, the notion refers to some point in time (or some fixed time interval); but again we leave this dependence implicit.

This reading makes the formal representation straightforward: a category is the set of objects that have been assigned to a concept, among the objects that come into view in a situation.[1]

Definition 8.1 (Category) *A category is the set of objects that a person categorizes as instances of a particular concept (given the information about the situation).*

$$\mathbf{cat}(c) \equiv \{o \mid \text{IS-A}(c, o)\}.$$

Think of the example of the artificial concepts of arrowhead styles that we have been using to illustrate the abstract model. In terms of definition 8.1, a participant's category for a style is the set of stimulus arrowhead drawings that she has categorized as instances of the style. This is a *list* of members. Her concept for the style, by contrast, is given by the concept likelihood of the kind shown in figure 4.2b.

Even if categorization is crisp at any moment in time, extensive research reveals that categorizations of the same object over occasions can and do vary. So it makes sense to view categorization probabilistically. That is, a categorization can be regarded as a realization of a probabilistic process (Ashby and Alfonso-Reese, 1995; Hampton, 2007; Sanborn et al., 2010; Verheyen et al., 2010).

The probabilistic nature of categorization makes categorical assignments potentially variable over occasions and thus fuzzy. In other words, we expect categories to be temporally unstable, especially at their edges, so that a second round of categorizations by the same person might yield a different list of members. Nonetheless concepts can be stable even if the associated categories are not. Understanding the probabilistic mechanism connecting concepts and categories holds the key to analyzing fuzziness.

Gaining a deeper understanding of these issues requires attention to (1) how objects get processed cognitively and (2) how people associate objects with concepts. We take up these two topics in turn.

8.2   Objects, Positions, and Mental Representations

In line with leading theories of categorization and with the perspective delineated in the previous chapter, we assume that the objects (i.e., the "stimuli") being categorized are described (represented) by their positions in a multidimensional feature space.

But what is a stimulus? In the experimental research that informs our work, stimuli are treated as externally given, as chosen and introduced by the experimenter. Subjects are assumed to mentally represent the stimuli in an orderly way. And the analysis relates the externally defined stimuli to some behavior, such as categorization decisions. We encountered this kind of structure in our report of the arrowhead experiments. We (the experimenters) created images that varied on a quantitative parameter, particularly the width of the arrowhead, and we related the categorization decisions to this parameter, bypassing the step of mental representation. Considerable psychological research supports the assumption of a simple mapping from the stimuli to mental representations. So the elision of the representation step might not be problematic for correct inference.

For the range of situations that we consider, these issues become more complicated. Consider the example of Impressionism discussed in chapter 3. For illustration we assume that the term refers to a genre, which is a concept. As such, it is a distribution over a semantic space. Now take a particular artwork, say Claude Monet's *Impression, soleil levant* (*Impression: sunrise*). We refer to this painting as an *object*. It has an external existence as a canvas in a frame on display in Musée Marmottan Monet in Paris (and in reproductions). So *Impression, soleil levant* plays the role of stimulus for a visitor to the museum or for someone looking at a digital image of it online.

The complicated part of the analysis lies in getting to the mental representation of this painting. What does someone perceive of this painting? We do not answer such a precise question. Instead, we assume merely that each person who is exposed to the painting and takes notice of it forms some representation of it and that this representation shapes judgment about it.

As we have already discussed, a vast number of features of an object could be incorporated in the representation. However, due to limits on human cognition, people likely do not pay attention to very large arrays of possible features. So there must be a powerful filtering of perception to obtain a mental representation. Concepts serve as the filters. A person's concepts designate the set of relevant features, what we call the semantic space. So two people with different repertoires of concepts, one containing Impressionism and one that does not, will likely develop different representations of the painting in question. For the person who does have the concept, her mental representation of *Impression, soleil levant* in a discussion of art genres can be regarded as a position in the semantic space for Impressionism.

The context decisively shapes mental representations. Some of the knowledge that someone has about an object does not enter into the mental representation in a context. For example, someone viewing *Impression, soleil levant* can take note of its dimensions, the material used in the frame, its placement and lighting in the museum, and so forth. But none of this information gets represented in the context of artistic genres. This is because the context primes certain concepts or makes them more cognitively available. When these concepts come to mind, attention is then drawn to particular features—those that define the semantic space for the concept.

Where does this leave us? We assume the existence of objects that are external to the mind of a person, and we use the convention of referring to objects in formulas with o. The objects and concepts that are relevant to a categorization decision depend on the context. The context in which a person makes a judgment establishes a certain domain as relevant, brings its concepts into the picture, and leads the person to represent objects as positions in a particular semantic space.

We think of a mental representation as a function that maps from objects to a semantic space. But what space? If there is only one concept in the picture, as we assume for most of this chapter, then obviously the space is given by this concept.

Representation Function

We define a representation function, $R_\mathbb{F}$, that maps objects to positions in the semantic space, $\mathbb{F}$. We express the function as

$$R_\mathbb{F}(o) = x.$$

> We will index the semantic space of representations as appropriate given the inference context, as we discuss below.

This view implicitly assumes that the individual perceives the object on all of the dimensions that form the semantic space, $\mathbb{F}$. In other words, we assume *full* perception of the object for the categorization task in the sense that there is no subjective uncertainty about its value on any of the dimensions of the space.

Sometimes the judgment task brings more than one concept into focus.[2] In these more general situations, the semantic space in which objects get mentally represented must have more dimensions. This issue introduces more realism but also more complexity in the analysis, and we address it formally in later sections.

8.3   Information about the Context

People do not generally apply concepts to objects in a vacuum; rather they apply concepts when facing some task in some context. Often the task is to make sense of the object in light of available concepts—sensemaking (Chater and Lowenstein, 2016). But it is unreasonable to think that all of a person's concepts become activated in this effort. The context in which the person encounters the object sets the boundaries of the sensemaking. Laboratory experiments generally try to teach artificial concepts to experimental subjects as a way to ensure that the subjects make minimal use of their existing sets of concepts and situational knowledge in making categorization decisions.

In the social world, nothing stops people from using such information. We want our models to apply in naturally occurring environments, and we devote more attention to specifying the inference context than is usual in experimental work on concepts and categorization. We start with a focus on the set of possible categorizations. Later in this chapter, we will add another key element of the inference context: the knowledge that enables the individual to form prior beliefs about the objects that can be encountered in the context.

It is helpful to think about what kind of information would have to be supplied to subjects in an experimental categorization study for responses to be meaningful. First, the experimenter must provide a set of possible categorizations. That is, the study must provide a choice set, which we denote by $\mathfrak{C}$. The idea is that this set presents a "menu" of possible categorizations. In the first part of the chapter, the menu contains a single concept. In later sections, the subject considers multiple concepts but makes exclusive categorization decisions. In the next chapter, the choices include multiple categorizations (i.e., the elements of $\mathfrak{C}$ are *sets* of concepts, some containing more than one concept). In either case, the idea is that the decision maker chooses one element from the menu.

In many, but not all, relevant contexts, the menu of choices includes the option of "no positive categorization." We represent this option in formulas as the emptyset, $\emptyset$. It is, of course, a residual choice; it means that none of the positive categorizations have been chosen. In other words, we do not think of $\emptyset$ as a concept.

Consider, for instance, the experimental study of categorization of images of arrowheads as instances of a style discussed in §4.2. In this experiment, participants were randomly assigned to begin with one style and learned each style in turn. In the first stage, subjects who began with the Akka style were given the menu of choices $\{\emptyset, \text{Akka}\}$ and were asked to assign each image to one of these options. In a second stage, described in detail in the next chapter, subjects were confronted with both styles. They were asked to classify the images given the choices "Akka style only," "Boko style only," "both styles," and "neither style."

Obviously, we are interested in categorizations that take place in naturally occurring environments. The context of the categorization will likely affect the "menu" of possible categorizations used by an individual. We discuss this extensively in the next chapter.

To describe how people use their conceptual knowledge to choose which concepts to apply to a particular object, we focus on the simpler situation: that of a decision about whether a particular concept c applies to an object o perceived to be at position x in the semantic space.

8.4   Single Concepts

We begin here with contexts in which there is a single concept to be considered. We denote the focal concept by c. We mark this single categorization task with the predicate $\text{SINGLE}(c)$, which reads as "the categorization task involves categorization (or not) of objects in the concept c".

Definition 8.2 (Single-categorization task)

$$\text{SINGLE}(c) \leftrightarrow \mathfrak{C} = \{\emptyset, \{c\}\}$$

That is, the categorization task is such that the individual categorizes an object either as a c or as not-a-c.[3]

Bayes' Theorem for Categorization

We follow the modern Bayesian approach by looking at categorization as a problem of statistical inference (Anderson, 1991; Tenenbaum and Griffiths, 2002). The key question is whether to regard an object—more precisely its mental representation—as an instance of a focal concept. We can express this formally with the instance-of predicate that we introduced in chapter 5. People use the available information about the object—its position in the semantic space—and their understanding of the context to evaluate the truth of the hypothesis that IS-A(c, o). The probabilistic perspective on categorization interprets the strength of a person's belief in the truth of this hypothesis as a subjective probability. Suppose that one has to answer "yes" or "no" to the question "Is the object o a c?" when the mental representation of the object is its position x in the semantic space associated with the concept c: $R_{\mathbb{F}_c}(o) = x$. The probabilistic approach on which we build holds that the probability that one would answer "yes" is given by the *categorization probability*

$$P(\text{IS-A}(c, o) \mid x) \equiv P(c \mid x).$$

The expression on the right in this equivalence gives the notational shorthand that we use throughout.

We would like to relate this categorization probability to the mental representation of the concept—the concept likelihood function, $\pi_{\mathbb{F}_c}(\cdot \mid c)$. This function specifies the distribution over the semantic space, $\mathbb{F}_c$, of the positions of the objects that are instances of the concept c (see §4.1). Consider a position, $x \in \mathbb{F}_c$. The quantity $\pi_{\mathbb{F}_c}(x \mid c)$ is the probability that an object that is a c finds itself at position x. We can rewrite this as

$$\pi_{\mathbb{F}_c}(x \mid c) \equiv P_{\mathbb{F}_c}(x \mid \text{IS-A}(c, o)) \equiv P_{\mathbb{F}_c}(x \mid c). \tag{8.1}$$

This notation suggests another formulation of our objective. We want to relate the probability that an object is a c given that it is at the position x, to the probability that an object is at the position x, given that it is a c. Bayes' theorem, a basic theorem in probability theory, is the tool that allows us to do so.

$$P(\text{IS-A}(c, o) \mid x) = \frac{P_{\mathbb{F}_c}(x \mid \text{IS-A}(c, o)) \, P(\text{IS-A}(c, o))}{P_{\mathbb{F}_c}(x)}.$$

To simplify notation, we replace "IS-A(c, o)" by "c" and rewrite the foregoing formula in terms of the concept likelihood

$$P(c \mid x) = \pi_{\mathbb{F}_c}(x \mid c)\frac{P(c)}{P_{\mathbb{F}_c}(x)}. \tag{8.2}$$

Equation 8.2 expresses the categorization probability in terms of the concept likelihood and also of two other constructs, $P(c)$ and $P_{\mathbb{F}_c}(x)$. These latter terms specify how knowledge about the context affects categorization. These expressions are called *priors* because they capture knowledge that the individual holds before facing the categorization decision. More precisely, these are beliefs, for arbitrary objects encountered in the context, about the probability that an object is an instance of the focal concept, $P(c)$, and the probability that the object is at a certain position in semantic space, $P_{\mathbb{F}_c}(x)$.

Context Dependence

The two prior beliefs depend on the context. To illustrate how the context affects these priors, suppose that the task is to categorize a film as a Western (or not Western). Let us consider two possible contexts. The first context concerns films that were directed by Quentin Tarantino, and the second context addresses films that were directed by Woody Allen.

How does the context affect the first of the priors, $P(c)$? That is, how does the context affect one's estimate that a film encountered in the context is a Western? The first context specifies that the categorization task is about the set of the twelve Tarantino films at the time of this writing: {*Reservoir Dogs, Pulp Fiction, Jackie Brown, Django Unchained, The Hateful Eight, ...*}. The prior probability that a film in this set is a Western is the subjective probability that a film about which nothing else is known turns out to be a Western. To make this concrete, consider how an experimenter could elicit this probability in an experiment. The experimenter would write the names of all the Tarantino movies on a piece of paper and put them in a hat. He then would ask the participant the following:

> This hat contains pieces of papers that list the titles of each of Quentin Tarantino's films. Suppose I pick a piece of paper, read the title of the film, put the piece of paper back and shuffle it with the other pieces in the hat. I repeat this sequence of operations 100 times. How many times do you think I would have picked the name of a film in this set that is a Western?

For people who are familiar with Quentin Tarantino's filmography, this subjective probability is likely to be in the vicinity of 0.17 because two of the twelve films directed by Tarantino are usually classified as Westerns: *Django Unchained* and *The Hateful Eight*.

The second context concerns Woody Allen films. The prior probability that a film in this context is a Western will likely be much lower than in the first context. This is because there is no Western in the dozens of movies Allen has directed. As these examples show, the context affects the prior probability that a not-yet-seen object is an instance of the concept.

Similarly, the context affects the prior probability that the object is at the position x in semantic space, $P_{\mathbb{F}_c}(x)$. Consider the feature value $x = the$ *hero is a female character who goes on a vengeance mission and kills opponents with a Japanese saber*. Suppose that the context is again Tarantino films. The prior probability that a film has this feature is the subjective probability that a film about which nothing is known, other than it was directed by Quentin Tarantino, turns out to have the feature value. For people who are familiar with Quentin Tarantino's filmography, this subjective probability will be around 17%; the two *Kill Bill* movies out of the twelve films directed by Tarantino have the focal feature.

By contrast, if the context concerns Woody Allen films, the prior probability of this particular feature value will presumably be very low—no Woody Allen has this feature. Just as the context affects the prior probability of categorization, it also affects the prior probability that an object has a given feature.

The information state $\mathcal{I}_0$. This example about how the context affects the priors suggests that we should mention it specifically in our notation. Henceforth, we will denote by $\mathcal{I}_0$ the information the focal individual has about the context. It includes knowledge of the menu of possible concept assignments $\mathfrak{C}$, the semantic spaces $\mathbb{F}_c$ for each of the available concepts and the information used to form the two priors, $P_{\mathbb{F}_c}(x)$ and $P(c)$. We assume that when someone makes an inference about the features of an object or about its categorization, the set $\mathcal{I}_0$ does not include any information about this specific object. We use the index zero to emphasize the fact that $\mathcal{I}_0$ refers to information about the priors—this is an initial information state that is updated when the individual learns that the object is at position x, that is, $R_{\mathbb{F}_c}(o) = x$.

With this notation, we can see the categorization probability as the subjective probability that an object is an instance of concept when the individual's information includes both $\mathcal{I}_0$ and the position of the object, $R_{\mathbb{F}_c}(o) = x$.[4] This suggests a revised notation for the categorization probability: $P(c \mid \mathcal{I}_0, x)$.

With all of the foregoing considerations in hand, we can specify the categorization probability implied by Bayes' theorem.

Postulate 8.1 (Bayes' theorem for a single-categorization task) *The probability that the focal person categorizes an object at a position as an instance of the concept equals the product of the concept likelihood and the ratio of the prior on the concept and the prior on the position.*

Consider an individual judging whether or not an object o is a c, that is, SINGLE(c) *is the case. The information about the context, including the fact that* SINGLE(c) *is the case, is denoted by* $\mathcal{I}_0$. *In addition, suppose that the focal individual knows the positions of the object in the semantic space associated with c: the person's information includes* $\{R_{\mathbb{F}_c}(o) = x\}$.

The subjective probability that an object o is an instance of the concept c (i.e., the person believes that the hypothesis IS-A(c, o) *is true), given that the object is at the position x in semantic space* $\mathbb{F}_c$, *is denoted by* $P_{\mathbb{F}_c}(c \mid \mathcal{I}_0, x)$. *It depends on three terms:*

1. *the subjective probability that the object is at the position in semantic space x given the information about the context and that it is a c,*

$$P_{\mathbb{F}_c}(x \mid \mathcal{I}_0, c);$$

2. *the prior that an object is a c given information about the context,*

$$P(c \mid \mathcal{I}_0);$$

3. *the prior that an object is at the position x given information about the context,*

$$P_{\mathbb{F}_c}(x \mid \mathcal{I}_0).$$

The categorization probability is given by

$$P(c \mid \mathcal{I}_0, x) = \frac{P_{\mathbb{F}_c}(x \mid \mathcal{I}_0, c) \, P(c \mid \mathcal{I}_0)}{P_{\mathbb{F}_c}(x \mid \mathcal{I}_0)}. \tag{8.3}$$

The formulation in equation 8.3 is the workhorse of Bayesian categorization studies. We have modified the standard representation by making explicit the individual's information state.

An Empirical Illustration

We can provide some empirical basis for postulate 8.1 using our experiment on the styles of arrowheads. In §4.2, we explained how we used typicality ratings to construct the concept likelihood associated with the Akka style (see also figure 4.2b). In this experiment, we also had the participants respond to categorization questions about all the stimuli. More precisely, the participants had to respond "yes" or "no" to the question, "Does the sample arrowhead belong to the Akka style?"

The context is provided by the experimental setup. The set of concept assignments is $\mathfrak{C} = \{\emptyset, \text{Akka}\}$. The feature space associated with Akka is the space of arrow widths, 25 values from 0.02 to 0.98 in steps of 0.04: $\mathbb{F}_{\text{Akka}} = \{0.02, 0.06, 0.10, ..., 0.94, 0.98\}$. The information about the context, $\mathcal{I}_0$, includes $\mathfrak{C}$ and the description of the experimental setup. In particular, it includes not only the representative set of arrowheads shown at the beginning of the experiment, but also the graphical display of the arrowheads and the text that describes the cover story of the experiment. By aggregating the data over all the participants, we compute the empirical probability of categorization for each position: $\hat{P}_{\mathbb{F}_{\text{Akka}}}(\text{Akka} \mid \mathcal{I}_0, x)$. These probabilities are depicted by the light gray line in figure 8.1.

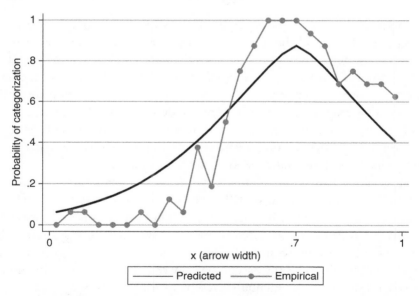

Figure 8.1 Probability of categorization of the stimuli as members of the Akka style (prototype at $x = 0.7$). The black line is the prediction made by of proposition 8.1. The gray line is the empirical categorization probability from the experimental data

In order to apply proposition 8.1, we assume that $P_{\mathbb{F}_{Akka}}(x \mid \mathcal{I}_0)$ has a uniform distribution because the participants saw one stimulus at each position before the experiment, and we set $P_{\mathbb{F}_{Akka}}(x \mid \mathcal{I}_0) = 1/25$, because there are twenty-five different stimuli in our space.

The instructions did not explicitly give the prior probability of categorization. But we can extract it on the basis of the aggregate behavior of the participants by relying on the law of total probabilities (see §8.7 for further discussion of category priors).

$$\hat{P}(\text{Akka} \mid \mathcal{I}_0) = \sum_{x \in \mathbb{F}_{Akka}} \hat{P}(\text{Akka} \mid \mathcal{I}_0, x) \, P_{\mathbb{F}_{Akka}}(x \mid \mathcal{I}_0) = 0.45. \qquad (8.4)$$

The predicted categorization probabilities are depicted by the black line in figure 8.1. As shown by the graphs, the predicted and empirical categorization probabilities are fairly close to each other. The correlation between these two quantities computed across positions in the space is about 0.95.

8.5   Context Independence of the Mental Representations of Concepts

An important aspect of our argument deals with the relation between the concept likelihood and the first item for the formula that gives the categorization probability (the right-hand side of equation 8.3), $P_{\mathbb{F}_c}(x \mid \mathcal{I}_0, c)$. This is the conditional (subjective) probability that an object that is a c would have the position x in the semantic space $\mathbb{F}_c$ when $\mathcal{I}_0$ is the information about the context. This reads *almost as if* it were the definition of the concept likelihood $\pi_{\mathbb{F}_c}(x \mid c)$. But there is a crucial difference: the term in the formula of equation 8.3 may depend on information about the context $\mathcal{I}_0$, whereas the concept likelihood *does not* depend on such information.

Our analytical objective in this section goes beyond the standard approach. We want to tie what we believe to be a somewhat stable knowledge structure (the concept) with context-dependent factors so as to explain how categorization decisions are affected by these two elements. More specifically, we want to connect concept likelihood and categorization probabilities. The concept likelihood is the psychologically relevant element of the model; it is our rendition of the mental representation of the concept. Therefore, we want to claim that $P_{\mathbb{F}_c}(x \mid \mathcal{I}_0, c) = \pi_{\mathbb{F}_c}(x \mid c)$. This amounts to positing that the information about the context affects the categorization probability only to the extent that it shapes the two priors.

We believe that this core assumption of our approach is reasonable because arguing otherwise would essentially amount to assuming that concepts are *context-dependent*. We think that building on concepts in sociological analysis requires that concepts be stable over contexts in terms of inference tasks and social interactions.[5] We formalize this assumption in the following postulate. In the interest of generality, we state the postulate in terms of an arbitrary semantic space that includes the semantic space associated with the concept. We will need this kind of construction when we bring the domain into focus and use a semantic space that spans those of the concepts in the domain. This general rendition shows that the claim applies to all kinds of categorization tasks, not just the single-concept task.

Postulate 8.2 (Relation of stable concepts and conditional probabilities) *The subjective probability that an object that is an instance of a concept finds itself at a certain position in the semantic space associated with the concept does not depend on the information about the context. Instead it is given by the concept likelihood, which is stable over contexts.*

Consider (1) a concept labeled c, whose semantic value is given by the concept likelihood $\pi_{\mathbb{F}_c}(\cdot \mid c)$, and (2) an arbitrary semantic space that includes the semantic space for the concept: $\mathbb{F}_c \subseteq \mathcal{F}$.

$$P_{\mathcal{F}}(x \mid \mathcal{I}_0, c) = \pi_{\mathcal{F}}(x \mid c),$$

where $\pi_{\mathcal{F}}(\cdot \mid c)$ is the uniform conceptual expansion of $\pi_{\mathbb{F}_c}(\cdot \mid c)$ to the space $\mathcal{F}$, that is $P_{\mathcal{F}} = uni(P_{\mathbb{F}_c}, \mathcal{F})$.

We can now re-express postulate 8.1 in terms of the concept likelihood using postulate 8.2; this provides our key claim about single categorization. The following proposition provides a way to achieve context-dependence of categorization decisions, while maintaining the context-independence of the mental representation of the concept. In this model, the context affects the two priors.

Proposition 8.1 *The categorization probability can be expressed as a product of the concept likelihood and terms that depend on information about the inference context.*

Under the specification of the categorization task given in the preamble of postulate 8.1,

$$P(c \mid \mathcal{I}_0, x) = \pi_{\mathbb{F}_c}(x \mid c) \frac{P(c \mid \mathcal{I}_0)}{P_{\mathbb{F}_c}(x \mid \mathcal{I}_0)}. \tag{8.5}$$

Here we see that the categorization probability factors into a component that depends only on the nature of the concept, $\pi_{\mathbb{F}_c}(x \mid c)$, and components (priors) that depend on information about the context, $P(c \mid \mathcal{I}_0)$ and $P_{\mathbb{F}_c}(x \mid \mathcal{I}_0)$.

We do not mean to suggest that concepts do not change. A broader theory of concepts must account for concept acquisition and loss, which presumably occurs over time horizons that extend beyond the limited time frame of a single categorization decision. In such an analysis, concepts would be indexed by time to allow exposure to new information over some time interval to shape the evolution of a concept. But this analysis falls beyond the scope of this book.

In our more limited focus, we consider judgments by individuals who have acquired stocks of concepts, and we treat those concepts as stable. What we treat as temporally unstable is not the presence of the concepts but the contexts in which the stable concepts are deployed. Because we define a concept as a distribution over a semantic space, both of these elements of the psychological construct should be stable over contexts.[6]

Proposition 8.1 provides a way for the analyst to recover concepts from categorization decisions. That is, suppose a researcher can empirically estimate the probability of categorization, $P_{\mathbb{F}_c}(c \mid \mathcal{I}_0, x)$, across what she assumes is the person's semantic space. Equation 8.5 allows the computation of the concept likelihood by reorganizing the terms:

$$\pi_{\mathbb{F}_c}(x \mid c) = P(c \mid \mathcal{I}_0, x) \frac{P_{\mathbb{F}_c}(x \mid \mathcal{I}_0)}{P(c \mid \mathcal{I}_0)}. \tag{8.6}$$

From an empirical standpoint, this means that we do not need typicality ratings to recover concepts. This will prove useful because the kind of data sociologists use frequently include the outcomes of categorization decisions but much less frequently list typicality ratings.

8.6   Categorization, Typicality, and Distance

The model as developed to this point implies that the probability of categorization increases with the typicality of the position, net of the effect of the prior on the position. We formalize this intermediate result in the following lemma:

Lemma 8.1 *In a single-concept context, the probability that an object will be categorized as an instance of a concept is an increasing function of its typicality* *in that concept. Let the categorization task be as described in the preamble to postulate 8.1. Then it follows that*

$$P(c \mid \mathcal{I}_0, x) = q_c(\mathcal{I}_0) \frac{\tau_c(x)}{P_{\mathbb{F}_c}(x \mid \mathcal{I}_0)},$$

where

$$q_c(\mathcal{I}_0) = \frac{P(c \mid \mathcal{I}_0)}{\sum_{x' \in \mathbb{F}_c} \tau_c(x')}.$$

In the simplest case, this lemma states that for two different positions with equal priors on position ($P_{\mathbb{F}_c}(x \mid \mathcal{I}_0) = P_{\mathbb{F}_c}(x' \mid \mathcal{I}_0)$), the objects at the position of higher typicality have higher probability of categorization than those represented at the position of lower typicality. More generally, comparison of any two positions needs to take account of differences in typicality and differences in the prior.

Similarly, we can express how the categorization probability depends on the distance between the mental representation of an object and a concept.[7] The Bayesian formulation of the categorization probability (proposition 8.1), when combined with the result relating typicality and distance in proposition 4.1, implies that the probability of positive categorization for an object decreases with its distance from the focal concept.

Proposition 8.2 *The probability of categorizing an object as an instance of a concept declines with the distance of (the mental representation of) the object from the center of the concept (conditional on the prior on the position remaining the same).*

Suppose the specification of the categorization task given in the preamble of postulate 8.1 holds and x and x' are two positions in $\mathbb{F}_c$. We have

$$\vec{d}_{\mathbb{F}_c}(x, c) > \vec{d}_{\mathbb{F}_c}(x', c) \wedge P_{\mathbb{F}_c}(x \mid \mathcal{I}_0) = P_{\mathbb{F}_c}(x' \mid \mathcal{I}_0)$$
$$\rightarrow P(c \mid \mathcal{I}_0, x) < P(c \mid \mathcal{I}_0, x'). \quad (8.7)$$

We can illustrate the implications of the proposition using the experimental data on classification of arrowheads. Figure 8.2 displays the relationship. It relates the average probability over subjects that a stimulus was categorized as an instance of the Akka style to the "objective" Euclidean distance between the stimulus and the prototype of the style. The dots depict the average probability and the smooth line gives a polynomial smoothing over the data. The dominant relationship is negative as predicted by proposition 8.2. Note that the prior probability of each position was the same at 1/25.

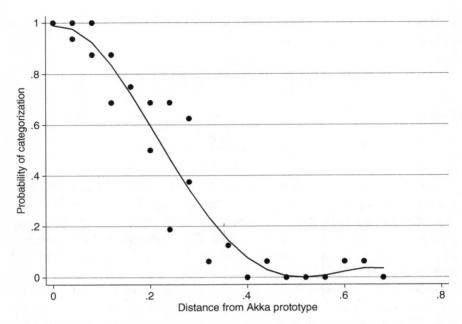

Figure 8.2 Relationship between the probability of categorization and the distance from the prototype—see the text for an explanation

8.7   Priors and Base Rates

We next raise the question of whether we should complicate the probabilistic model of categorization by more formally specifying the priors, $P(c \mid \mathcal{I}_0)$ and $P_{\mathbb{F}_c}(x \mid \mathcal{I}_0)$. This is an issue because the Bayesian framework on which we build does not restrict how people form priors. We have to assume that people have some information about the situation that allows them to construct such priors. We have denoted this information by $\mathcal{I}_0$. But what one person would find a sensible prior might not be sensible to another. Analysis of the matter cannot proceed absent more structure.

The relevant research in cognitive psychology often deals with this issue by assuming that priors are set to base rates. The base rate is the frequency of an "event." This is the probability that the event will occur independent of knowledge of the more detailed facts other than the information about the context captured in $\mathcal{I}_0$. In the categorization problem, the base rate that corresponds to the prior on the position, $P_{\mathbb{F}_c}(x \mid \mathcal{I}_0)$, is the proportion of objects at the position x among objects encountered in the setting. For example, in the arrowhead experiment discussed above, the participants saw exactly one arrowhead at each position before starting to categorize arrow-heads as Akka or not. They saw a total of twenty-five arrowheads. Therefore, their experienced base rate for each position was 1/25.

Similarly, the base rate that corresponds to the prior on the concept, $P(c \mid \mathcal{I}_0)$, is the *relative prevalence of a concept* in the categorization setting. So, for instance, in the case of films, the base rate of drama is much higher than that of documentary: there are just many more films classified as drama than films classified as documentary.

In the context of experiments, the experiment designer often creates ar-tificial environments to control the prior knowledge that participants bring to the categorization task. This is exactly what we did with our arrowhead experiment: we created a setting that would be entirely new for the vast ma-jority of participants. Therefore, the only knowledge that one can reasonably bring to bear is the base rates that we controlled, for example, by showing just one arrowhead at each position before the categorization task. The set of relevant objects for computation of the base rate of each position x was the set of arrowheads shown at the beginning of the experiment.

In naturally occurring environments, it is much trickier to know what set of relevant objects serves as a basis for computation of base rates. We can say more about this by bringing to the forefront an issue that we suppressed to this point in the interest of simplicity. This is the domain in which the focal concept(s) sit. Recall that chapters 5 and 7 built up an imagery and a corresponding formal model of local structure in a conceptual space, sets of concepts in domain (root concepts and their first-order subconcepts). We argued that concepts inherit information from their "parent(s)," including feature dimensions. Moreover, as the root is a concept in its own right, peo-ple with that concept form expectations (concept likelihoods) that inform the priors associated with the subconcepts. Moreover, information about the objects likely to be encountered in the task of deciding what things are instances of the root concept also provides information about what kinds of objects one will likely encounter in making judgments about a focal concept from the domain.

People presumably estimate a category base rate as the proportion of all of the objects that they have encountered in a domain that they have posi-tively categorized as instances of the focal concept. With the definition of a category introduced in the previous section as the set of objects that get cat-egorized, this proportion can be formulated as the cardinal of the category divided by the cardinal of the set of objects perceived in the domain. For example, think of the concept as a film genre and the set of relevant objects as the set of films already viewed.

The formation of priors is likely not only a function of relative prevalence as captured by a person's previous categorization experiences in a domain. A large body of work in cognitive psychology points to a variety of object-level and situational factors that shape how a given experience or object is perceived, encoded in a person's memory, and subsequently recalled.[8] Among these factors are an object's salience, which describes the extent to which it stands out from its environment, and vividness, which captures inherent or non-context-dependent features of an object that make it stand out regardless of context. While research suggests that these factors do not necessarily affect the sheer amount of memory devoted to an object or experience, they do likely influence how memories get stored. This might cause them to vary in terms of accessibility, that is, the ease with which they come to mind.

Through the process of priming, some mental representations of experience or objects become activated more readily than others and might then influence how novel stimuli get perceived. For example, if a person has been primed to think of crime, she is more likely to categorize a person she observes struggling with the lock on a car as a thief who is attempting to break in rather than as an owner attempting to get into her own car. To the extent that an experience like this then becomes remembered in a particular way (i.e., a crime or not), it can enter into a person's priors for the concept of crime going forward. While we acknowledge the role of these processes in shaping priors, we do not specify them formally beyond noting their contribution to the formation of one's priors.

Notwithstanding the role of various factors that shape encoding and recall, we make the assumption that the prior probability is a nondecreasing function of the category base rate. Let N_{cr} denote this ratio for the concept c in the domain with root r. We assume that base rates are established within domains, (e.g., if one is thinking about films, it does not matter how many fruits and cars that person has seen). Similarly, let N_{xr} denote the number of objects for which the individual has a mental representation at the positions x in the semantic space $\mathbb{F}_r$, that is, objects for which $R_{\mathbb{F}_r}(o) = x$.

With these, we can rewrite the probabilities of categorization in a form more amenable to empirical analysis by substituting the relative frequencies. For example, the probability of categorization in a single-concept context (equation 8.5 in proposition 8.1) becomes

$$P(c \mid \mathcal{I}_0, x) = \pi_{\mathbb{F}_c}(x \mid c) \, \frac{N_{cr}}{N_{xr}}. \tag{8.8}$$

All of the other Bayesian formulas in the foregoing sections can be restated in similar terms.

Modeling the prior probability in this fashion is not always reasonable. For example, the superordinate concept (e.g., fruit) probably has a higher base rate than many of what Rosch called the *basic-level* concepts (e.g., apple). But the basic level has greater diagnosticity and there are many situations in which we will categorize foods in terms of basic-level concepts. So we have seen more fruit (N is larger), but the $P(\text{fruit} \mid \mathcal{I}_0)$ might not be as high as the probabilities for the basic-level concepts. This discussion suggests that the prior probability will vary strongly with context, as we argued above.

8.8 Exclusive Categorization

In many settings, people have to choose one concept among a set of candidate concepts to categorize each item. For example, much—perhaps most—experimental research on categorization asks subjects to choose between two concepts (for instance, to tell which of two children drew a stick-figure after learning the two styles). The online auction website eBay.com restricts sellers to list an item in only a single category; the seller does the exclusive categorization. Some research journals demand that submitting authors choose one of a set of disciplinary categories for processing the submission. For most of its history, the United States Census restricted census takers to choose one of a set of ethnic/racial categories for a respondent.

We mark this kind of context with the predicate EXCLUSIVE($\mathfrak{C}$), which reads as "the categorization task involves assigning an object to one element in $\mathfrak{C}$, a list of single-categorization alternatives."

Definition 8.3 *A categorization task is exclusive if the set of possible concept assignments contains two or more items and each item is a single concept, meaning that there are no joint categorization possibilities allowed and that the empty set is not a possible assignment.*

$$\text{EXCLUSIVE}(\mathfrak{C}) \leftrightarrow \mathfrak{C} = \{\{c_1\},...,\{c_K\}\}.^9$$

To specify a Bayesian model of categorization in this setting, we need to assume that the individual has some information about the context that allows him to form the necessary priors. In particular, he needs a set of prior probabilities on the concepts $c_1,...,c_K$. We denote the prior on concept c_k by $P(c_k \mid \mathcal{I}_0)$. This is the subjective probability that an arbitrary object encountered in the context turns out to be a c_k. We will denote the expanded semantic space associated with the menu of possible categorizations as $\mathbb{G} = \cup_{k=1}^K \mathbb{F}_{c_k}$. We specify the concept likelihoods and priors on positions over this space because we need the probabilities to be expressed over the same space if we want to use them in the same mathematical expression.

The first step toward expressing the categorization probability is to establish the priors on concepts and positions. In this particular setting, we can express the prior on the position on the basis of the priors on the concepts by using the law of total probability:[10]

$$\text{EXCLUSIVE}(\mathfrak{C}) \rightarrow P_{\mathbb{G}}(x \mid \mathcal{I}_0) = \sum_{c_k \in \mathfrak{C}} P_{\mathbb{G}}(x \mid c_k, \mathcal{I}_0) \, P(c_k \mid \mathcal{I}_0). \quad (8.9)$$

And by applying postulate 8.2, we can rewrite this formula in terms of the concept likelihoods:

$$\text{EXCLUSIVE}(\mathfrak{C}) \rightarrow P_{\mathbb{G}}(x \mid \mathcal{I}_0) = \sum_{c_k \in \mathfrak{C}} \pi_{\mathbb{G}}(x \mid c_k) \, P(c_k \mid \mathcal{I}_0). \quad (8.10)$$

These developments imply that, in this exclusive categorization setting, a prior on positions is not needed to specify the categorization probability. This is because the prior can be reconstructed on the basis of the priors on the concepts and the concept likelihood functions. Therefore, the information about the context, $\mathcal{I}_0$, only needs to include information that allows for the formation of priors over concepts. We can now specify a postulate that parallels postulate 8.1.

Postulate 8.3 (Bayes' theorem for exclusive categorization) *The categorization probability of an object at a position equals the product of the concept likelihood and the ratio of the two priors (on the concept and on the position).*

Consider an individual facing the task of categorizing an object o as an instance of one concept among $c_1, \ldots, c_K$: EXCLUSIVE($\mathfrak{C}$) is the case and $\mathfrak{C} = \{\{c_1\}, \ldots, \{c_K\}\}$. In addition, suppose that

1. *the information about the context, including the fact that EXCLUSIVE($\mathfrak{C}$) is the case, is denoted by $\mathcal{I}_0$;*
2. *the expanded semantic space associated with the menu of possible categorizations is $\mathbb{G} = \cup_{k=1}^{K} \mathbb{F}_{c_k}$; and*
3. *the individual knows the position of the object in the expanded semantic space: the person's information includes $\{R_{\mathbb{F}_{\mathbb{G}}}(o) = x\}$.*

The subjective probability that object o is an instance of the concept c_k (i.e., the person believes that the hypothesis IS-A(c_k, o) is true), given that the object is at the position x in semantic space $\mathbb{G}$, is

$$P(c_k \mid \mathcal{I}_0, x) = \frac{P_{\mathbb{G}}(x \mid \mathcal{I}_0, c_k) \, P(c_k \mid \mathcal{I}_0)}{P_{\mathbb{G}}(x \mid \mathcal{I}_0)} = \frac{P_{\mathbb{G}}(x \mid \mathcal{I}_0, c_k) \, P(c_k \mid \mathcal{I}_0)}{\sum_{j=1}^{K} P_{\mathbb{G}}(x \mid \mathcal{I}_0, c_j) \, P(c_j \mid \mathcal{I}_0)}.$$

This postulate is Bayes' theorem adapted to a particular inference context, as in postulate 8.1. We can use our postulate that links stable concept likelihoods and conditional probabilities (postulate 8.2) and the law of total probability (equation 8.9) to rewrite the categorization probability in terms of the concept likelihoods.

Proposition 8.3 (Bayes' theorem for exclusive categorization in terms of the concept likelihood) *Under the specification of the categorization task given in the preamble of postulate 8.3, it follows that*

$$P(c_k \mid \mathcal{I}_0, x) = \frac{\pi_{\mathbb{G}}(x \mid c_k) \, P(c_k \mid \mathcal{I}_0)}{\sum_{j=1}^{K} \pi_{\mathbb{G}}(x \mid c_j) \, P(c_j \mid \mathcal{I}_0)}. \tag{8.11}$$

Discussion

In this chapter, we delineated a model of categorization, the process by which concepts get applied to objects. We view categorization as crisp at a moment in time (i.e., an object either gets categorized as an instance of a concept or it does not), but it is clear that categorizations of the same object by the same person can and do vary over occasions. As a result, we modeled categorization as a probabilistic process, giving special attention to the role of the local context. Key elements of our specification are summarized and discussed below.

Analogous to our representation of concepts as existing in a semantic space, we also represent objects as positions within such a space. An object's position encapsulates a person's perception of the object. Importantly, we view the context as decisively shaping perception by priming certain concepts and thereby drawing a person's attention to a subset of the object's potentially numerous features. For the purpose of this chapter, we treat perception as "full," meaning we assume that a person has no uncertainty as to the object's values on any features of the semantic space.

An important aspect of our model involves specifying the role of the inferential context. One way in which the context shapes categorization is by specifying the set of possible categorization options (e.g., the set of concepts that are available for assignment). In this chapter, we model categorization in two kinds of contexts: first, contexts in which a person has to choose to categorize an object as an instance of a single concept (or not), and second, contexts in which a person has to categorize an object as belonging to one out of a set of several candidate concepts.

For both contexts, our model of categorization is built upon Bayes' theorem. We specify the probability of categorizing an object as an instance of a concept as a function of three factors: the concept likelihood, and two prior probabilities, namely the subjective probability that a randomly encountered object in the context belongs to the category and the subjective probability that a randomly encountered object in the context exists at a particular position (i.e., has a specific set of feature values).

An important assumption of our model is that concepts remain stable over different contexts. That is, the meaning that a person associates with a given concept does not change over situations. Formally, this means that the concept likelihood enters our model in a way that is not conditional on the local context. In contrast, the context plays an important role in shaping the two prior probabilities involved in categorization. We model the concept and position priors, respectively, as nondecreasing functions of base rates, which capture the relative prevalence of concepts and positions in a person's previous experiences of the domain. Of course, other psychologically relevant aspects of a person's previous experiences (e.g., the salience of objects encountered) also shape these priors.

We also relate categorization to typicality. The probability that an object will be categorized as an instance of a concept is an increasing function of the object's typicality in a given context. However, modeling categorization in the Bayesian fashion described above, and specifying that the concept likelihood is stable, together imply that researchers can use data on a person's categorization behaviors in a context to recover his or her concept likelihood. In other words, relying on typicality ratings is not the only way to obtain a person's concept. This is an attractive feature of our model, given the type of data to which sociologists typically have access.

Given the central role that Bayes' theorem plays in our model, it is worth discussing the justification for this approach. Reliance on Bayes' theorem is central to a large number of probabilistic theories of cognition (Ashby and Alfonso-Reese, 1995; Sanborn et al., 2010). These theories differ with respect to the assumptions they make regarding how people compute the various components of this ratio rule.[11] Much attention has been given to the concept likelihood. A vast amount of research has discussed how this function is represented in memory and how people can learn it on the basis of observations. Multiple perspectives have been developed in the form of a variety of prototype and exemplar models. Our purpose here is not to decide which of these is the most realistic model of the mental representation of categories. Instead, we build on this work to develop models of categorization that fit the notion of concept laid out in chapters 2 and 4 and that let us build bridges to sociological and cultural analysis. In addition, we note that our own experimental examination of categorization behaviors, which we reported earlier in this chapter, provides strong evidence of the correspondence between predictions derived from a Bayesian model and our observations of people's actual categorization behaviors.

CHAPTER NINE

Free Categorization

SO FAR, WE HAVE AIMED to demonstrate that much can be gained by drawing upon the cognitive psychology literature to better specify the foundations for sociological analysis. Yet, in the interest of focusing on detailed mechanisms involving mental representations, research on concepts and categories in psychology and related fields often purposefully avoids some of the messy (and in our opinion fascinating) realities of how people deploy concepts in everyday life. For example, outside of the lab a person might say that a music album sounds emo, indie, and punk, or that a software product provides business intelligence and management systems integration. Existing research has generally treated the learning and deployment of concepts one at a time. As a result we know little about how multiple categorization works and what consequences it has. While the complications of concept use outside the lab certainly raise challenges to the study of meaning-making processes, tackling such issues is important for sociological application.

9.1   Ubiquity of Multiple Categorization

Typical laboratory tests of categorization models ask participants to assign a series of visual or verbal stimuli (objects) to just one of a menu of concepts. Often, the procedure involves naming a concept and then presenting a picture or a word, and participants must decide whether or not the object is an instance of the category. Alternatively, participants are presented with objects, one at a time, and are asked to choose which of two possible concepts is the most appropriate for the object. For instance, a common experimental design displays stick-figure drawings said to be produced by two children; participants are first taught the style of each child and then are asked to judge for a set of stimulus drawings which child produced the drawing. In other studies, participants see pairs of objects and must choose which is more typical of a given concept.

But when they are unconstrained, people frequently give multiple categorizations to objects. Consider illustrative examples from three market contexts.

The first is music. We describe the pattern of categorizations of albums by the website allmusic.com, which offers descriptive and editorial content to consumers, although it also provides data to online and traditional music stores.[1] The entries are generally signed by an individual critic. Allmusic.com categorizes albums using genre and stylistic tags to describe the aesthetic characteristics of the music. Genres describe broad aesthetic categories, such as blues, country, jazz, pop/rock, and rap.[2] Genres are further subdivided into various musical styles. In the case of the most common genre, pop/rock, these include many subgenres ranging from experimental to new wave and punk.

Figure 9.1 shows the distribution of categorizations of 146,635 music albums by style on allmusic.com during the period 1991–2009. Our understanding is that the set of styles can be regarded as standing at the same level, constituting a single cohort. Categorization with only one style has been fairly rare (roughly 20% of the albums); the modal number of styles

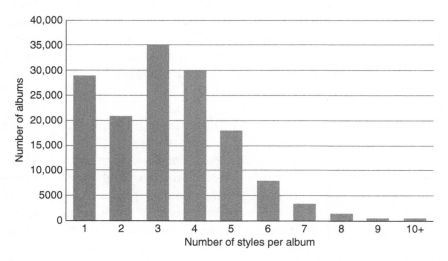

Figure 9.1 Distribution of style assignments to music albums on allmusic.com, 1991–2009

applied is three (57.8% of the albums). Clearly, this set of music critics commonly makes multiple categorizations of artistic works.

We next consider the pattern for feature films as provided by the American Film Institute Catalog of Motion Pictures (AFI).[3] We focus on feature films, defined as motion pictures of running time long enough to fill an exhibition program, typically forty minutes or more. AFI had a team of film scholars issue a collective assignment of these films based on a clear set of genre definitions it has internally researched and developed. The major genres are the common ones such as comedy, drama, fantasy, war, and western.

Figure 9.2 presents the distribution of the number of major genre assignments for 30,523 films by the Institute's curators from 1912 to 1970. Single categorization is by far the most common case, with nearly 59% of the films assigned to one genre. Still, the AFI curators assign a substantial percentage (32%) of films two genres and three or more to 9% of the films.

Finally consider the self-categorizations by software producers in press releases. Claiming affiliation with an industry (sub)category indicates a market in which the firm competes.[4] Figure 9.3 shows the distribution of the number of subindustries claimed each year during the period 1990–2002 (Pontikes, 2008). While single categorization is most common, with nearly

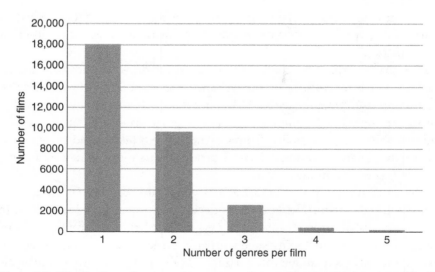

Figure 9.2 Distribution of genre assignments to feature films by the American Film Institute, 1912–1970

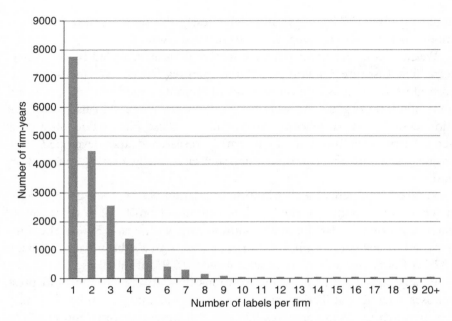

Figure 9.3 Distribution of assignment of subindustries claimed by software producers, 1990–2002

43% of the organizations claiming one subindustry, 33% claim three or more. A handful of producers claim membership in as many as forty different subindustries.

A similar distribution characterizes categorizations by industry analyst Gartner, which covers firms in software and other high technology industries. Gartner releases "magic quadrant" reports that evaluate producers in different market segments, using an industry category structure that they create and maintain.[5] Data compiled from Gartner's subindustry reports over time reveals that analysts assigned 25% of producers to more than one market category, as shown in figure 9.4.

The pattern seen in these illustrations is typical of free social categorization. Multiple categorization does not seem a mistake or residual noise in a statistical distribution. Instead it is a common phenomenon in social discourse. Individuals, including such market intermediaries as curators, do not restrict themselves to single categorizations of objects that they judge as fitting multiple concepts to some nontrivial degree. So now we adapt the formulation that we developed in the previous chapter to deal with the more complex reality of social categorization.

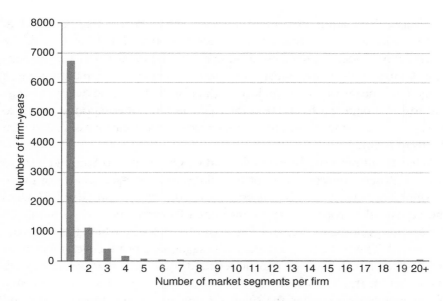

Figure 9.4   Distribution of software submarket assignments by Gartner, 1996–2010

9.2   Concept Sets versus Compound Concepts

Before turning to the model, we briefly address a potentially important complication. Some situations of multiple categorization involve assigning together a set of distinct concepts, such as post-punk, new-wave, and alternative (all subcategories of rock). Other situations, however, involve combining multiple concepts. For instance, AFI treats romantic comedy as a stand-alone film genre, defining it as "a genre in which the development of a romance leads to comic situations." Similarly, the Script Lab defines as romantic comedy "a genre that attempts to catch the viewer's heart with the combination of love and humor." How can we address situations in which a particular combination of concepts has become conceptualized?

Should romantic comedy be read as a concept *list* (i.e., set) or as a compound concept? In the case of noun-plus-noun pairs, the most relevant type for our comparison, a compound constitutes a linguistic unit in which one word operates as the "head" noun of the expression and the other word modifies it (in more extreme form the nouns are combined as in airport). In English, the head noun generally comes after its modifier. Consider another compound: cellar door. Here the modifier tells the kind of door.

Clearly, these kinds of compounds narrow down the kinds referred to by the head nouns. There are many kinds of doors, and cellar door is one specific type. Indeed, such a compound should be regarded as a *single* concept. Compounds do not satisfy the criterion that calling something, say, a hedge fund means that one thinks that the object is to some degree a hedge and to some degree a fund. We think that this kind of compound ought to be regarded as a single concept, a subconcept of the concept associated with the head noun.

What about pet fish, the example used by Osherson and Smith (1981) to criticize Rosch's interpretation of typicalities as (fuzzy-set) grades of membership? The issue at stake is *compositionality*, the desideratum that languages should have the property that the meaning of an utterance depends only on the meanings of the elementary terms and the rules by which the terms are composed. This is the property that makes language productive: if meanings are compositional, then we can understand utterances that we have never encountered. If, as Rosch suggested, typicalities are grades of membership (fuzzy memberships), then the rules of fuzzy logic apply. In this kind of set theory, the intersection set of grade of membership functions is defined as the minimum of the set. Here something seems to go wrong with pet fish. The most typical exemplars of this term are things like goldfish and guppies. But these are both highly atypical pets and highly atypical fish. So by this arithmetic, compositionality fails.

But it is not exactly clear what is going on in this famous example. It is tempting to think of pet fish as a compound: it narrows down the kinds of fish that qualify as typical instances. But one could as well think of the term as narrowing down the kinds of pets (even though the reverse wording sounds weird). Indeed, Hampton (1987) argues and shows experimentally that people can form prototypes of the intersection in such situations. Participants sometimes judge stimuli to have higher typicality in the intersection of a pair of concepts than in the component concepts. So, for instance, participants judge a picture of an apple that happened to be brown as more typical of brown apple than as apple.

This is an instance of what is termed an overgeneralization of the intersection or the conjunction fallacy. Tversky and Kahneman (1983) report a similar pattern for probability judgments using the well-known story of "Linda"; the experimenters told participants that Linda had radical feminist views as a college student and was employed as a bank teller. These participants report that the probability that "Linda is a feminist bank teller" is higher than that of "Linda is a bank teller." Hampton (1997, p. 145) argues that both categorization judgments and judgments of typicality in these cases "depend on an assessment of the similarity of the instance to representation of the conjunctive category, and a corresponding tendency to over-extend the boundaries of the conjunction, or overestimate the probability that an individual belongs to it." Hampton's (1987) composite-prototype model shows how people can form prototypes of the conjunction using the feature profiles associated with the conjoined concepts.

These lines of research suggest some caution for analysts interpreting multiple categorization in social situations. One needs to distinguish two quite different cases:

1. a particular combination of concepts has been conceptualized, and
2. a combination of concepts is applied to objects that "sit between" concepts in semantic space in positions that have not (yet) been conceptualized.

Compound concepts (case 1) should not be treated as multiple concepts since they are in effect a single concept. An indication that a noun-plus-noun unit forms a compound is that reversing the terms changes the meaning, perhaps making it meaningless (e.g., door cellar). Another indication, following Hampton's work, is that assessments of objects' typicality can be higher for a joint concept than for each of its constituents.

Notice that disambiguating the compounds requires background knowledge of the context and the domain in both cases. This makes things tricky. Someone without knowledge of modern financial organization would not know that the hedge in hedge fund refers to a particular investment strategy (hedging bets). So, the meaning of the compound is indeed compositional but only to those with detailed knowledge of the local language fragment.

Our experience in studying the application of genres and other social concepts is that combinations are not commonly used as compounds and that the combinations of genres have generally not been conceptualized. When Yelp.com categorized a San Francisco restaurant as {Mexican, Vietnamese}, it did not intend, in our view, to signal that this establishment was a special kind of Vietnamese restaurant. We interpret this as a categorization decision that the establishment is to some degree an instance of the two genres. This is an instance of what we mean by multiple categorization. We treat these concepts as an unordered set for which each element is a "stand alone" concept.

We restrict attention to situations in which the context imposes a domain and its cohort of concepts. We do not treat classification of an artwork as, say, {symphony, music} as a multiple categorization because one concept is a subconcept of the other. In general, the context fixes the relevant set of concepts. For instance, each of the data sources we sketched above pertains to a specific context. It would be redundant for AFI, say, to classify items as film.

To conclude, we consider as instances of multiple categorization only those in which

1. each component concept qualifies as a "stand-alone" concept;
2. the combination of concepts has not been conceptualized; and
3. none of the concepts refers to a concept that is a subconcept of one of the other concepts.

A structure that satisfies these desiderata is a *cohort of concepts*, as defined in chapter 5. So we restrict that argument in this chapter to apply to situations in which the context focuses attention on a cohort.

9.3   Free-Categorization Probability

The demand to choose a single exclusive concept strikes us as highly artificial. A requirement that objects have to be sorted into categories such that every object is made an instance of a unique concept often generates tension. The question of whether what we experience now is snow or rain could sometimes more naturally be answered as "a bit of both."

Now we are ready to build a model in which people can freely apply one or several concepts to an object. Multiple categorization of an object reflects the judgment that it satisfies the IS-A relation for several concepts but not for others.[6]

Definition 9.1 (Free categorization) *A categorization task that focuses on the domain $\mathfrak{D}_r$ is free if and only if the menu of possible categorizations includes any combination of concepts in the cohort associated with the domain (these are all of the elements in the powerset of the cohort).*

$$\mathrm{FREE}(r) \leftrightarrow (\mathfrak{C} = \wp(\kappa)) \wedge (cohort(r, \Lambda) = \kappa).$$

We now need to introduce some notation regarding categorization in sets of concepts. Consider a set of concepts $\mathbf{C}$. We will denote by $P(\mathbf{C})$ the probability that the object has been categorized in all concepts in $\mathbf{C}$ but no other in the cohort.

We can now specify the categorization probability in a way that parallels what we did when the menu of concept assignments was constrained (postulates 8.1 and 8.3).

Postulate 9.1 (Bayes' theorem for free categorization) *Consider an individual facing the following categorization task and context:*

1. *categorization in the domain $\mathfrak{D}_r$ is free;*
2. *the information about the context, denoted by $\mathcal{I}_0$, includes knowledge of the domain $\mathfrak{D}_r$—that is, it includes information about the distribution of positions of objects that are r's, the list of concepts in the cohort κ associated with the domain, the fact that the categorization is free ($\mathfrak{C} = \wp(\kappa)$), and information that allows the individual to have priors about all the possible concept assignments;*
3. *the expanded semantic space associated with the menu of possible categorizations is $\mathbb{G} = \cup_{c \in \kappa} \mathbb{F}_c$; and*
4. *the individual knows the position of the focal object in the expanded space: the person's information includes $\{R_{\mathbb{G}}(o) = x\}$.*

The probability of categorizing an object o with exactly the set of concepts $\mathbf{C} \in \mathfrak{C}$, given that the object is at the position x in semantic space $\mathbb{G}$, is

$$P(\mathbf{C} \mid \mathcal{I}_0, x) = \frac{P_{\mathbb{G}}(x \mid \mathcal{I}_0, \mathbf{C})\, P(\mathbf{C} \mid \mathcal{I}_0)}{\pi_{\mathbb{G}}(x \mid r)}. \tag{9.1}$$

Although we see nothing wrong with the claim of the postulate as an implementation of Bayesian categorization in the free-categorization context, we do find it problematic to associate it with a clear cognitive process. To understand the difficulties encountered in using the postulate as a cognitive rule, compare this formula with the corresponding formula for single-concept contexts in postulate 8.1.

For free categorization, $P(\mathbf{C} \mid \mathcal{I}_0)$ is the prior probability that the object has been categorized as an instance of exactly the concepts in $\mathbf{C}$ (all of them and no other). This closely matches $P(c \mid \mathcal{I}_0)$ in the single-concept context. The prior on the position is unproblematic as well. In the free categorization, it is given by $\pi_{\mathbb{G}}(x \mid r)$, which is just another way of writing $P_{\mathbb{G}}(x \mid \mathcal{I}_0)$ by using the knowledge that the object is an r. This matches the prior probability on positions for single concepts, $P_{\mathbb{F}_c}(x \mid \mathcal{I}_0)$.

The problematic difference between the two formulas concerns the remaining term. In single-concept contexts, it is $P_{\mathbb{F}_c}(x \mid \mathcal{I}_0, c)$, which denotes the probability that the object lies at the position x given that it is a c. The corresponding term for free categorization is $P_{\mathbb{G}}(x \mid \mathcal{I}_0, \mathbf{C})$. For single concepts, we could substitute $P_{\mathbb{F}_c}(x \mid \mathcal{I}_0, c)$ by the concept likelihood—the mental representation of the concept (using postulate 8.2). No similar substitution is possible for free categorization.

For free categorization, unlike our analysis of single concepts, we do not want to assume pre-existing mental representation for the *set* of multiple concepts, following the desideratum we stated in §9.2. If a particular combination has been conceptualized, for example, romantic comedy (today), then it should be treated as a concept in its own right. No issues arise. We are trying here to make sense of multiple categorizations in which the combinations are not compound concepts.

9.4   Categorization under Conditional Independence

We can make a start on the analysis by considering a tractable baseline formulation, which we call conditional independence. To fix ideas, consider a domain with only two concepts in the cohort: c_1 and c_2. In this case, $\mathscr{P}(\kappa) = \{\emptyset, \{c_1\}, \{c_2\}, \{c_1, c_2\}\}$. Suppose an individual believes that an object is an instance of both concepts. We can use the law of total probability for this simple example to write

$$P(\text{IS-A}(c_1, o) \wedge \text{IS-A}(c_2, o) \mid \mathcal{I}_0, x)$$

$$= P(\text{IS-A}(c_1, o) \mid \mathcal{I}_0, x) \cdot P(\text{IS-A}(c_2, o) \mid \mathcal{I}_0, x, \text{IS-A}(c_1, o)). \quad (9.2)$$

In our model, the relevant information about an object–concept pair is represented by the object's position x in the semantic space in which the concept embeds. Suppose that (perceived) position is all that matters. Then, the decision that an object is a c does not change a person's information about the object because she made this assignment exclusively on the basis of her information about feature values. When people can categorize objects with as many concepts as they want and information about objects consists *only* of feature values, the likelihood of multiple categorizations is the product of the likelihoods of the separate categorizations.[7] If the categorization of an object as an instance of c_1 does not change the information state about the object, then

$$P(\text{IS-A}(c_2, o) \mid \mathcal{I}_0, x, \text{IS-A}(c_1, o)) = P(\text{IS-A}(c_2, o) \mid \mathcal{I}_0, x). \quad (9.3)$$

This implies that

$$P(\text{IS-A}(c_1, o) \wedge \text{IS-A}(c_2, o) \mid \mathcal{I}_0, x)$$

$$= P(\text{IS-A}(c_1, o) \mid \mathcal{I}_0, x) \cdot P(\text{IS-A}(c_2, o) \mid \mathcal{I}_0, x). \quad (9.4)$$

In this setup, the likelihood that the object at the position x gets assigned both c_1 and c_2 equals the product of the likelihood of the belief that the object is a c_1 and the likelihood of the belief that it is a c_2. In other words, the elementary categorization events are independent conditional on the position of the object in semantic space.

The crucial step that allowed us to move ahead and write the probability of receiving two categorizations as a function of the component concept likelihoods was the realization that we could write this probability as the *product* of two categorization probabilities (see equation 9.4). We call this property *conditional independence*.

For notational simplicity, we assume there are K concepts in the cohort κ and that $\kappa = \{c_1, ..., c_K\}$.

Definition 9.2 (Conditional independence) *The conditional independence property is a potential property of a free categorization task.*

$$\mathrm{IND}(\kappa) \leftrightarrow \mathrm{FREE}(r)$$

$$\wedge\, P(\mathrm{IS\text{-}A}(c_1, o), ..., \mathrm{IS\text{-}A}(c_K, o) \mid \mathcal{I}_0, x) = \prod_{k=1}^{K} P(\mathrm{IS\text{-}A}(c_k, o) \mid \mathcal{I}_0, x). \quad (9.5)$$

This definition has an interesting implication for the likelihood that an object receives an *additional* categorization and that it gets categorized, say, as c, in addition to all of its other categorizations.

Proposition 9.1 *Suppose an object o has received a set of categorizations $c_1, ..., c_J (J < K)$. The probability that the individual also categorizes object o as a c_{J+1} has the following form, provided that conditional independence holds:*

$$\mathrm{IND}(\kappa) \to P(\mathrm{IS\text{-}A}(c_{J+1}, o) \mid \mathcal{I}_0, x, \mathrm{IS\text{-}A}(c_1, o), ..., \mathrm{IS\text{-}A}(c_J, o))$$

$$= P(\mathrm{IS\text{-}A}(c_{J+1}, o) \mid \mathcal{I}_0, x). \quad (9.6)$$

Adding Constraints

Sometimes cultural conventions rule out some combinations of assignments. For instance, the English-speaking community appears to agree that an object cannot be categorized as both sacred and profane. One way to accommodate such constraint is to define the set of possible concept assignment, $\mathfrak{C}$, as a subset of $\wp(\kappa)$ that excludes the impermissible assignments.

9.5   Testing Conditional Independence

We introduced conditional independence in categorizations as a simple base-line. It is not at all clear that it approximates well how people conduct free categorization. So we conducted a series of experiments to address the fit of the baseline to behaviors in controlled categorization situations.

Arrowhead Experiment

We used the general setup of the experiments with styles of arrowheads, described in chapter 4, to explore the predictive power of the conditional independence assumption. In a second stage of the experiment described previously, the participants were told the following:

> Experts have concluded that some arrowheads of the
> West African collection belong clearly to the Akka
> style and others clearly belong to the Boko style.
> However, they concluded that some arrowheads have
> influences of both styles. Next, you will be shown a
> series of arrowheads and you will be asked to choose
> the description that best fits each of the
> arrowheads.

The participants saw each stimulus arrowhead along with *both* prototypes. Figure 9.5 shows an example.

The participants were asked, "Which of the following best describes the sample arrowhead?" We provided radio buttons for

- Akka style,
- Boko style,
- Akka style and Boko style, and
- neither style.

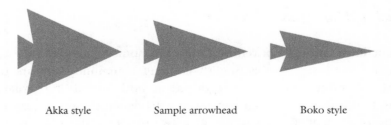

Akka style   Sample arrowhead   Boko style

Figure 9.5 An example of the comparisons made in the second stage

(The program allowed participants to click only one of the available responses.) The responses are the stage-two categorization decisions. Finally, the participants were asked, "How typical is the sample arrowhead of each style?" They were presented with two sliders, one for each style, and asked to give a typicality rating with respect to each style. These are the *second-stage typicality judgments*.

Next we use our estimates of the concept likelihoods from Stage 1 and definition 9.2 to form predictions of categorization behavior in Stage 2, assuming that conditional independence holds. It is worth emphasizing that these are *out-of-sample* predictions because parameter estimations are made at a stage prior to collection of categorization data.

Remember that we denoted by $\mathbb{F}_{\text{Akka}}$ the semantic space associated with the Akka concept. The semantic space associated with the Boko concept is the same: $\mathbb{F}_{\text{Boko}} = \mathbb{F}_{\text{Akka}}$. To maintain notational consistency with earlier developments, we denote this common semantic space by $\mathbb{G}$. (Thus, $\mathbb{G} = \mathbb{F}_{\text{Akka}} = \mathbb{F}_{\text{Boko}} = \mathbb{F}_{\text{Akka}} \cup \mathbb{F}_{\text{Boko}}$.)

Recall that participants can give one of four categorical assignments. First, consider instances of categorization of an arrowhead only as an Akka. Equation 9.5 gives[8]

$$P(\text{Akka only} \mid \mathcal{I}_o, x) = \frac{P_{\mathbb{G}}(x \mid \mathcal{I}_o, \text{Akka}) \, P(\text{Akka} \mid \mathcal{I}_0)}{P_{\mathbb{G}}(x \mid \mathcal{I}_0)}$$
$$\left(1 - \frac{P_{\mathbb{G}}(x \mid \mathcal{I}_o, \text{Boko}) \, P(\text{Boko} \mid \mathcal{I}_0)}{P_{\mathbb{G}}(x \mid \mathcal{I}_0)}\right).$$

Figure 9.6 compares the model predictions with the average behavior over the space (with polynomial smoothing). We see a very close fit in the more complex situation of Stage 2. We get a very similar pattern for the Boko style (not shown).

We are interested in the both-style and neither-style responses. Figures 9.7 and 9.8 show that the model predictions do not fit well the data in the portion of the space that lies in between the two prototypes. By contrast, the fit is good on the "outside." Let us focus on the probability of being categorized as an instance of both styles (figure 9.7). Between the prototypes, participants were much more likely to assign both styles than our model predicted. In other words, the likelihood of assigning the two styles was much higher than the products of the individual categorization probabilities implied by the conditional independence assumption. Correspondingly, figure 9.8 shows that the probability of "neither" is greatly suppressed relative to the expectation under conditional independence in the region

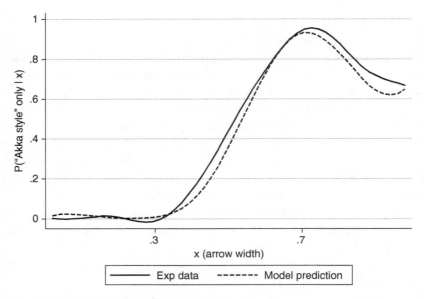

Figure 9.6 Likelihood of assigning only the Akka style

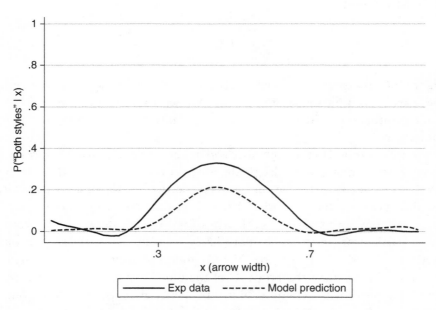

Figure 9.7 Likelihood of selecting the button "Akka style and Boko style"

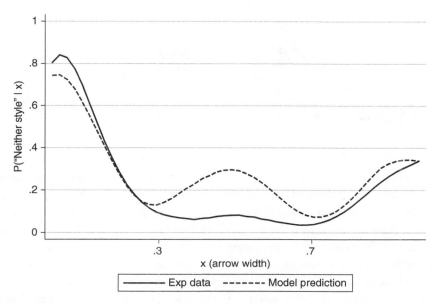

Figure 9.8 Likelihood of choosing "Neither style"

between the concepts but reasonably approximates the expectation outside this range.

The Earring Experiment

Le Mens et al. (2016) replicated this study in a different context to learn whether something about the setup of the arrowhead experiments created misleading results. The overall structure of this study closely followed that of the arrowhead experiment. But participants were told that they were to categorize stylized earrings by style (an "East-island" style and "West-island" style). Unlike the one-dimensional real-valued stimuli created to represent arrowheads, the stylized earrings were constructed from four binary features: outer shape (triangle or circle), insert shape (crescent or star), color (blue or orange), and fill (whole figure or outer band only). This results in sixteen stimuli.

The stimuli were positioned in a four-dimensional Boolean space. The maximal (city-block) distance between them was four (every feature of one has to be switched to get the other). The prototypes were three steps apart (the only common feature is outer shape.) What does it mean to be "inside" or between the prototypes in this kind of Boolean space? We propose that this

West style   East style

Figure 9.9 Prototypes used in the earring study

is the case when a position lies closer to each prototype than the prototypes are to each other. Given that the prototypes were set to be three steps apart, a position is inside if it is one step from one prototype and two steps from the other. Likewise, a position lies outside the space spanned by the prototypes if it is further from one of the prototypes than they are from each other. In the case in hand, this means that the position would have to differ on all four features from one of the prototypes. The discrete space allows ambiguous positions that lie on the boundary separating "inside" and "outside." We call these boundary positions.

In a preliminary study, participants gave similarity ratings to all pairs of stimuli. Multidimensional scaling analysis of the matrix of similarities reveals that the participants generally perceived the stimuli as four-dimensional objects.[9]

In the main study, another group of participants learned (in random order) the two prototypes depicted in figure 9.9 and categorized stimuli as instances or not. They also gave typicality ratings as we described for the arrowhead experiments. In the second stage, participants saw each stimulus and were asked to indicate whether it was "East style only," "West style only," "both styles," or "neither style."

If the conditional independence property holds, then categorization of a stimulus as an instance of the East style and categorization of the same stimulus as an instance of the West style are independent of each other.

To evaluate conditional independence, we rely on the data collected in the two stages of the experiment. From the first stage, we obtain the probability that an object is (at least) from the East style, $\hat{p}_1(\text{East} \mid x)$ and the probability it is (at least) from the West style, $\hat{p}_1(\text{West} \mid x)$. From the second stage, we obtain the probability that an object is from both styles, $\hat{p}_2(\text{both} \mid x)$. If the conditional independence property holds, then the following equation should hold:

$$\hat{p}_2(\text{both} \mid x) = \hat{p}_1(\text{East} \mid x) \times \hat{p}_1(\text{West} \mid x), \tag{9.7}$$

where the right-hand side is the "predicted" probability of categorization in both styles under conditional independence and the left-hand side is the observed probability of categorization in both styles. For each object, we calculated t-tests comparing the left-hand side and the right-hand side of equation 9.7. Finding a significant difference between the left-hand side and the right-hand side would indicate a violation of conditional independence. We found evidence for such violation for the positions "between" the prototypes and on the "boundary." Comparison of observed and predicted probabilities indicate a statistically significant higher likelihood of being categorized as "both styles" than is predicted by conditional independence. A similar analysis comparing the observed probability of "neither style" from stage 2 and the prediction based on the stage 1 categorization probabilities indicates a statistically significant lower likelihood of being categorized as "neither style" than is predicted.[10] However, the model of conditional independence fits reasonably well in the region "outside" the prototypes.[11]

Discussion of the Experiments

We examined whether the probability of joint categorization would be well modeled by the product of the probabilities of categorization in two sets of experiments. This strategy seems intuitive. But, in fact, this is an oversimplification that amounts to assuming conditional independence. This puts constraints on expected categorization behavior that are not borne out in our experiments.

The likelihood of assigning a collection of concepts is not multiplicatively separable. This suggests that people attend to considerations other than the fits in concepts considered in isolation when deciding on making a categorical assignment. Participants seem to behave in a qualitatively different fashion, depending on the location of the stimulus relative to the concepts.

We learned much more than the failure of the simple baseline of conditional independence to characterize empirical categorization behavior. Specifically, the likelihood that the baseline fails varies strongly by position. If we distinguish the positions that lie "between" the prototypes and those that lie "outside," both sets of experiments find substantial deviation of categorization behavior from the model in the "middle." And these are patterned. We see much more categorization of stimuli as instances of *both* concepts and much less as *neither* than is predicted by the baseline model of conditional independence.

After the fact, it seems obvious that the information content of the responses differs. If one learns that an object is an instance of neither of the applicable concepts, then all that is known is that it is reasonably far from both concepts. But it can be far from both in the middle (if the concepts are far enough apart) or somewhere on the outside of the space between the concepts. On the other hand, the categorization of an object as an instance of both concepts tells us that it is not too far from either of them but not much closer to one than to the other. The places in semantic space that satisfy this condition lie in the middle. So the joint classification (when appropriate) is much more informative.

The empirical research that stimulated our interest in free categorization used data in which objects generally received one or more concept assignments. For instance, all of the films in a compendium are assigned one or more genres. So these data do not provide information on objects without a positive classification. One way to look at this is that the categorization task faced by those who produced the data was not exactly free categorization as we defined it but instead categorization that is free but does not offer the choice of "none." In data produced under this kind of categorization task, multiple categorization (as contrasted with singleton categorizations) signals that an object lies between concepts. Perhaps the participants have so much experience with the output of the free-but-forced categorization (in normal interaction, from what they read, and so forth) that they have learned to use multiple assignment in this informative manner. It seems clear that joint categorizations for objects in positions that fall between concepts provide information about position.

Discussion

In this chapter, we noted that, in naturally occurring environments, people frequently use several concepts to characterize objects. This happens in domains as diverse as everyday conversations, review websites, reports by stock analysts, typologies of cultural production by experts, and so forth. Key elements of our discussion are summarized below.

We draw a distinction between two kinds of instances for which several concept labels are applied to an object: concept sets and compound concepts. Compound concepts use a combination of more than one label (e.g., romantic comedy) but have been conceptualized: the meaning of such a concept combination cannot be reconstructed on the basis of the component concepts (e.g., romantic and comedy). By contrast, a concept set is a concept combination that has not been conceptualized: its meaning can be derived based on the meanings of the component concepts and the rules of compositionality of the language.

We define a free categorization situation as a context that allows an agent to apply concepts to an object without restriction on the maximal number of concepts that can be applied. The set of candidate concepts is given by the categorization domain (a root concept and its immediate descendent in the concept hierarchy held by the agent—see chapter 5).

A possible way to predict the probability that an object will be categorized in a set of concepts is to assume *conditional independence*: if the position of the object in semantic space is known, knowing that the object is a c_1 does not change the belief that the object is a c_2. In other words, when the position is known, concept assignments are independent from each other. Under this assumption, the probability that an object at position x is a c_1 and a c_2 is the product of the two elementary categorization probabilities. These categorization probabilities can be deducted from the priors on each concept, the prior on the position, and the concept likelihoods for c_1 and c_2.

In experiments designed to test the conditional independence assumption, we found limited support for it. At positions outside of the area between the centers of two candidate concepts, the probability that an object received two categorizations was close to the product of the categorization probabilities. This is consistent with the conditional independence assumption. In between the two concept centers, support for the conditional independence assumption was weaker: the probability that an object received the two categorizations was substantially higher than the product of the categorization probabilities. Of note, the probability of joint categorization was increasing with the product of the categorization probabilities.

More work is needed to develop a model that captures beliefs about the positions of objects that have received more than one categorization. Such a model will have to be based on studies of the violation of the conditional independence assumption. Understanding the systematic patterns of such violations is an exciting avenue for future research.

CHAPTER TEN

Concepts, Perception, and Inference

THE PICTURE DRAWN SO FAR takes the perspective of a person who first perceives an object and then categorizes it depending on how closely his or her representation of the object fits to a concept. Now we turn the process around and consider how conceptualization and categorization affect perception and feature inference (Harnad, 1987a).

Previous research shows that conceptualization affects how objects are perceived. A key aspect of this work is that it casts perception as an inference process, as demonstrated in studies analyzing people's discrimination of speech sounds. As Liberman, Safford, Hoffman, and Griffith (1957) note:

> In listening to speech, one typically reduces the number and variety of the many sounds with which he is bombarded by casting them into one or another of the phoneme categories that his language allows. Thus a listener will identify as *b*, for example, quite a large number of acoustically different sounds.

The fact that some differences occur along an acoustic continuum allowed these researchers to test whether the presence of a phoneme affects perception of the sounds. They do so by comparing the quality of discrimination of sounds that lie on opposite sides of a phoneme boundary from those that lie within a phoneme category.

10.1   The Perceptual-Magnet Effect

Similar patterns have been found in experiments conducted by Patricia Kuhl (1991) on the effects of typicality on generalization in speech, leading her to introduce the idea of a perceptual magnet. The set of experiments took the following form. The first experiment asked subjects to rate the "goodness" of a series of utterances of the \o\vowel (as in *know*). Kuhl identified the sound frequency that was judged as best by a sample of adult speakers of the language; she calls this sound the prototype.[1] She also chose another that was viewed as a relatively poor rendition of \o\but was still perceived to be an instance of that vowel. In the second experiment, the subjects heard a series of sounds and were instructed to press a button when they heard a sound that differed from the one that preceded it. As predicted, the subjects were more accurate in these judgments when the referent (preceding) sound was not a prototype. When the referent was the prototype, they judged other members of the category as more similar (they were less likely to indicate a difference). Kuhl (1991, p. 99) summarizes the working hypothesis of the study as

[a] prototype acts like a perceptual "magnet": Surrounding members of the category are perceptually assimilated to it to a greater degree than expected on the basis of real psychophysical distance. Relative to a non-prototype of the category, the distance between the prototype and surrounding members is effectively decreased; in other words the perceptual space appears to be "warped," effectively shrunk around the prototype.

Effects that can be attributed to the perceptual magnet have been shown to hold in diverse domains and not only in auditory perception, although different terminology is used. For example, studies have explored these patterns in color perception by exploiting differences in perceptions by speakers of languages that do and do not linguistically discriminate between particular pairs of colors. Kay and Kempton (1984) compare English-speaking subjects to speakers of Tarahamura, a language from Northern Mexico that lacks the lexical distinction between blue and green. They found that English speakers exaggerate distances between color hues close to the blue-green border, while Tarahamura speakers showed no such distortion. Davidoff, Davies, and Roberson (1999) compared Berinmo- (a hunter-gatherer tribe from Papua New Guinea) and English-speakers. The Berinmo lack terms distinguishing blue and green but do have a boundary separating nol and wor, which does not have a parallel distinction in English. Nol is a color name defining a blueish hue, while wor defines a green-ish hue. Subjects from each linguistic group were shown a color sample and, after a delay, were asked to recall it from a pair of color samples. Each group was substantially better at discriminating over their linguistic boundary than within (a magnet effect). Moreover, this discrimination advantage did not work for the other group's linguistic boundary. Similarly, Winawer, Witthoft, Frank, Wu, Wade, and Boroditsky (2007) compared English to Russian speakers, exploiting the fact that Russian has two different words for what English speakers call blue: goluboy for light blue and siniy for dark blue. Russian speakers were faster to discriminate between colors in these linguistic categories, but there was no such effect for English speakers (who use one linguistic category for blue).

Applying concept labels to object representations accentuates the effects of concepts on perception.[2] But the magnet effect does not necessarily depend on label application. Evidence of perceptual distortion due to concepts has been found in studies that use unlabeled artificial categories.

For instance, Goldstone, Lippa, and Shiffrin (2001) created a series of bald faces by morphing between two categorized faces as well as a neutral, non-categorized one. In the first stage, subjects saw pairs of faces selected from a set of faces that belonged to two constructed categories and another unrelated face that did not belong to the categories and were asked to rate their similarity. The neutral face was chosen such that its similarity to each of the stimulus faces was within 20% of their similarities to each other. In this stage, the subjects were not given the categories. In the categorization task, subjects were shown a set of faces and were asked to put them in category A or B, and they were given feedback for their responses; the third stage is the same as the first. The experimenters then measured the differences between similarity ratings for categorized faces relative to the neutral face for faces that belonged to the same category or to different categories. They found that the differences among within-category faces significantly decreased after categorization compared to before categorization, but the differences for between-category faces did not. Goldstone et al. (2001) call this effect an altered object description.

10.2   How Concepts Affect Feature Inference

The important finding that concepts shape perception has stimulated search for mechanisms. One promising analytic approach relies on the probabilistic perspective on categorization on which we build. Feldman and Griffiths (2007) and Feldman, Griffiths, and Morgan (2009) developed a Bayesian model for the perceptual-magnet effect. They proposed that people make optimal statistical inferences when confronted with a noisy perception of an object's position in semantic space, along with a concept assignment that also conveys information about its position. We build a model that uses their formulation for multiple concepts.

What happens when someone makes an inference about the position of an object in a semantic space? One ubiquitous cause of noise in inference is partial perception: some relevant features might not be observable. For instance, one might observe the architecture and interior decoration of a restaurant and have access to its menu but not yet have sampled the food that it offers.

We are interested in modeling the inference made about the position of an object when the individual observes some possibly unreliable information about its position. We model the situation as follows. Let X denote the random variable[3] that records the true position of the object o in the semantic space $\mathbb{F}_c$. The individual observes a noisy signal z_o about this true position of the object. In this context, a signal is a function of the true position; it is a random variable whose mean equals the true position and has positive variance. The noise (the variance of the distribution of the signal) characterizes a broad array of factors that preclude observation of the true position. For example, when assessing the personality of another person, we obtain information about what they do and what they say. The situation affects these observable signals, as well as their stable personality traits. But each instance of observed behavior does not perfectly reveal the personality of the target: somebody who scores high on agreeableness might be very annoying and disrespectful in some particular situation.

Known Categorization

We start by considering a possibly unrealistic setting: the individual knows that the focal object is a c. As in §8.4, we denote the information that the individual possesses about the inference context by $\mathcal{I}_0$. Here, we use the same notation despite the differences in the tasks facing the decision maker. Whereas in §8.4, the individual was categorizing the object on the basis of knowledge of its position in feature space, here the individual does not know the position of the object, but she has already categorized it. In addition to knowing the applicable concept, she also possesses a noisy signal about the position of the object, z_o. This is the realization of a random variable denoted Z_0.[4] So that we can represent how the individual interprets this signal, we have to assume that she knows how it relates to the true position of the object. More precisely, we assume the individual knows the distribution of the signal, conditional on the true position. This knowledge forms part of her information about the context, $\mathcal{I}_0$.

In summary, the information specific to the object is the signal z_o; and the relevant information about the situation is the knowledge of the distribution of Z_0 conditional on the true position x.

We want to establish how the mental representation of the concept affects the belief about the position of the object. More precisely, we want to specify how the subjective probability distribution about the position of the object in semantic space $\mathbb{F}_c$ depends on the concept likelihood function $\pi_{\mathbb{F}_c}(\cdot \mid c)$. The following postulate gives the assumed relationship.

Postulate 10.1 (Feature inference based on a noisy signal: single-concept case) *Consider an individual who infers the position x of an object o known to be a c in semantic space $\mathbb{F}_c$. Information about the context is denoted by $\mathcal{I}_0$. In addition, suppose that the focal individual*

1. *knows the distribution of Z_0 given the true position of the object (x): $P_{\mathbb{F}_c}(z_0 \mid \mathcal{I}_0, x)$ and that this distribution is independent of the concept: $P_{\mathbb{F}_c}(z_0 \mid \mathcal{I}_0, x) = P_{\mathbb{F}_c}(z_0 \mid \mathcal{I}_0, x, c)$; and*
2. *has partial information about the position of the object in the expanded semantic space: a signal, z_0, about the position of the object.*

The subjective probability that the object o is at the position x given that it is a c and signal z_0 about its position is

$$P_{\mathbb{F}_c}(x \mid \mathcal{I}_0, z_0, c) = \frac{P_{\mathbb{F}_c}(z_0 \mid \mathcal{I}_0, x)\, \pi_{\mathbb{G}}(x \mid c)}{\sum_{x' \in \mathbb{G}} P_{\mathbb{F}_c}(x')\, P_{\mathbb{F}_c}(z_0 \mid \mathcal{I}_0, x')}. \tag{10.1}$$

For the purpose of illustration, we now assume that the concept likelihood comes from the normal family of distributions (thus concepts have a single center). We denote the mean of the concept likelihood by μ_c and its variance by σ_c^2:

$$X \mid c \sim \mathcal{N}(\mu_c, \sigma_c). \tag{10.2}$$

We also assume that the signal Z_0 follows a normal distribution centered on the true position x, with variance $\sigma_{z_0}^2$:

$$Z_0 \mid x \sim \mathcal{N}(x, \sigma_{z_0}). \tag{10.3}$$

This later distribution is part of the information the individual has about the inference context, $\mathcal{I}_0$. With these distributional assumptions, we have (Feldman et al., 2009)

$$X_o \mid \mathcal{I}_0, z_0, c \sim \mathcal{N}\left(\frac{\sigma_c^2 z_0 + \sigma_{z_0}^2 \mu_c}{\sigma_c^2 + \sigma_{z_0}^2}, \frac{\sigma_c^2 \sigma_{z_0}^2}{\sigma_c^2 + \sigma_{z_0}^2} \right). \tag{10.4}$$

In other words, the posterior distribution about the position of the object in the semantic space is a normal distribution, with a mean that is a function of both the prototype (μ_c) and the signal about the position of the object (z_o). To see this more clearly, we can rewrite the mean as follows:

$$E(X_o \mid \mathcal{I}_0, z_o, c) = \psi z_o + (1 - \psi)\mu_c, \tag{10.5}$$

where

$$\psi = \frac{\sigma_c^2}{\sigma_c^2 + \sigma_{z_o}^2}. \tag{10.6}$$

Substituting equation 10.6 into 10.5 gives the mean of the normal distribution on the right-hand side of equation 10.4.

The expected location of the object is a weighted average of the signal and the mean of the given concept. The terms in this sum are products of weighted likelihoods of the concepts given the signal. These weights show how much the inference of a rational person depends on the signal and on the concept mean. The weights have a familiar variance component form. Note that as the variance of the concept (the spread of its pdf) increases, the relative weight given to the concept—the strength of its magnet—declines. We will build on this notion in chapter 12 where we develop the implications of the entropy of a concept.

Figure 10.1 illustrates the warping of perceptual space induced by the perceptual-magnet effect. The density of the normal distribution gives the concept likelihood for the applicable concept. The points at the top of this figure refer to the "objective" space, which would be perceived by someone who lacks any applicable concept. The spacing of the points at the bottom are those that the individual perceives when she does have the concept. In this case all points in the space are pulled toward the center of the concept. And those furthest from the center of the concept are warped the most.

Uncertain-but-Exclusive Categorization

The magnet effect also operates when an object has not been categorized and there are several candidate concepts but the categorization is understood to be unique, as in a context of exclusive categorization. Then the information about the situation $\mathcal{I}_0$ includes knowledge necessary to form category priors, as in postulate 8.3. We formulate how the magnet effect operates in this slightly more realistic situation in the following postulate.

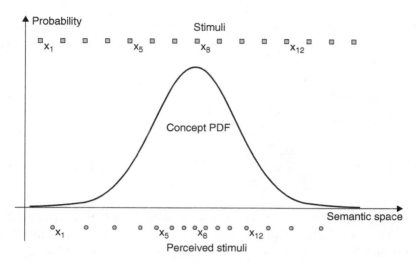

Figure 10.1 Illustration of the warping of perceptual space due to the perceptual magnet when the context makes only one concept relevant

Postulate 10.2 (Feature inference based on a noisy signal: uncertain-but-exclusive categorization) *Consider an individual who infers the position x of an object o. In addition, suppose that this individual*

1. *has not categorized the object, but regards it as one concept among $c_1, \ldots, c_K$:* EXCLUSIVE($\mathfrak{C}$) *is the case and* $\mathfrak{C} = \{\{c_1\}, \ldots, \{c_K\}\}$;
2. *knows the distribution of Z_o given the true position of the object x in expanded semantic space: $P_{\mathbb{G}}(z_o \mid \mathcal{I}_0, x)$. For all $c \in \mathfrak{C}$, this distribution is independent of the categorization, $P_{\mathbb{G}}(z_o \mid \mathcal{I}_0, x) = P_{\mathbb{G}}(z_o \mid \mathcal{I}_0, x, c)$. The knowledge of this distribution is part of $\mathcal{I}_0$, the information about the context; and*
3. *has partial information about the position of the object in the expanded semantic space: a signal z_o about its position.*

The subjective probability that the object o is at the position x in the semantic space given the signal z_o about its position is

$$P_{\mathbb{G}}(x \mid \mathcal{I}_0, z_o) = \sum_{k=1}^{K} P_{\mathbb{G}}(x \mid \mathcal{I}_0, z_o, c_k) \, P(c_k \mid \mathcal{I}_0, z_o), \qquad (10.7)$$

where the expanded semantic space associated with the menu of possible categorizations is $\mathbb{G} = \cup_{k=1}^{K} \mathbb{F}_{c_k}$.

Both $P(c_k \mid \mathcal{I}_0, z_0)$ and $P_{\mathbb{G}}(x \mid \mathcal{I}_0, z_0, c_k)$ can be expressed as functions of the concept likelihoods, the priors on the concepts, and the distribution of the signal conditional on the position:

$$P_{\mathbb{G}}(x \mid \mathcal{I}_0, z_0, c_k) = \frac{P_{\mathbb{G}}(z_0 \mid \mathcal{I}_0, x) \, \pi_{\mathbb{G}}(x \mid c_k)}{\sum_{x' \in \mathbb{G}} \pi_{\mathbb{G}}(x' \mid c_k) \, P_{\mathbb{G}}(z_0 \mid \mathcal{I}_0, x')}, \tag{10.8}$$

and

$$P(c_k \mid \mathcal{I}_0, z_0) = \frac{\sum_{x' \in \mathbb{G}} P_{\mathbb{G}}(z_0 \mid \mathcal{I}_0, x') \, \pi_{\mathbb{G}}(x' \mid c_k) \, P(c_k)}{\sum_{l=1}^{K} \sum_{x' \in \mathbb{G}} P_{\mathbb{G}}(z_0 \mid \mathcal{I}_0, x') \, \pi_{\mathbb{G}}(x' \mid c_l) \, P(c_l)}. \tag{10.9}$$

For the purpose of illustration, we again assume that the concepts likelihoods are normal distributions, and so too is the distribution of the signal conditional on the true position of the object (equations 10.2 and 10.3). Moreover, we assume that all of the candidate concepts have the same semantic space (a one-dimensional real line). Then the mean of the posterior is given by

$$\mathrm{E}(X_o \mid \mathcal{I}_0, z_0) = \psi z_0 + (1 - \psi) \sum_{c \in \mathbb{C}} P(c \mid \mathcal{I}_0, z_0) \mu_c, \tag{10.10}$$

with ψ given by equation 10.6 from the exclusive-categorization case.

Note the mean of posterior on the position of the object is a weighted average of the signal and the positions of the centers of the concepts (the prototypes). The weight of each concept is its categorization probability (based on the signal z_0). This equation formalizes the perceptual-magnet effect: the averaging process pulls the perception toward the centers of the concept likelihoods.

Figure 10.2 illustrates the perceptual-magnet effect when two concepts in a cohort are relevant. The densities of the normal distribution give the concept likelihoods for the two concepts. Again the points at the top of this figure refer to the "objective" space, and those at the bottom are those that the individual perceives when she has the two concepts. Now warping has a different pattern. Positions in the space are generally pulled toward the closer concept. However, the positions in the middle, those that lie nearly equidistant from the two concept centers, are stretched. The overall picture is one in which:

Under the assumptions of this model, then, the optimal solution for a rational perceiver is to shrink perceptual space near [...] category centers and expand perceptual space near category boundaries (Feldman and Griffiths, 2007, p. 260).

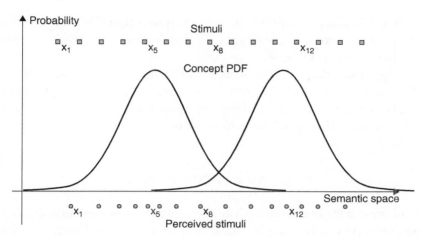

Figure 10.2 Illustration of the warping of perceptual space due to the perceptual magnet when the context makes two concepts relevant

Free Categorization

Suppose that the artificial constraint of exclusive categorization is removed and that the person making the inference faces what we called free categorization. We can work out the Bayesian formula that expresses this kind of situation in parallel to what we did for exclusive categorization. However, as we pointed out in chapter 9, we cannot reduce the probability of the position given the concept assignment to a concept likelihood. Nonetheless, it is clear that people do make inferences based on free categorization—virtually all social interaction allows this possibility, and people appear to make inferences with ease.

The interesting cases are those with multiple categorization such as the films *M⋆A⋆S⋆H* and *Stripes* that get categorized as comedy, war. Can we, upon learning the joint categorization, make inferences about the position of these films in a semantic space? It appears that we can and that these inferences are shaped by our concepts of comedy and war in the film domain.

Our categorization experiments show that people tend to categorize as instances of a pair of concepts the objects that lie near the center of the space between them. If we assume that people interpret such categorizations in the same way that they make them, then we predict that someone who is told that an arrowhead has been categorized as Akka & Boko will infer that its feature value position is roughly midway between the prototypes for these two styles. Likewise, we expect that someone who is told that a film has been categorized as comedy, war will expect its position in the joint feature space for the two concepts to lie between them.

We regard the theory and research on the perceptual-magnet effect as fundamental. It shows that the presence of concepts distorts perception from what it would be in the absence of the concepts. Moreover, the magnet effect depends on the structure of the cohort of concepts.

10.3   Experimental Evidence

We now present experimental evidence regarding whether and how concepts shape perception as in the perceptual-magnet effect. Two related experiments examine the effect of category labels on similarity judgments. Previous research shows that labeling affects judgments of similarity. Object representations are judged to be more similar when they are given a label that evokes feature relationships, and more different when different labels are applied (Yu, Takashi, and Schumacher, 2008) Studies of facial similarity using morphed photographs show that when labels convey categorical meaning, such as food eaten, disease acquired, or beliefs, then sharing a similar label increases perceived similarity, while having different labels decreases it (Lara, Hahn, Yu, and Yamauchi, 2012).

We reinterpret these prior studies in terms of the perceptual-magnet effect. According to Shepard's law, similarity is inverse to distance in semantic space. If the magnet warps the semantic space, then it alters perceived similarity from what it would be in a concept-free perception. If the magnet effect shrinks the space near the concept center, then it follows that positions in this part of the space will be perceived as more similar to each other and to the concept prototype. If the warping increases distances in some region, then perceived similarities will fall. If so, a plot of similarity against distance from the prototype will be steeply negative in the region.

We report the results of two studies that illustrate this effect. Previous research typically uses either meaningful labels or objects. We use a simpler design and apply nonsense labels to artificial objects, thereby minimizing the effects of background knowledge.

Study 1

The first study employs a widely used triad task: subjects are presented with three images and asked how similar they are to each other. Each triad is

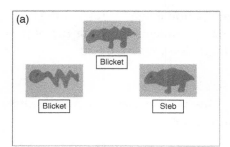 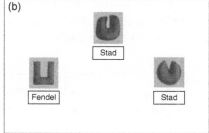

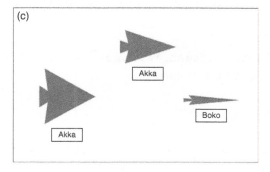

Figure 10.3 Objects used in the experiments: (a) clay objects from Landau and Shipley (2001), labeled "Blicket" or "Steb" or presented without labels; (b) felt objects from Landau and Shipley (2001) labeled "Fendel" or "Stad" or presented without labels; (c) Arrowheads from experiments in chapter 2, labeled "Akka" or "Boko" or presented without labels

arranged with one image on top and two images, which we call the anchor images, at the bottom (Lara et al., 2012). The center image is a morphed composite of the two anchor images, equidistant from each other.

We use three sets of images of novel objects.[5] We chose novel objects to ensure that subjects had not formed concepts for them prior to the experiment. In each set the images are the same size and constructed of the same materials but have different shapes.[6] Figure 10.3 depicts the three sets of objects. The images are either (1) unlabeled, or (2) the left and right objects bear different nonsense labels. When labeled, the center image either bears the label of either the left image or the right image. In all experiments, participants are shown three images and asked to indicate how similar is the middle image to those to its right and left (they are also asked to rate its similarity with the left and right images).[7]

Subjects were recruited to give their opinion about representational objects. In the no-label condition, for the experiments involving the objects depicted in panels a and b in figure 10.3 the subjects were told

> ```
> We are interested in your reactions to
> representational images. The following sketches are
> representations of fictional creatures.
> ```

For the experiments involving the objects depicted in panel C in figure 10.3, they were told

> ```
> The following images represent arrowheads from an
> archaeological museum.
> ```

Then, the subjects were told

> ```
> You will be asked about the sketches once you have
> seen them.
> ```

In the label condition, subjects were additionally told that `"Each sketch is labeled."` In the label conditions, the objects were marked by a single word, "Blicket" or "Steb" for the first set, "Fendel" or "Stad" for the second set, and "Akka" or "Boko" for the third. The manipulation involved randomly assigning the label of the top object to one of the two labels.

Participants were asked to rate the target object similarity to the right and left standard objects of each target-standard object pair on a scale ranging from 1 (not at all similar) to 7 (very similar). Therefore, each participant contributes two observations: similarity ratings for objects with the same label and objects with different labels (in the label condition).[8]

RESULTS: In order to examine how labeling changes perception, we compare the perceived similarity between the center object and the left/right objects based on whether they were assigned the *same label*, a *different label*, or *no label*. Figure 10.4 reports the mean similarity between objects by condition. For all three sets of objects, similarity is greatest when the objects are assigned the same label and lowest when they are given different labels. The

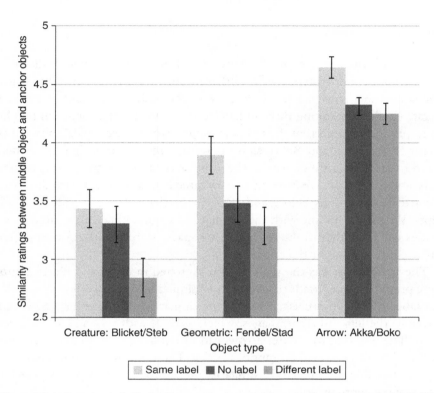

Figure 10.4 Perceived similarity between pairs of objects in Study 1, single label (The thin bars mark a two standard-deviation interval around the mean)

difference between the same-label and different-label conditions is significantly different from zero for all three sets of objects.[9] For all sets of objects, perceived similarity in the no-label condition lies between same-label and different-label conditions.[10]

These results show that "mere labeling" changes rated similarities, even when the labels do not convey an obvious meaning. Objects bearing the same label are perceived as more similar than those bearing different labels. Overall, the experiment supports the idea that applying nonsense labels alters the perceptual space—even if the labels are not associated with a meaningful concept. In particular, an object equally "distant" from two others representing two distinct concepts is pulled closer to the object with which it shares the same label. These effects are broadly consistent with the perceptual magnet mechanism.

Study 2

The second study investigates how perceived similarities vary with distance from a concept prototype under different labeling conditions. This study builds on the arrowhead study described previously. Participants are asked to rate similarities among three unlabeled arrowheads. They are then taught concepts and are told that the two anchor arrowheads are typical of two different tribes, Akka and Boko, as we described in chapter 4. They are then asked to rate similarities between the same arrowheads, with the anchor objects labeled by type. We investigate how rated similarities vary with distance, comparing conditions before and after the participants are taught the concepts. We expect, in line with the perceptual-magnet effect, that rated similarities will be higher in the region of the space nearest to the concept after participants are taught the concepts.

The basic setup was the same as that sketched in chapter 8. Participants were presented with triads of arrowheads, similar to figure 10.3(c) but without labels.[11] They were asked to rate the similarity of the center arrowhead image to the left and right images, which were of width 32 and 72, respectively. The width of the center arrowhead varied from 8 to 96 in increments of 8 and were presented in random order. These ratings were intended to capture baseline or "objective" similarity perceptions, free from any possible effect of conceptualization.

Participants were told that curators at the museum had classified the arrowheads into two styles. They were presented the arrowhead of 32 width and told it was the "Akka style" and then they were presented with the arrowhead of 72 width and told it was the "Boko style" (the order of presentation was randomized across trials). The participants were then asked to rate similarities of the same triads, but with the anchor objects labeled as "Akka style" and "Boko style." The center arrowhead remained unlabeled.

RESULTS: Figure 10.5 provides graphical evidence of the effects. The horizontal axis represents the width of the center arrowhead. The left graph is rating of similarity to the width-72 arrowhead (the Boko prototype), and the right graph is the similarity to the width-32 arrowhead (the Akka prototype).[12] The thick-dotted dark gray line demarcates the width of the Akka and Boko prototypes. The dotted gray line gives the average of the similarity judgments before participants were taught these concepts. The solid black line gives the average rated similarity of the same arrowheads after

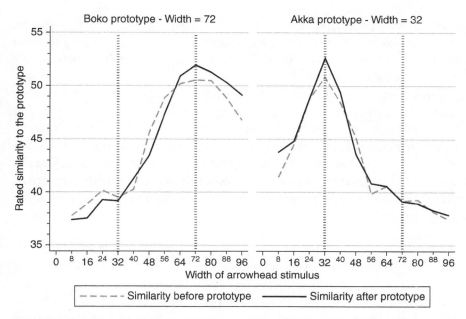

Figure 10.5 Perceived similarity between stimuli and the prototypes as a function of arrow width

participants are taught that the anchor images are prototypes of the respective styles, with the anchors labeled. In the no-concept condition, similarity ratings are not linear with distance but increase sharply for arrowheads that are a close distance to each anchor. This pattern is even stronger after participants are taught that the anchors are concept prototypes, in line with the perceptual-magnet effect.

We compare differences in similarity ratings between the pre-concept and post-concept conditions for arrowheads at close and far distances from the prototypes. We first compute the difference in rated similarity between the concept and baseline (pre-concept) conditions for each participant and each arrowhead width. We then separate evaluations by the distance in arrowhead width between the rated image and each prototype for distances close to the prototype and distances far from the prototype.[13] Close to a concept, similarity ratings in the concept condition are higher than the baseline condition, and far from a concept there is not a large difference in similarity ratings.[14]

Interestingly, the effect of the concept seems to extend farther for arrowheads on the outside of the feature space, positions that are either thinner than the Akka prototype or wider than the Boko prototype.[15] This asymmetry is consistent with the findings in chapter 9 that multiple categorization predicts behavior in the range of feature space outside each prototype, but not between them.

These patterns are consistent with the perceptual-magnet effect. Learning concepts affects similarity ratings of objects that are close to the concept in semantic space. After participants are taught that a location in the space is typical of a concept, they rate objects at small distances as even more similar to the location of the prototype, as compared to similarity ratings before the concepts were taught. This pattern is generally consistent with perceptual-magnet effects, where the magnet "pulls" more strongly at closer distances from a prototype.

10.4   Perceptual Magnets and Threshold Effects

The general inference story behind the perceptual-magnet effect casts new light on two threshold models, one from psychology and the other from sociology. The key process is that the warping of perceptual space creates a region around a conceptual core within which it is difficult for a person to discriminate between prototypes and nearby positions in the semantic space.

Such a process appears to underlie James Hampton's (1987; 2007) threshold model for typicality. As we developed a representation of typicality in chapters 2 and 4, we followed previous research in assuming that typicality falls monotonically with the distance of a position from the center of the concept. Hampton argued and showed empirically that typicality functions are flat within a region above a threshold distance from the concept (Verheyen et al., 2010). This is exactly the pattern expected from the warping of perceptual space under a magnet effect.[16]

The sociological process, middle-status conformity, seems at first glance to be far removed from the issues under discussion. A body of research in anthropology and sociology documented a pattern of heightened conformity to prevailing norms by those in the middle of status distributions. Phillips and Zuckerman (2001) provided an interpretation of this pattern as an issue of category membership. They argue that, for members of the relevant audience, some social actors have a secure membership in a market category, others have a tenuous membership, and yet others have at best a negligible membership. The incentive to take actions consistent with expectations for members of the focal concept is, they argue, strongest in the middle. Those with secure memberships are free to take actions that modestly lower their fit to categorical expectations; those with negligible membership will not in-cur any costs from the audience if they lower their fit still further—they have little or nothing to lose. But those with a middling degree of membership risk being included in the category if they deviate from expectations. If ac-tions follow incentives, then those in the middle will be less likely to take actions that run against audience expectations of category members. Phillips and Zuckerman (2001) present a diagrammatic representation of their argu-ment with two explicit thresholds that separate the middle from the top and from the bottom.

This sociological argument is pitched in terms of status, hence the label middle-status conformity. But for the argument to apply to a conceptual structure, status must map monotonically to the probability of categoriza-tion (and hence to scaled typicality). The actions in question are those that might lower typicality by increasing the distance of a revised position in the semantic space from the concept relative to the status-quo distance. The rel-evant distance is that perceived by members of the audience. If the concept warps the perceptual space, then we are back to the analysis of the threshold effect in typicality functions. Agents are free to move within a region around a concept (by changing the values of certain features) without losing their indiscernibility from the nearest prototype.

Discussion

In previous chapters, we modeled how semantic space similarities affect cat-egorization. In this chapter, we provide evidence for the reverse relationship: that concepts affect judgments of similarities in semantic space. We build on research that proposes and finds a perceptual-magnet effect: the presence of concepts causes people to perceive objects as more similar to conceptual cores than would be expected based on their "real" distances from these positions (the distances that one would perceive lacking the concepts).

This research provides a strong refutation of the view, mentioned in chap-ter 1, that agents rely on concepts only when they lack information about relevant feature values. This view depends on the implicit assumption that information about feature values can be concept-free. Learning that percep-tual magnets shape perception and inferences belies this assumption.

The influence of concepts on perception and inference can take several forms. For contexts that involve a single concept, inference about the po-sition of an object in semantic space is a function of its categorization and observable yet incomplete information about the object's position (signal). The inference is an average of the concept's location in the space and the information we receive about the object (the signal). The presence of the concept warps the perceived space and pulls objects toward the concept.

The general free-categorization context is more complicated. Each concept exerts some magnetic attraction, and objects are not pulled as strongly to nearly concepts. Nonetheless, inference is still affected by the warping of the space.

In two experiments, we find evidence consistent with the perceptual-magnet effect. The studies examine the effect of nonsense category labels on similarity judgments of artificial objects to minimize the effects of background knowledge. A first study examines variation in the signal while keeping the position of the objects constant. Using a triad task and three sets of images of novel objects, the experiment shows that the same pairs of objects are perceived as most similar when they are assigned the same label and least similar when they are assigned different labels. The mere application of labels increases similarity judgments of objects at the same position in the space. A second study varies the position of the objects. Using image pairs, the experiment shows that, prior to concept learning, similarity ratings increase for objects close to an anchor object. The pattern is even stronger after participants are taught that the anchor objects are prototypes. Judged similarity increases for objects closer to the concept after the participants have been taught the concepts associated with the labels.

The model we delineated in this chapter focused on one-dimensional semantic spaces. Yet, it is possible to extend the magnet-effect model to semantic spaces with several features (Konovalova and Le Mens, 2016, 2018). Doing so allows the study of how concepts shape inferences about unobserved features of objects. The model developed in the aforementioned papers considers settings where an individual perceives a feature of an object that belongs to a particular domain and makes a prediction about the value of an unobserved feature of the object. Moreover, the category of the object is uncertain, as in the setting of postulate 10.2. The person thus obtains a noisy signal about the position, but in this case, the "noise" has a different structure: observation of one dimension provides some information about the feature value on another, unobserved, dimension. The adaptation of the magnet-effect model to this setting predicts that the concepts structure people's representations of the relation between the observed and unobserved features. Inferences about the value of the second feature tend to vary more strongly with the first feature at positions that lie between candidate concepts and less strongly with the first feature at positions close to concept centers. In this case, what is being warped is not the perceptual space but the belief about the relation between feature dimensions.

The valuation model we propose in chapter 12 applies these ideas to a different setting, one in which valuation takes the place of the "unobserved dimension" in the multidimensional magnet-effect model. In that chapter, we will propose that concepts shape valuation in a way that is similar to how they shape perception and feature inferences.

PART THREE

Bridges to Sociological Application

THIS PART OF THE BOOK continues developing connections between our framework and sociological applications. We address two issues that are core to many contemporary sociological analyses of concepts and categories. In chapter 11, we discuss how conceptual ambiguity could lead to the difficulty of interpreting the objects, positions, persons, or organizations. We propose that conceptual ambiguity can be understood as the entropy of the vector of an object's categorization probabilities over a cohort of concepts. We argue that conceptual ambiguity makes objects less easy to process, that we experience cognitive disfluency in trying to make sense of them. We then revisit the notion of category contrast, which has previously been used in the literature but has had limited foundation in cognitive research. In our proposed framework, we argue that categorical contrast can be understood as the degree to which a category stands out from its cohort.

Chapter 12 connects these notions to valuation. We argue that concepts influence the valuation of objects via three factors: valence, conceptual ambiguity, and uncertainty. We believe that evaluation is inextricably linked to categorization. First, for reasons of cognitive economy, people generally do not attempt to discern every single feature of an object. Rather, the set of concepts that a person holds dictates which features are considered germane, drawing attention to those particular features. Second, beyond their role in focusing attention on particular features, concepts shape how features are seen (via perceptual-magnet effects). Third, concepts represent people's understandings of feature-value combinations, and their liking for those combinations might not straightforwardly reflect their liking of the underlying features in isolation. Rather, concepts have a valence that encapsulates their liking for feature-value combinations.

We examine three key ways in which concepts can shape the evaluation of objects. First, concepts themselves have valences, which get transferred to objects through categorization. This inherited valence, in turn, shapes affective reactions to objects, in proportion to their typicality. Second, objects vary in terms of how easy they are to comprehend in light of one's conceptual understandings, and this ease of comprehension affects evaluation. In chapter 11, we refer to objects that are more difficult to make sense of in terms of a set of concepts as having greater conceptual ambiguity. Such ambiguity complicates the process of combining the separate valuations pertaining to the concepts that apply to an object. For instance, suppose that a musical piece is both classical and electronic. How do we combine the typicality-weighted valuations according to the two genres? Third, uncertainty about which, if any, potentially applicable concepts actually apply to an object can affect valuation over and above the effect of ambiguity. When a person does not know which concepts apply to an object, the process of aggregating valuations of the potentially applicable concepts is more complicated.

We build a formal framework for expressing the three kinds of effects, beginning with the case in which only a single concept is relevant. Then we deal with more complicated multiple-concept cases.

Taken together, we believe that the framework we propose can help us understand the widely documented valuation discount imposed on objects, persons, and organizations that span categories.

In these two chapters, we provide sociological examples of calculating conceptual ambiguity and category contrast, and testing its effect on valuation. Specifically, we walk readers through detailed analyses of genres in film and rap music, demonstrating how conceptual ambiguity and category contrast can be calculated, and how these affect critics' evaluations. We hope that these analyses provide guidelines for future empirical research about the antecedents and consequences of conceptual ambiguity, contrast, and evaluations.

CHAPTER ELEVEN

Conceptual Ambiguity
and Contrast

AT THIS POINT, we shift almost entirely from the roots in cognitive science to sociological considerations. Sociological applications of models of concepts have focused on issues concerning the difficulty of interpreting categorical assignments. To build a bridge for such analysis, this chapter uses the framework developed to this point to characterize objects/positions by ease of interpretation, ambiguity. Then we use this notion of ambiguity to characterize the degree to which a category stands out from its cohort, its contrast.

11.1   Conceptual Ambiguity of Objects

We have proceeded from the assumption that people perceive objects, form mental representations of them, and try to make sense of them in light of their concepts. This becomes more complicated when we consider that some feature-value configurations (i.e., positions in semantic space) lie between concepts or occupy positions where concepts have nontrivial overlap. Objects whose mental representations coincide with such configurations are ambiguous: it is not clear which, if any, concepts apply to them. Obviously, this problem does not arise for crisp (classical) concepts. The prevalence of the issue of conceptual ambiguity increases as concepts become increasingly fuzzy (the concept likelihoods flatten) or as concepts overlap more with one another in the conceptual space.

We assume that people can easily make sense of objects that they can definitively associate with a particular concept but might have great difficulty interpreting others that fit partially with many concepts but not one in particular. For example, a movie that has elements of horror and romance might be more difficult to interpret than movies that have elements of just one of the genres. We formalize this notion in terms of *conceptual ambiguity*. An object is conceptually ambiguous to someone who finds it hard to make sense of it in terms of their concepts.

To devise a formal notion of conceptual ambiguity, we deploy a general intuition from previous research, beginning with Hsu (2006) and Hsu et al. (2009). This research conceptualized vectors of typicalities in concepts as defining niches in conceptual space. The core idea is that an object with a strong typicality in one concept and low typicality in all others has a narrow categorical niche. By virtue of its specialized position, it has strong appeal to a narrow band of the audience. And an object with equal typicality in each concept has the broadest possible categorical niche. Standard niche theory makes the assumption of a trade-off between breadth and strength of appeal (Hannan and Freeman, 1983; Hsu, 2006).

Kovács and Hannan (2015) translated the niche-theoretic intuition in terms of interpretability. They argue that interpretability is a monotonically decreasing function of the width of an object's categorical niche. Moreover, objects with positive typicality in multiple concepts are relatively more interpretable if these concepts are closer in conceptual space and less interpretable if these concepts are more distant. Here we focus on the inverse of interpretability, our notion of conceptual ambiguity. We take advantage of the model developed so far, and we use the more direct notion of conceptual ambiguity instead of that of categorical niche.

Before getting into some technical details, we sketch our approach. We focus on positions that characterize the mental representations of objects and analyze the distribution of categorization probabilities of a position for the various concepts in a cohort. We propose that objects represented as positions with a high categorization probability for only one concept have low conceptual ambiguity; positions that have an even distribution of categorization probabilities have maximal conceptual ambiguity.

We define the conceptual ambiguity of a mental representation in terms of entropy, a widely used measure of unpredictability. In the context of communication, as introduced by Shannon (1948), entropy characterizes the information content of a message. In our context, the message is the mental representation of an object as a particular position in semantic space. We apply the entropy notion to the vector of categorization probabilities for a focal cohort of concepts made salient by the context. We think that an ambiguous object representation is one that might well be classified under many concepts in the cohort. So we want to examine the distribution of an object's categorization probabilities over the concepts in the cohort.

It seems intuitive that we should only experience conceptual ambiguity if our interpretations of objects get structured by a set of concepts. If someone does not make any conceptual distinctions in some aspect of life, perhaps due to lack of any knowledge about a domain, then conceptual ambiguity should not arise. For example, a person who sees someone using a baseball bat to swing at a football should not experience any ambiguity about whether the game is football or baseball if he or she knows nothing about either sport. We capture this notion in our model through our treatment of categorization probabilities by specifying that the IS-A(c, o) predicate in the categorization probability is undefined if an individual has not formed the concept c. This allows us to account for the extreme—but perhaps common—situation in which someone makes no conceptual distinctions in a domain. One could further specify how the extensiveness of a person's knowledge structure in a given domain can shape the experience of conceptual ambiguity—for example, whether a person who makes more fine-grained conceptual distinctions in a domain tends to experience ambiguity more frequently. But we do not do it here.

Figure 11.1 gives a simple example of the situations we want to consider. It depicts a one-dimensional conceptual space with two concepts with centers of **cen**$_1$ and **cen**$_2$. We mark two positions x_a and x_b at equal distance (in opposite directions) from c_1. These positions are equally typical as instances of c_1. If the second concept, c_2, were not present in the space, the two positions would not differ in any interesting way. However the presence of the second concept does make a difference: the conceptual ambiguity of the position in the middle, x_a, is higher than that of x_b.

As we build toward a definition of conceptual ambiguity, we assume that the focal person's information about the context, denoted by $\mathcal{I}_0$, includes knowledge of the domain $\mathcal{D}_r$—that is, it includes information about the distribution of positions of objects that are r's, the list of concepts in the cohort κ associated with the domain, the set of possible concept assignments ($\mathfrak{C}$), and information that allows the individual to have priors about all the possible concept assignments. In cases that involve more than one object, we assume that the information states contain the same kind of knowledge for each object.

We will consider two information states based on $\mathcal{I}_0$. One concerns the person's knowledge of the position of the focal object. When the person has this knowledge, we write the information state in the form $\{\mathcal{I}_0, x\}$. The second concerns categorizations. If the object has already been a set of categorical assignments **C**, we write the information state as $\{\mathcal{I}_0, \mathbf{C}\}$ or $\{\mathcal{I}_0, \mathbf{C}, x\}$, depending on whether the position is known. Crucially, the

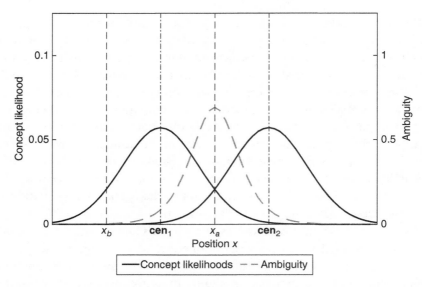

Figure 11.1 Concept likelihoods of two concepts (solid lines) and the conceptual ambiguity of positions (dashed line centered on x_a) in a one-dimensional semantic space. Ambiguity is high at positions between the concept centers ($\mathbf{cen}_1$ and $\mathbf{cen}_2$) and low at positions that are close to one concept center or on the sides of the semantic space. The graph is constructed assuming that the category priors are both equal to 0.5. The concept likelihoods follow normal distributions with means $\mathbf{cen}_1$ and $\mathbf{cen}_2$

absence of $\mathbf{C}$ in an information state means that the object has not (yet) been categorized—categorization is uncertain.

To fix ideas, we start with the simple example of a cohort that contains two concepts: $\mathfrak{D}_r = \{c_1, c_2\}$. Table 11.1 displays illustrative summaries of categorization decisions for four scenarios. The entries are the proportion

TABLE 11.1
Illustrative categorizations of a set of objects at a focal position for a two-concept domain: four scenarios

Scenario	Proportion of categorizations		
	c_1-only	c_2-only	c_1 and c_2
A	1.0	0	0
B	.75	.20	.05
C	.25	.25	.50
D	.33	.33	.33

TABLE 11.2
Illustrative construction of the measure of conceptual ambiguity for objects at a focal position for two concepts in four scenarios

Scenario	P(at least c_1)	P(at least c_2)	$P^*(c_1)$	$P^*(c_2)$	Ambiguity
A	1.0	0	1.0	0	0
B	.80	.25	.76	.24	.55
C	.75	.75	.50	.50	.75
D	.67	.67	.50	.50	.75

of decisions of the various kinds. (For purposes of illustration we assume that there are no empty assignments.) These are the raw data to be used in calculating conceptual ambiguity.

The first issue to consider is how to deal with the joint categorizations in scenarios B–D in table 11.1. We want to capture the probability that an object at the focal position is judged to be an instance of each concept. That is, we want to record the judgments that an object is *at least* an instance of a concept (and might, as well, be judged as an instance of the other). In table 11.2, the first two columns of data make this simple calculation. For instance, in scenario B, the proportion of judgments that an object at the position is at least a c_1 is $.75 + .05$ given the data in table 11.1. Notice that the two "at least" probabilities do not sum to one. So we cannot treat them as estimates of probabilities. So we rescale: dividing each by the sum of the two. We denote these calculations as P^*. These are the estimated probabilities on which we base the measurement of conceptual ambiguity.

Now we write a general expression for the calculations that we just discussed in the context of the illustration in tables 11.1 and 11.2. Note that in our formal renditions, the probability that an object is *at least* a c is $P(\text{IS-A}(c, o) \mid \mathcal{I})$, where $\mathcal{I}$ refers to the information the agent possesses about the object. It could include the position of the object ($\mathcal{I} = \{\mathcal{I}_0, x\}$), but this is not necessary. In this second case, the relevant categorization probabilities would be the priors on the concept. Our framework can also accommodate intermediary cases where the information state includes a noisy signal about the position of the object. We do not address these cases explicitly here.

Definition 11.1 (Scaled probability that an object is at least an instance of a concept) *The probability that the set of concepts assigned to an object includes a focal concept scaled relative to those of the other concepts in the domain's cohort is defined as follows.*

[A.] Uncertain categorization:

$$P^*(\text{IS-A}(c,o)\mid \mathcal{I}) = \frac{P(\text{IS-A}(c,o)\mid \mathcal{I})}{\sum_{c'\in\kappa} P(\text{IS-A}(c',o)\mid \mathcal{I})}, \qquad (11.1)$$

[B.] The object has been categorized in a set of concepts **C**:

$$P^*(\text{IS-A}(c,o)\mid \mathcal{I},\mathbf{C}) = \frac{P(\text{IS-A}(c,o)\mid \mathcal{I})}{\sum_{c'\in\mathbf{C}} P(\text{IS-A}(c',o)\mid \mathcal{I})}, \qquad (11.2)$$

where IS-A(c,o) *can be read as "o is at least a c (and might also be a c')"* *and* $\mathcal{I}$ *equals* $\mathcal{I}_0$ *or* $\{\mathcal{I}_0,x\}$.

In the special case of exclusive categorization, the scaled categorization probabilities are exactly the categorization probabilities given by postulate 8.3.

Now we turn to conceptual ambiguity, a problem of interpretation that arises in contexts of uncertain categorization or known categorization in multiple concepts. We use a real-valued non-negative function $A(o\mid \mathcal{I})$ that maps from objects and information states to the level of conceptual ambiguity. According to our intuition, an object is ambiguous if it could be considered an instance of more than one concept in a cohort. This issue arises when (1) the object has not yet been categorized or (2) it has already been given multiple categorical assignments. To represent this intuition, we calculate conceptual ambiguity in terms of the scaled categorization probabilities (P^*s) for each concept in the cohort for the case of an uncategorized object or in terms of the scaled probabilities for the concepts in the multiple assignment for already categorized objects.

Definition 11.2 (Conceptual ambiguity of an object) *The conceptual ambiguity of an object is given by the entropy of the vector of the (scaled) categorization probabilities.*
[A.] Uncertain categorization:

$$A(o\mid \mathcal{I}) = -\sum_{c\in\kappa} P^*(\text{IS-A}(c,o)\mid \mathcal{I}) \ln P^*(\text{IS-A}(c,o)\mid \mathcal{I}). \qquad (11.3)$$

[B.] The object has been categorized in a set of concepts **C**:

$$A(o\mid \mathcal{I},\mathbf{C}) = -\sum_{c\in\mathbf{C}} P^*(\text{IS-A}(c,o)\mid \mathcal{I}) \ln P^*(\text{IS-A}(c,o)\mid \mathcal{I},\mathbf{C}), \qquad (11.4)$$

where $\mathcal{I}$ *equals either* $\mathcal{I}_0$ *or* $\{\mathcal{I}_0,x\}$.

Note that the definition of conceptual ambiguity conditions on the person's information state. This information state includes information about the concepts available. Clearly the ambiguity of a position depends on what concepts are in the picture. Moreover, it also depends on the distances among the concepts in a cohort via the scaled categorization probabilities. As the distance between a pair of concepts decreases, the probability that an object close to one concept center will be get categorized in the (now nearer) other concept rises. As a result the ambiguity of the position will rise.

In the special case where the object has been categorized in just one concept (e.g., $\mathbf{C} = \{c\}$), there is no conceptual ambiguity—it equals zero; equation 11.3 reduces to $A(o \mid \mathcal{I}, c) = 0$.

Conceptual ambiguity equal to zero also obtains in settings where the object has not been categorized but has a categorization probability of (nearly) one for a particular concept and (nearly) zero probability of categorization for any of the other relevant concepts. High levels of conceptual ambiguity result from an even distribution of categorization probabilities. That is, an object that is, in some small respect, an instance of every concept has maximum conceptual ambiguity. The right-most column of table 11.2 reports the value of conceptual ambiguity for a position under the four scenarios.

We can illustrate the effect of multiple concepts on the conceptual ambiguity of the stimuli at the positions that lie between them using data from the arrowhead experiments described earlier. We do so in figure 11.2, which

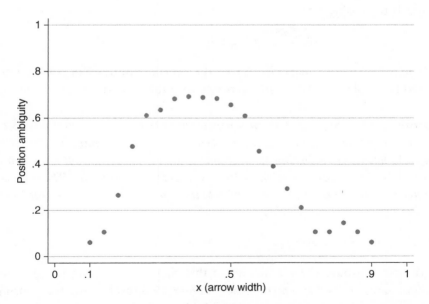

Figure 11.2 Conceptual ambiguity of an arrowhead stimulus in the setting with the prototype of the Akka style set at 0.1 and the prototype of the Boko style set at 0.9

plots the ambiguities of the stimuli that lie between styles whose centers are set to 0.1 and 0.9. As we would expect, stimuli that lie between the two styles are more ambiguous than those close to the prototypes. Participants' behavior revealed the highest levels of conceptual ambiguity when they perceived stimuli that were approximately equidistant from the two prototypes.

11.2   Conceptual Ambiguity and Multiple Categorization

Our construction of the measure of conceptual ambiguity creates the expectation that objects with mental representations at positions of high ambiguity are more likely to be assigned multiple concepts. Indeed, if categorization follows conditional independence as defined in chapter 9, this expectation does follow. Consider the simplest case: a cohort with two concepts. The position of maximal ambiguity has probability of categorization equal to one-half for each concept. Under independence, the probability of joint categorization is the product of the separate single-concept categorization probabilities, $.5 \times .5 = .25$.

We cannot see a way to prove a general results about the implications of conceptual ambiguity for multiple categorization. So we instantiate our intuition as a postulate, an empirical claim. We denote the set of concepts assigned to an object as

$$\ell_\kappa(o) \equiv \{c \mid (c \in \kappa) \wedge \text{IS-A}(c, o)\}.$$

The following postulate claims that the expected number of concepts assigned to an object, $E[|\ell_\kappa(o)|]$, increases with the ambiguity of its position.

Postulate 11.1 *Suppose that an agent observes two uncategorized objects o_1 and o_2 at positions x_1 and x_2 in a free-categorization situation. The background knowledge including the fact this is a free-categorization situation is denoted by $\mathcal{I}^f$. The two positions differ in conceptual ambiguity. The expected number of concepts the agent will assign to the objects is the greater for the object at the more ambiguous position.*

$$A\big(o_1 \mid \mathcal{I}^f, x_1\big) < A\big(o_2 \mid \mathcal{I}^f, x_2\big) \rightarrow E[|\ell_\kappa(o_1)|] < E[|\ell_\kappa(o_2)|]. \quad (11.5)$$

We can illustrate the plausibility of this claim again, using the data on categorization of stylized arrowheads. Figure 11.3 displays the relationship between the estimated conceptual ambiguity and the proportion of participants who assigned the stimulus at this position to both of the potentially

Figure 11.3 Illustration of the relationship between the likelihood of a double categorical assignment of arrowheads (to {Akka,Boko}) as a function of the conceptual ambiguity of the stimulus arrowhead

applicable styles. We see that the expected number of joint categorizations increases at an increasing rate with ambiguity.

11.3   Conceptual Ambiguity and Fluency

Conceptual ambiguity has important implications for cognitive processing that matter in sociological applications, such as valuation in market contexts, as analyzed in the next chapter. Ambiguous objects are processed less fluently. An object representation is said to be *fluent* when it is cognitively easy to process. Fluency can stem from a variety of factors, such as familiarity and clarity of representation. For example, Winkielman, Schwarz, Faziendeiro, and Berber (2003) showed images of common objects to study participants and manipulated fluency by preceding the images with exposure to a matched word in the high-fluency condition (e.g., showing the participant a picture of a lock preceded by the word lock) and with an unrelated word (e.g., snow) in the low-fluency condition. Pictures preceded by matching words were liked more than those preceded by unrelated words. And subjects presented with images of a single two-dollar bill or of two one-dollar

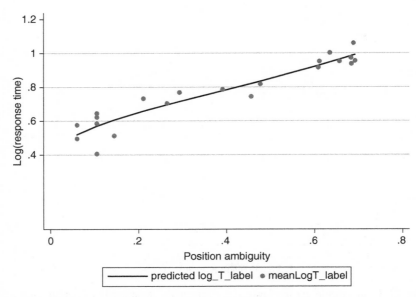

Figure 11.4 The relationship between conceptual ambiguity of a position and the natural log of response time from the experiment using arrowhead stimuli in the setting where the prototype of the Akka style is set at 0.1 and the prototype of the Boko style is at 0.9

bills estimate that they can purchase more standard items (such as paper clips) when shown the image of the more familiar one-dollar bills.

Experimental research reveals that subjects find prototypes more appealing than less typical instances because they are processed more fluently (Winkielman et al., 2006). By extension, conceptual ambiguity ought to generate an experience of disfluency. Our experiments on categorization provide evidence for this kind of process. Specifically, participants took longer to categorize objects that lied between concepts, indicating that these positions were more difficult for them to process. As can be seen in figure 11.4, the log of the response time in categorizing a stimulus increases roughly linearly with the ambiguity of the position calculated as indicated in definition 11.2. Longer processing time corresponds to more effort, and more effort means a lack of fluency.

We represent fluency in our model using the function $\phi(o \mid \mathcal{I})$, which records the level of fluency that the focal individual experiences in processing the object o given the information state $\mathcal{I}$. Over a range of domains, experimental research shows that fluency affects emotional reaction (Reber, Schwarz, and Winkielman, 2004) and, in turn, valuation (Alter and Oppenheimer, 2008; Vogel, Carr, Davis, and Winkielman, 2017). Lower fluency is a negative experience, translating into more negative affect, which gets transferred to objects in evaluation. We exploit this association in chapter 12. At this stage, we incorporate the role of conceptual ambiguity into our model by formally specifying the relationship between conceptual ambiguity, typicality and fluency.

Notation

We introduce notations for average typicality in candidate concepts in settings with potentially multiple concept assignments. There are several situations to consider depending on whether or not position is known and whether or not categorization is known.

[A.] Known categorization in $\mathbf{C}$, unknown position:

$$\mathbf{T}(o \mid \mathcal{I}_0, \mathbf{C}) = \sum_{c \in \mathbf{C}} P^*(\text{IS-A}(c, o) \mid \mathcal{I}_0, \mathbf{C}) T_c; \tag{11.6}$$

where T_c is the expected typicality (implied by the concept likelihood for c) of an object with unknown position:

$$T_c = \int_x \tau_c(x) \, d\pi_{\mathbb{F}_c}(x \mid c). \tag{11.7}$$

[B.] Known categorization in $\mathbf{C}$, known position, x:

$$\mathbf{T}(o \mid \mathcal{I}_0, \mathbf{C}, x) = \sum_{c \in \mathbf{C}} P^*(\text{IS-A}(c, o) \mid \mathcal{I}_0, x, \mathbf{C}) \tau_c(x). \tag{11.8}$$

[C.] Uncertain categorization, unknown position:

$$\mathbf{T}(o \mid \mathcal{I}_0) = \sum_{\mathbf{C} \in \mathcal{C}} P(\mathbf{C} \mid \mathcal{I}_0) \mathbf{T}(o \mid \mathcal{I}_0, \mathbf{C}). \tag{11.9}$$

[D.] Uncertain categorization, known position, x:

$$\mathbf{T}(o \mid \mathcal{I}_0, x) = \sum_{\mathbf{C} \in \mathcal{C}} P(\mathbf{C} \mid \mathcal{I}_0, x) \mathbf{T}(o \mid \mathcal{I}_0, \mathbf{C}, x). \tag{11.10}$$

The following postulate formalizes the associations between typicality, conceptual ambiguity, and fluency discussed in the previous paragraphs. It claims that fluency increases with average typicality and decreases with conceptual ambiguity.

Postulate 11.2 *Consider an agent and an object o. The fluency of the object for the agent increases with average typicality and decreases with conceptual ambiguity. There exists $a < 0$ and $b > 0$ and an error term ϵ independent of conceptual ambiguity and average typicality such that*

$$\phi(o \mid \mathcal{I}) = a\,A(o_1 \mid \mathcal{I}) + b\mathbf{T}_C(o \mid \mathcal{I}) + \epsilon, \qquad (11.11)$$

where $\mathcal{I}$ equals $\mathcal{I}_0$, $\{\mathcal{I}_0, x\}$, $\{\mathcal{I}_0, \mathbf{C}\}$, or $\{\mathcal{I}_0, \mathbf{C}, x\}$.

In the special case where an object has been categorized in just one concept and its position is known, equation 11.11 reduces to $\phi(o \mid \mathcal{I}_0, c, x) = b\mathbf{T}_c(o \mid x) + \epsilon$. It says that the fluency of the object increases with typicality in the focal concept.

Figure 11.5 depicts how conceptual ambiguity, average typicality, and fluency vary with position in the two-concept setting of figure 11.1, in an exclusive categorization context. We see that positions in between the two concepts have low fluency due to the impact of high conceptual ambiguity and low average typicality. Fluency is also low at for small and large values of x. Such positions have low conceptual ambiguity and thus the low fluency is driven by the low average typicality.

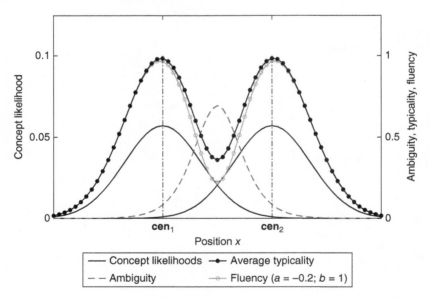

Figure 11.5 Fluency, conceptual ambiguity, and average typicality as a function of position in an exclusive categorization context, with the same concept likelihoods used in figure 11.1. Fluency computed using postulate 11.2, with $a = -.2$ and $b = 1$

11.4   Measuring Conceptual Ambiguity

We now consider how conceptual ambiguity can be measured empirically, and we provide examples. There are two cases to consider. In one, the researcher has access to measurements of the positions of the objects in the semantic space; in the other, the researcher knows *only* the categorizations of the objects.

Uncertain Categorization and Known Position

The estimated conceptual ambiguity for an uncategorized object with known position in semantic space is given by equation 11.3 with fitted probabilities. More formally, let $\widehat{P}(c \mid \mathcal{I}_0, x)$ denote the estimated categorization probability in concept c when the position of the object is known. We can construct an empirical estimate of conceptual ambiguity as

$$\widehat{A}(o \mid \mathcal{I}_0, x) = -\sum_{c \in \kappa} \widehat{P^*}(c \mid \mathcal{I}_0, x) \ln \widehat{P^*}(c \mid \mathcal{I}_0, x), \qquad (11.12)$$

where $\widehat{P^*}(c \mid \mathcal{I}_0, x)$ is defined by equation 11.1 based on the estimated categorization probabilities $\widehat{P}(c \mid \mathcal{I}_0, x)$.

We return to the rap music to provide an example. To compute the conceptual ambiguity of a rap album, (equation 11.12), we need to calculate the probability that an album, at a given position in semantic space, will be categorized as an instance of each style in the cohort of styles (here a style plays the role of a concept). To review, we have already placed each album and style in semantic space, based on their lyrical content. In chapter 3, we applied topic modeling to a corpus of rap lyrics to create a semantic space, which uncovered seven meaningful dimensions. In subsequent chapters, for tractability, we considered a reduced three-dimensional feature space $\mathbb{G}_{rap3}$ where a position is defined by a 0 to 1 score on three features: *swagger*, *street violence*, and *romantic love*. We restrict our analysis to the twelve largest styles and albums with ten or more tracks. In chapter 4, we used distances in the space to calculate the positions of each album and style. Finally, in chapter 7, we computed the concept likelihood for each style, as well as priors on positions in the semantic space. We build on this work to compute the conceptual ambiguity of an album in the three-dimensional space.

TABLE 11.3
Descriptions of albums with low versus high conceptual ambiguity

Artist	Album	Description from AllMusic.com
Low Ambiguity		
Mobb Deep	*The Infamous*	One of the cornerstones of the New York hardcore movement, *The Infamous* is Mobb Deep's masterpiece, a relentlessly bleak song cycle that's been hailed by hardcore rap fans as one of the most realistic gangsta albums ever recorded. ...The product of an uncommon artistic vision, *The Infamous* stands as an all-time gangsta/hardcore classic.
High Ambiguity		
A Tribe Called Quest	*The Low End Theory*	One of the closest and most brilliant fusions of jazz atmosphere and hip-hop attitude ever recorded. ...The trio also takes on the rap game with a pair of hard-hitting tracks ...the latter a lyrical soundclash with Q-Tip and Phife plus Brand Nubian's Diamond D, Lord Jamar, and Sadat X. ...It's a tribute to their unerring production sense that, with just those few tools, Tribe produced one of the best hip-hop albums in history, a record that sounds better with each listen. The Low End Theory is an unqualified success, the perfect marriage of intelligent, flowing raps to nuanced, groove-centered productions.

According to equation 11.12, we need to estimate probabilities of categorization in a style s given a position x in semantic space. We use Bayes' theorem:

$$\widehat{P}(s \mid x) = \frac{\widehat{P}(s)\, \widehat{P}_{\mathbb{G}_{\text{rap3}}}(x \mid s)}{\widehat{P}_{\mathbb{G}_{\text{rap3}}}(x)}. \qquad (11.13)$$

Recall that, in chapter 7, we computed empirical estimates of $\widehat{P}_{\mathbb{G}_{\text{rap3}}}(x \mid s)$, the probability of a position given that the object is an instance of a style (equation 7.2), and $\widehat{P}_{\mathbb{G}_{\text{rap3}}}(x)$, the prior on the position in the semantic space (equation 7.3). What remains to be estimated is the concept prior $\widehat{P}(s)$, or the probability that an album with unknown features belongs to a style. We calculate this as the number of albums assigned to the style, N_s, divided by the total number of album-style pairs, N:[1]

$$\widehat{P}(s) = \frac{N_s}{N} \tag{11.14}$$

We use the estimated $\widehat{P}(s \mid x)$ to calculate $\widehat{P^*}(s \mid x)$ according to equation 11.1, to complete the measurement.

What do we find? Table 11.3 contains excerpts of descriptions from All-music.com's music critics of a pair of albums by well-known artists. One album has low ambiguity ($A = 1.35$), and the other has high ambiguity ($A = 3.11$). These descriptions illustrate the pattern of interest: the album with low ambiguity has a clearer style classification, while the high-ambiguity albums is more difficult to pin down.

We computed conceptual ambiguity based on the features of the albums (in this case, lyrical content). With this in hand, we can investigate how album positions in semantic space relate to categorizations. By postulate 11.1, we expect more ambiguous albums to have more style assignments. Figure 11.6 plots the relationship between levels of album ambiguity and (average) number of style categorizations.[2] It shows the expected positive trend.

Known Categorization and Unknown Position

In non-experimental research on concepts and categories, researchers frequently have access to categorizations of objects but not to the semantic spaces and perceptions of the positions of the objects in those spaces that governed the categorizations. For instance, much of the research discussed in the next chapter uses archival data that give categorizations of objects such as books, films, and restaurants. This kind of data structure can also arise in experiments that elicit categorizations without knowledge of the semantic spaces of the subjects.

We defined the conceptual ambiguity of objects in terms of the categorization probabilities in the concepts in the focal domain in equation 11.3. The categorization probabilities depend on the information state about the object. If the position in feature space is known, we can use the categorization probabilities defined in chapters 8 and 9. When the position is not known, we need to specify the categorization probabilities differently.

What can a researcher do? We propose to combine two kinds of information to approximate the underlying structure. The first step uses information on the categorical assignments to estimate typicalities of objects.

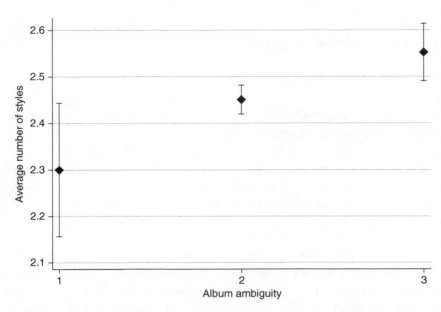

Figure 11.6 The relationship between conceptual ambiguity of a rap album and the number of styles an album is assigned

(Below we report several ways this has been done in prior empirical research.) We want our notation to distinguish the typicality of an *object* from that of a *position* because sometimes people can judge (or learn from others) the typicality of an object without knowing its position in the semantic space. We let $t_c(o)$ denote the object's typicality, specifically the typicality of o as a c.

The second kind of information concerns the priors on concepts and position. We propose setting priors to the observed (or estimated) based rates. As we described in §8.7, much research estimates priors from so-called base rates (relative frequencies observed by a person). The information on base rates available in the situations we consider consists of N, the number of objects perceived, and $N_c = |\mathbf{cat}(c)|$, the number of objects in the category c (for the focal person). The relevant statistic is $p_c = N_c/N$, the ratio of the number of objects categorized as a c the agent observed in the setting to the number of objects the agent observed in the setting.

We approximate the categorization probabilities for the situation in which only categorizations are known as

$$P^*(\text{IS-A}(c,o)\,|\,\mathcal{I}_0,\mathbf{C}) \approx \widetilde{P}^*_c(o) \equiv \frac{t_c(o)\,p_c}{\sum_{c'\in\kappa} t_{c'}(o)\,p_{c'}}. \tag{11.15}$$

To see the similarity with the formulation of the categorization probability that we used earlier in the book, note that the right-hand side of equation 11.15 is very similar to the right-hand side of equation 8.10 for exclusive categorization. We rewrite it here for convenience:

$$P(c \mid \mathcal{I}_0, x_o) = \frac{\pi_{\mathbb{F}_c}(x_o \mid c') \, P(c \mid \mathcal{I}_0)}{\sum_{c' \in \kappa} \pi_{\mathbb{F}_{c'}}(x_o \mid c') \, P(c' \mid \mathcal{I}_0)}. \tag{11.16}$$

Note that p_c in equation 11.15 corresponds to the category prior, $P(c \mid \mathcal{I}_0)$, in equation 8.10, and that $t_c(o)$ in equation 11.15 corresponds to the concept likelihood in equation 11.16. The first correspondence makes sense because the proportion of objects in the setting that are cs is the base rate, as we discussed in §7. The second correspondence also makes sense because both $\pi_{\mathbb{F}_c}(x \mid c)$ and $t_c(o)$ characterize the similarity of the object to the concept.

The approximation of the categorization probabilities in equation 11.15 allows us to form a measure of the ambiguity of the position of the focal object based only on categorical assignments to objects:

$$\widetilde{A}(o \mid \mathcal{I}_0, \mathbf{C}) \approx -\sum_{c \in \mathbf{C}} \widetilde{P}_c^*(o) \ln \widetilde{P}_c^*(o). \tag{11.17}$$

The key issue for measurement concerns typicalities. If the researcher has access only to objects' categorizations and not their feature values, one can still construct typicality measures. In analyses with only categorizations, the researcher can estimate typicalities from sets of concept assignments.

EMPIRICAL ESTIMATES OF TYPICALITY FROM CATEGORIZATIONS: We summarize a set of empirical proposals for using categorizations to approximate typicality. We discussed empirical measurement of typicality in §4.5, for the example of rap music, in which a semantic space was constructed using rap lyrics. In that example, we assumed that the style assignments captured default categorization in the domain. But different people might place styles in different locations within the space. Empirically, typicality measures could be calculated for the categorizations of a focal person, or a population of people who use similar concepts in a domain.

In the situations of interest, a researcher has access to the categorizations of each object with respect to the concepts in the focal cohort. The relevant data come in two forms in the empirical research. In the first form, the data provide a weighted assessment of the extent to which an object is an instance of different concepts. For example, the data might record multiple assignments by the same agent, as when firms claim association with labels in a series of press releases during the specified period (the application studied by Pontikes (2008)). Or assignments might be made by multiple agents during the period. For instance, goodreads.com reports that reviewers of Mario Puzo's novel *The Godfather* categorized it as mystery/crime (448 times), classics (418), thriller (188), historical fiction (104), mystery (101), and a set of other labels with less frequent assignment. In a third example, an agent explicitly assigns weighted membership of an object to different concepts. For example, the United States Patent Office assigns patent applications to primary and secondary technology classes. Researchers can derive weighted categorizations from these different assignments to technology classes.

In the second data form, concept labels are assigned but there are no weights that tell how well the label applies. This can occur when a market intermediary, such as a website curator or regulator, assigns labels or provides a fixed set of labels from which sellers can choose. So we learn from IMDB.com, say, that Francis Ford Coppola's film version of *The Godfather* is classified simply as crime and drama. In such cases, due to lack of information on weights, researchers can reasonably assume that the object is half-way between the concept centers of the applied labels, and therefore has the same level of typicality in each assigned concept. Note that this means that when an object is equally typical in each of the applied concepts. As a result, $t_c(o)$ will be constant and will drop from equation 11.15. In other words, when label weights are not available, typicality information is not needed to calculate ambiguity.

With data of the first (general) form, one can form a vector that records the proportion of times that an object was classified as an instance of each concept in the cohort. We introduce a function $\eta(c,o)$ that maps pairs consisting of concept and objects to the $[0,1]$ interval. For data with the second (binary) form, we use the function $v(c,o)$ that maps pairs of concepts and objects to $\{0,1\}$. Prior research has built measures of typicality using these two functions.

In the first and largely implicit step, the analyst assumes that objects with only one categorical assignment generally fit better to the concept than those assigned two concepts. For instance, a film classified as comedy/horror likely lacks some of the typical features of either genre. Similarly, a restaurant categorized as Mexican/Thai can hardly typify either concept.[3] The reasoning then makes a similar assertion about dual categorization versus triple categorization, and so forth.

Following this reasoning, an object's typicality as an instance of any concept generally declines with its number of concepts assigned from the focal cohort. In particular this reasoning suggests that the typicality in any assigned concept decreases monotonically with the number of concepts assigned subject to the condition that it remain non-negative.

In what has become the standard approach, Hsu et al. (2009) proposed the following functional form for relating categorizations and typicalities that satisfies these desiderata:[4]

$$t_c^b(o) = \frac{v(c,o)}{\sum_{c' \in \kappa} v(c',o)}. \tag{11.18}$$

For example, if an object gets categorized as an instance of three concepts, then its typicality equals one-third for each of them, and its typicality in all other concepts in the cohort equals zero.

For the generalized case, Pontikes (2008) proposed the following:

$$t_c(o) = \frac{\eta(c,o)}{\sum_{c' \in \kappa} \eta(c',o)}. \tag{11.19}$$

For example, reviewers apply the concept c_1 to an object eight times and apply the concepts c_2 and c_3 each one time, then $t(c_1,o)=0.8$ and $t(c_c,o)=0.1=t(c_3,o)$.

As noted above, an object whose feature values cause it to be assigned to two distant concepts generally has low typicality in each. But one that gets assigned two close concepts might be quite typical of each. Kovács and Hannan (2015) proposed that typicalities be defined in a way that incorporates metric information about the distances among concepts:

$$t_c^g(o) = \frac{\eta(c,o)}{1 + \sum_{c' \in \kappa} \eta(c,o)\,\vec{d}(c,c')};$$

$$t_c^{gb}(o) = \frac{v(c,o)}{1 + \sum_{c' \in \kappa} v(c,o)\,\vec{d}(c,c')},$$

where $\vec{d}(c,c')$ denotes the distance from the concept c to the concept c', as defined in chapter 6. This definition, like the discrete one in equation 11.18, sets $t_c(o)=1$ if c is the only concept in the cohort assigned to o, and it sets $t(c',o)=0$ for $c' \neq c$ in such cases. The addition of each concept lowers empirical typicalities, but it does so much more when the added concept lies far from the others.

Recall that $\vec{d}(c,c')$ denotes the distance from the concept c to the concept c'. In chapter 7 we rendered this distance in terms of the two concept likelihoods. Lacking information on the positions of objects, a researcher likely cannot get empirical estimates of concept likelihoods. How can we measure the distance between concepts for data with categorizations but not positions in semantic space? Recent sociological research has constructed a measure from categorization co-occurrences. Completing the definition proposed above requires specification of perceived distance in the sociocultural space of categories. A basic intuition, backed by research in cognitive psychology, holds that similarity and distance are inversely related as we discussed in chapter 2. Researchers can accordingly calculate distance between concepts by first calculating pairwise similarity based on overlaps in the objects categorized, and then translating these similarity measures to distances using Shepard's law.

Sociological research has used a simple measure of category similarity due to Jaccard (1901).[5] Formally, if $|\mathbf{cat}(c) \cap \mathbf{cat}(c')|$ denotes the cardinality of the set of objects categorized as both c and c', and $|\mathbf{cat}(c) \cup \mathbf{cat}(c')|$ denotes the cardinality of the set of objects categorized as c and/or c', then their Jaccard similarity is

$$J(c,c') = \frac{|\mathbf{cat}(c) \cap \mathbf{cat}(c')|}{|\mathbf{cat}(c) \cup \mathbf{cat}(c')|}. \qquad (11.20)$$

This index takes values in the $[0,1]$ range, with 0 denoting perfect dissimilarity and 1 denoting perfect similarity. For example, the dataset on restaurants analyzed below contains nine restaurants categorized as Malaysian and eleven categorized as Singaporean. Four of these restaurants are categorized as both. Thus, the similarity of Malaysian and Singaporean in these data is $4/(9+11-4)=0.25$.

Finally, estimated similarities of categories can be used to estimate the distances between the associated concepts. Using the standard form of Shepard's law, we can write:

$$\widehat{d}(c,c') = e^{-s\,J(c,c')}, \quad s > 0, \qquad (11.21)$$

for some suitably chosen value of the free parameter s.

With this step in hand, we have an empirical form of the proposed typicalities:

$$\widehat{t^{\vartheta}}_c(o) = \frac{\eta(c,o)}{1 + \sum_{c' \in \kappa} \eta(c,o)\,\widehat{d}(c,c')}; \qquad (11.22)$$

$$\widehat{t^{\vartheta b}}_c(o) = \frac{\nu(c,o)}{1 + \sum_{c' \in \kappa} \nu(c,o)\,\widehat{d}(c,c')}, \qquad (11.23)$$

The estimated $\widehat{t^{\vartheta}}$ or $\widehat{t^{\vartheta b}}$ can be rescaled and inserted into equation 11.15 and used to complete the measurement of ambiguity.

11.5   Category Contrast

Finally, we use our formal definition of ambiguity to go from the object level to the category level. We propose a new rendering of the sociologically important notion of the contrast of a category.

Recall that we defined the distinctiveness of a concept as a measure of the difference between the mental representation of the concept and the mental representations of related concepts (those in the cohort of the domain, definition 7.2). When we introduced distinctiveness, we proposed that it could replace the notion of contrast, which has played a central role in empirical research on sociological implications of concepts and categories. We pointed out that Hannan et al. (2007) had introduced contrast as an extensional construct: as the average grade of membership (typicality in our terms) of the objects in the extension of a concept. If all of the elements in the category (the extension) are full members, then the contrast equals unity. As the fit to the concept by members of the concept declines, then contrast falls.

We noted that the contrast combines information about a concept (the variability of its concept likelihood and its position in semantic space) with information about the objects that a focal person happens to have observed and categorized. Two individuals with exactly the same concepts might experience different sets of objects and by virtue of this alone might have categories that differ in contrast. Therefore, contrast cannot be seen as a characteristic of a concept, which is a weakness in some applications. This is why we introduced the notion of distinctiveness.

Although we think this reasoning is sound, it has not settled the issue for us. As we wrote the book and discussed its arguments, we often found ourselves reverting to the original notion of contrast. Our intuitions hold that what kind of category emerges makes a difference and that this difference does not get fully represented by distinctiveness. So here we revive the extensional idea of contrast. We propose that contrast is an extensional version of the intensional notion of distinctiveness. A concept is distinctive if it lies far in the expanded semantic space from the other concepts in its cohort. Given the relationship between distance and categorization probability, we suggest that a distinctive concept is unlikely to be combined with others in categorizations. That is, the more distinctive a concept is, the less likely it is that the objects that are included in its category are also included in categories for the other concepts in the cohort.

We think that our formulation of ambiguity well represents this intuition because high ambiguity means high likelihood of multiple classification (postulate 11.1). In simple terms, we suggest that the contrast of a category, the

degree to which it stands out from its cohort, is (essentially) inversely proportional to the average conceptual ambiguity of its members. We denote
the contrast of (an unspecified) person's category associated to the concept
c as $\Gamma(c)$. We propose the following definition.

Definition 11.3 (Contrast of a category) *The contrast of a category associated
with a concept in a cohort is the inverse of one plus the average level of conceptual
ambiguity of the members of the category.*[6]

$$\Gamma(c) = \frac{1}{1 + \overline{A}(c)}, \tag{11.24}$$

where

$$\overline{A}(c) = \frac{1}{|\mathbf{cat}(c)|} \sum_{o \in \mathbf{cat}(c)} A(o \mid \mathcal{I}_0, \mathbf{C}, x).$$

11.6   Measuring Contrast

We turn to our empirical examples to calculate contrast. First, we calculate
contrast for styles in rap music. We have already computed the object ambiguity of each album in the domain (see §11.4). We calculate the contrast of
style categories using equation 11.24, with conceptual ambiguity replaced
by our empirical estimates. Table 11.4 lists the contrast for the top styles.

TABLE 11.4
Contrast of the twelve largest styles
in rap music

Style	Contrast	No. tracks
Alternative rap	.29	2743
Dirty south	.34	2496
East Coast rap	.30	6729
G-Funk	.32	924
Gangsta rap	.33	5819
Golden age	.29	1194
Hardcore rap	.32	9863
Political rap	.29	750
Pop-rap	.28	1858
Southern rap	.33	3358
Underground rap	.30	3254
West Coast rap	.31	3106

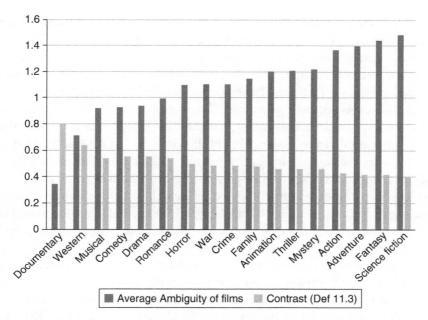

Figure 11.7 Average conceptual ambiguity and genre-level contrast among Hollywood feature films, 2001–2003

Figure 11.7 compares conceptual ambiguity and contrast at the genre level for 458 feature films released in the United States during 2001–2003. The calculations use genre assignments by IMDB, and contrast is calculated using definition 11.3. Among the seventeen genres listed in figure 11.7, documentary has the lowest average ambiguity and highest contrast. On the other end of the spectrum, genres such as action, adventure, fantasy, and science fiction have the lowest levels of contrast. This is consistent with the fact that films classified under the latter set of genres tend to be combined much more extensively with other genres compared to documentaries.

Discussion

The central issue of this chapter is how to represent formally the sociologically important notion of conceptual ambiguity. We build on the idea that ambiguous objects are those that might well be instances of multiple concepts in a cohort. This way of thinking about it makes conceptual ambiguity domain-specific. A natural way of expressing this uses the entropy of the categorization probabilities over the concepts in a cohort. Conceptual ambiguity is high when the vector has higher entropy.

This construction has an interesting implication that can be exploited in empirical research: multiple categorization in a domain is a signature of conceptual ambiguity. The usual language in sociological research for multiple categorization is *category spanning*. This signature serves as a warrant for the common practice of assuming that multiple categorization signals that an object is ambiguous (Hsu et al., 2009; Pontikes, 2012; Olzak, 2016).

Why does conceptual ambiguity matter? Our answer ties ambiguity to cognitive fluency. Trying to interpret objects with high entropy of categorization takes cognitive effort. Extensive research reveals that such effortful reasoning gives rise to a sense of disfluency. In turn, disfluency depresses affect. We will exploit this connection in the next chapter where in our analysis of valuation.

The analysis of conceptual ambiguity and categorization probabilities allows us to revisit the construct of category contrast, which we used in previous research. In the earlier research, the contrast of a category was measured as the average typicality of the members for the concept, and typicality was an explicit function of the frequency of overlaps in memberships with other categories associated with the domain. A category, by these measures, has a contrast of one if no member of the category is also an instance of another category (in the domain). Contrast declines with the number of categorical overlaps (possibly weighted by the distance between categories). So there is a link between contrast as measured and conceptual ambiguity. We seized on this link to propose a theoretically grounded definition of the contrast of a category as the average conceptual ambiguity of its members.

Throughout the chapter, we presented some empirical applications of conceptual ambiguity and contrast. We showed that researchers can examine these issues with data when they measure positions of the objects in the semantic space but also when they know only the categorizations of the objects (as is common in sociological research).

CHAPTER TWELVE

Valuation

OUR WORK THUS FAR has focused on explaining how concepts enable people to identify and interpret what they encounter, thereby mediating their experiences. We modeled the process of categorization and showed how conceptualization shapes inference and perception. In this chapter, we turn to analyzing how the concepts through which people comprehend their world also influence their value judgments, such as ratings of movies, assessments of teachers, or choice among job candidates. We begin the chapter by tying valuation to fluency, typicality, and conceptual ambiguity by building on ideas developed in chapter 11. Then we note that this approach imposes severe limitations because it cannot accommodate the observation that people see some concepts more positively or negatively than others. We propose that such concept valences affect the valuation of particular objects. When an object has been categorized in just one concept, concept valence will affect valuation more strongly for typical objects than for atypical objects. When categorization is uncertain, or when an object has been categorized in multiple concepts, it is unclear to the agent which concept is most relevant. The contribution of the concept valence of candidate concepts will depend on the categorization probabilities. In this chapter, we propose a model for this process. As we discuss at the end of this chapter, this model can be linked to a substantial body of work within sociology on the relationship between categorization processes and evaluation in markets.

12.1 Fluency and Valuation

Research reviewed in the previous chapter (pp. 172–173) provides evidence that objects that are processed more fluently tend to be evaluated more positively. We formulate this claim in terms of the function, $\mathcal{V}(o \mid \mathcal{I})$, that gives the focal person's valuation of an object.

Postulate 12.1 (Valuation of categorized objects increases with fluency under deliberate cognition) *Suppose the agent's information state is $\mathcal{I}$. There exists a constant $\beta > 0$ such that*

$$\mathcal{V}(o \mid \mathcal{I}) = \beta \, \phi(o \mid \mathcal{I}) + \epsilon_1, \qquad (12.1)$$

where ϵ_1 is an error term.

In the previous chapter, we have proposed that fluency increases with typicality and decreases with conceptual ambiguity (postulate 11.2). When the object has been categorized as a c, what matters is the typicality of the object in the focal concept c. When the object has not been categorized, or has been categorized in multiple concepts, what matters is the average typicality of the object in the relevant concepts, $\mathbf{T}(o \mid \mathcal{I})$. These two postulates jointly imply that the valuation of an object increases with the average typicality of the object and decreases with its conceptual ambiguity.

Proposition 12.1 *Overall valuation declines with conceptual ambiguity and increases with average typicality.*
There exist constants $\beta_A < 0$ and $\beta_T > 0$ such that

$$\mathcal{V}(o \mid \mathcal{I}) = \beta_A A(o \mid \mathcal{I}) + \beta_\mathbf{T} \mathbf{T}(o \mid \mathcal{I}) + \epsilon_2, \qquad (12.2)$$

where ϵ_2 is an error term, and $\mathcal{I}$ equals $\mathcal{I}^f$, $\{\mathcal{I}^f, x\}$, $\{\mathcal{I}^f, \mathbf{C}\}$ or $\{\mathcal{I}^f, \mathbf{C}, x\}$.

Although proposition 12.1 captures important aspects of evaluation, we believe it is overly simplistic. First, the valuation implied by this proposition is not sensitive to the valence of concepts, a fortiori to the possibility that candidate concepts might have different valences. In the case of film for instance, some might place much higher value on drama than on action, while others might have a different ordering of valences. Moreover, it ignores that valuation likely differs according to whether people rely on automatic or deliberate cognition. In the remaining sections of this chapter, we address these shortcomings and propose a much more comprehensive model of how concepts affect valuation.

12.2   Valuation and Cognition

Structured by Concepts

Before getting into the details of our approach, it is important to consider how and why concepts affect valuation. One perspective on this issue holds that concepts and categorization only play a role in valuation when people lack full information on the objects that they are evaluating. That is, people use concepts to "fill in the blanks" about the unobserved features of objects. But if a person has full information on all relevant features, then he or she would evaluate the object on the basis of their liking and disliking of the combination of those particular features relative to their tastes; categorization would provide no additional information and therefore would have no effect on valuation net of the valuations of the feature values.

Based on our modeling in earlier chapters of how concepts shape inference and perception, it should not be surprising that we view concepts as playing a more fundamental role than this. We see valuation as inextricably linked to categorization for at least two reasons. First, because of limited attention, people generally do not attempt to discern every single feature of an object. Rather, the set of concepts that a person holds and get activated at the time of judgment dictates which features are germane, and draws attention to those particular features. In other words, even if a person were to evaluate an object on the basis of its features alone, the concepts that the person holds would determine the weight that each feature warrants in valuation.

Second, even if people paid attention to every feature, a person's valuation of an object would often diverge from what might be obtained from a straightforward summing or averaging of the person's liking for various features individually. At the same time, there exists evidence from cognitive psychology that people are unlikely to possess mental representations of complicated functions in multi-dimensional spaces. We thus find it unlikely that people would possess mental representations of highly nonlinear mappings between feature combinations and valuations for all possible sets of features that might be considered in coming up with a valuation.

Where does this leave us? Our idea is that concepts are at the core of people's *structured* understandings of feature-value combinations: people have valuations associated with concepts and ascribe value to objects by relying on the valuations of the relevant concepts. The weight of each relevant concept depends on the typicality of the object in the concept.

This perspective allows us to derive predictions for a variety of settings that differ in terms of the information available to the evaluator: settings in which the agent knows the features of the objects but not the categories to which they belong, settings in which she does not know the features but knows the categories to which the objects belong, and settings in which she knows both the features and the categories. We are not aware of any such general treatment of concepts and valuation.

That concepts can shape how people affectively respond to what they encounter is evident from both casual observation of the world and scholarly work. The reason for these differential responses is that concepts themselves often vary in terms of whether they are associated with positive or negative interpretations—what psychologists call *valence* (Lerner and Keltner, 2000). The valence of a concept gets transferred to specific objects when they are recognized as instances of the concept. Through this process, a concept's valence shapes affective responses to objects (i.e., material objects, persons, social situations, organizations, and so forth).

Our approach builds on an active research program within cognitive psychology on inferences about unobserved features of objects when position is known on some feature dimensions but the category of the object is unknown (Murphy and Ross, 1994; Griffiths, Hayes, and Newell, 2012; Konovalova and Le Mens, 2016, 2018). A fundamental premise of this research program is that people do not possess mental representations of the relationships between all possible feature combinations of objects (e.g., about the extent to which movies that contain more violence tend to have more suspense). Rather, the concepts people have in mind would shape, "on the fly", feature inferences. Our proposal that people do not possess mental representations of a hypothetical mapping between feature combinations and valuation is similar to this premise.

Within sociology, the idea that the conceptual understandings used to delineate various types of persons, objects, and events shape affective responses via the process of categorization has been widely recognized. For example, the large body of work on occupational prestige shows that individuals' conceptualizations of various occupations include a hierarchical component, with some occupations being widely viewed as more prestigious and thereby garnering more positive reactions (Blau and Duncan, 1967; Treiman, 1977; Zhou, 2005). Recent work by Sharkey (2014) indicates that people similarly view the industries into which organizations are often classified as being associated with more or less status and that industry-based status differences shape how specific organizational actions are interpreted and evaluated. Sociologist William J. Goode (1978) captured the process in general terms in *The Celebration of Heroes: Prestige as a Control System*:

> Much interaction is made up of exchanges and valuations among social categories. …Because people first perceive one another as "members" of such social units, their initial behavior and attitudes are determined most by the respect or dispraise they usually give to such social categories or groups. [p. 101]

Concepts often evoke affective reactions that cause the stakes of categorization to be high. This, in turn, can lead to fierce contention over the boundaries or formal borders within classification systems (Lamont and Molnár, 2002) and can help explain why actors engage in substantial efforts to shape the positive or negative meanings associated with different concepts (e.g., abortion, gentrification, transgender).

Hannan et al. (2007) define positively valued concepts as those for which individuals tend to find more appealing the more typical members of the associated category. In comparison, other concepts, such as pedophile and plagiarist have a general negative valence, meaning that a good fit to the concept lowers valuation.

MODES OF COGNITION: In this chapter, we build a model of valuation linked explicitly to categorization. A central consideration is the mode of cognition on which the agent relies to perform her evaluation. Psychological research distinguishes between two modes of cognition. The first is automatic (or implicit), when people use well-established associations to respond to an object through non-conscious, unintentional processes. The second is deliberate (or controlled): when responses result from an individual's active attention to consciously respond to a stimulus (Bargh, 1994; Kahneman, 2011). Implicit or automatic processing underlies spontaneous judgments and nonverbal reactions, whereas explicit or deliberate cognition predicts evaluative judgments and deliberate behaviors (Dovidio, Kawakami, Johnson, Johnson, and Howard, 1997; Galinsky, Martoran, and Ku, 2003). Studies of stereotyping and prejudice make clear that both modes play a role in judgment, including valuation. Stereotypes of social categories affect how people judge others primarily through automatic processing, while conscious processing can interact with automatic responses to change overall reactions (Dovidio, Evans, and Tyler, 1986; Bargh, 1997; Kawakami, Dovidio, Moll, Hermsen, and Russin, 2000). Vaisey (2009) has initiated sociological analysis of the implications of the distinction between the two modes.

Kahneman (2011) gives us the flavor of the distinction between these two modes:[1]

> System 1 does not keep track of alternatives that it rejects, or even of the fact that there were alternatives. Conscious doubt is not in the repertoire of System 1; it requires maintaining incompatible interpretations in mind at the same time, which demands mental effort. Uncertainty and doubt are the domain of System 2.

For our purposes, the key insight is that automatic cognition ignores variability and uncertainty. When agents rely on automatic cognition, we propose that they categorize the object in one of the candidate concepts and apply the associated valuation. By contrast, we propose that, when relying on deliberate cognition, agents integrate over the valuations associated with the candidate concepts. This deliberate cognition case is similar to the model of expected utility, which assumes that choice is sensitive to valuations associated with alternative outcomes as well as to outcome uncertainty (Bernoulli, 1738; Savage, 1972).

In line with this distinction, we make different predictions for valuation under these different modes of cognition. We argue by cases, depending on which system applies. We refrain from specifying the conditions that make people more or less likely to rely on intuitive versus deliberate cognition. A large literature in psychology has addressed this issue (Kahneman (2011) provides an overview.) The main pattern that becomes evident in this stream of research is that people rely by default on automatic cognition unless the situation triggers deliberate thinking. Factors that lead people to engage in deliberate thinking include (but are not limited to) an objective to be accurate, facing a threat, providing an explicit justification for one's judgment or decision, and facing a confusing situation (that lacks fluency).

Before turning to the specification of the predictions, we need to clarify the background assumptions we make regarding the setting of the valuation and what the agent knows about it.

CONTEXT OF THE VALUATION: In previous chapters, we developed the intuition and a formal rendering that judgments depend on the context in which they are made. One crucial part of the context is the domain. We continue with this theme in this chapter by indexing functions by the information about the background, the domain. In all of the cases we analyze, the information state includes $\mathcal{I}_0$, which contains the information that the focal object is an instance of the root of the domain $\mathfrak{D}_r$. In formal terms,

$$\mathcal{I}_0 = \{\text{"the focal domain is } \mathfrak{D}_r\text{"}\} \cup \{\text{IS-A}(r, o)\}.$$

We assume that all of the information states considered contain this information.

12.3   Valence and Typicality

In general, valuation involves both categorization (what kind of object is this?) and the assignment of value based on fit to a category (how appealing is the object in light of the relevant concepts?). In the interest of building intuition and connecting with prior research, we begin with the simple setting in which there is no uncertainty about whether a particular concept applies to an object.

Our analytic structure builds on a foundation that treats valuation of an object in a context that makes a single concept relevant. This is the parallel to our building a model of categorization that starts with the single-concept case in chapter 8. Once we have established the foundation, we move to more general cases in which the context makes all of the concepts in a cohort relevant.

As we have explained above, a central claim of this chapter is that objects derive value from the concepts to which they are associated. We thus need to introduce a notation for the valence of a concept. If c is a concept, we denote its valence by $\mathfrak{v}_c$. Our analysis ties valuation to conceptualization *within* a domain characterized by a root concept, which we denote by r. Note the root of the domain is itself a concept. As such, it too has a valence, $\mathfrak{v}_r$ that will play an explicit role when an object is not categorized in one of focal concepts. It seems reasonable to regard the valence of a concept to include (much or all of) the valence of the root. However, we do not constrain this to be so in our formalization.

Suppose that the evaluator knows the position of the object in the semantic space for the focal concept, c. In this case, the evaluator can assess how typical the object is of concept c. We propose that the more typical the object, the more it inherits of the concept valence, $\mathfrak{v}_c$. Conversely, highly atypical objects are seen as very different from the focal concept and thus should gain little of the concept valence. We capture these intuitions by assuming that the valuation of the object as an instance of concept c is given by the product of concept valence and the object's typicality. This claim is consistent with the research that has shown that fluency increases with typicality and that a higher fluency leads to more positive valuations.

We also consider the case where the only information the evaluator possesses about the object is its categorizations. In this case, the evaluator cannot assess the typicality of the object as an instance of the focal concept. Then the valuation is given by the concept valence adjusted by the average typicality of positions, computed over the semantic space. Informative concepts tend to have "peaked" typicality functions such that the average typicality will be relatively high. By contrast, uninformative concepts tend to have flat typicality functions. In this case, the average typicality will be much lower than one. The valuation of an instance of an uninformative concept will be strongly discounted as compared to the valence of the concept itself. In this case, the agent realizes that no strong conclusions about value can be derived on the basis of categorizations alone.

We formalize these claims in the following postulate.

Postulate 12.2 (Valuation as an instance of one concept) *If an object is known to be an instance of a concept, then its valuation depends on the valence of the concept and object's typicality.*

[A.] Position is not known:

$$\mathcal{V}(o\,|\,c) = \mathfrak{v}_c\, T_c, \tag{12.3}$$

where T_c is expected typicality (implied by the concept likelihood for c) of an object with unknown position (equation 11.7).

[B.] Position is known:

$$\mathcal{V}(o\,|\,c,x) = \mathfrak{v}_c\tau_c(x). \tag{12.4}$$

An immediate implication of this postulate is that the valuation of the prototype is exactly the concept valence, $\mathfrak{v}_c$. This can be seen by taking $\tau_c(x) = 1$ in equation 12.4.

As we build the model, we assume that objects (known to be instances of the root of the domain) get valued as instances of the root when they are not categorized in any of the available concepts in the cohort associated with the root. We denote the categorization of such an object as Ø, for "empty concept assignment."

Postulate 12.3 (Valuation under empty concept assignment) *If the object is not judged to be an instance of any of the concepts in the cohort, then it is valued as a known instance of the root of the domain.*

[A.] Position is not known:

$$\mathcal{V}(o \mid \emptyset) = \mathfrak{v}_r T_r, \tag{12.5}$$

where T_r is expected typicality (implied by the concept likelihood for r) of an object with unknown position:

$$T_r = \int_x \tau_r(x) \, d\pi_{\mathbb{F}_r}(x \mid r). \tag{12.6}$$

[B.] Position is known:

$$\mathcal{V}(o \mid \emptyset, x) = \mathfrak{v}_r \tau_r(x). \tag{12.7}$$

These postulates state that the valuation of an object of very low typicality is close to zero. Notice that if both $\mathfrak{v}_r$ and $\mathfrak{v}_c$ are positive, an object judged to be a very atypical of c might receive a lower valuation than if it were not categorized as a c. For instance, a restaurant known to be Italian but judged to have low typicality in this genre might get lower ratings than an otherwise identical restaurant that does not categorized as anything but restaurant.

12.4   Valuation in a Single-Concept Context

Now we examine a series of situations in which the domain of the objects being evaluated contains just one single concept c in addition to the root of the domain, r. Each situation is characterized by a particular information state regarding the object. In all of the information states we consider here, the person knows that the focal object belongs to the domain—it is an instance of concept r. Moreover all the information states contain the background knowledge of the domain, which we discussed extensively in earlier chapters. To refer to the background knowledge and the fact that the context is one in which only a single concept is relevant, we use $\mathcal{I}^s$.

At one extreme, the information state includes both categorization (in c) and its position in feature space. At the other extreme, the information state tells very little about the object, as when it neither includes the position in feature space nor positive categorization (other than the object belongs to the domain). In the intermediate cases, the information case includes either categorization as a c or position in feature space, x, but not both.

As an illustration, consider a member of a departmental committee charged with doing preliminary assessment of "rookie" candidates (recent graduates of PhD programs) for a position as sociologist. The call for application specified that candidates should hold (or soon hold) a PhD in Sociology or other related fields within the social sciences. The root of the domain is thus social scientist, and the focal concept is sociologist. Before reading the application file, the evaluator might only know that an applicant is a sociologist, based on the fact that she is enrolled in a sociology PhD program. In this case, the information state is $\{\mathcal{I}^s, c\}$. Based on this information about the category, the evaluator might decide it is worth reading the research papers of the applicant, or not (if she knows the applicant is not a sociologist, as when the applicant indicated she was from a Physics PhD program). Sometimes disciplinary categorization is uncertain, as when a candidate has studied in an interdisciplinary program. In this case, the information state is $\mathcal{I}^s$. For example, if the candidate was trained in an organizational behavior department, it could be unclear if he is a sociologist or not. Some candidates might get rejected without further consideration based on this information about the field. In these two information cases ($\{\mathcal{I}^s, c\}$ and $\mathcal{I}^s$), the first-stage valuation proceeded solely on the basis of the category of the candidate.

Those who survive the initial hurdle get more scrutiny. The evaluator might study the research papers and attend a job talk, thereby gaining knowledge about the relevant feature values of the research. In other words, the evaluator comes to know the position of the candidate in the semantic space associated with the concept sociologist. We consider two cases that parallel the two cases without knowledge of the position in semantic space. First, if the evaluator sees the candidate as a sociologist without any uncertainty about it (categorization is known), then the information state is $\{\mathcal{I}^s, c, x\}$. Second, if the evaluator is uncertain about a candidate's discipline, then the information state is $\{\mathcal{I}^s, x\}$.

The reader might wonder about the empirical relevance of the cases where the information state includes categorization but not information about the position. How can a person arrive at a belief that an object is an instance of a concept without knowing anything about its feature values? This information must come externally, and the person must believe it. Obvious external sources of categorization are the people we interact with, the media, and, in situations in which the objects have agency, self-claims advanced by the object or the agent that created it. For instance, a concert poster might claim that the bands performing are heavy metal, or a review of a restaurant might refer to it as Peruvian. In chapter 14, we develop a model of social effects. At this point, all we need to do is to postulate the consequences of a focal person developing a belief about the category membership of an object or a judgment of typicality without telling where these come from.

Uncertain Categorization in the Single Concept

What happens when the evaluator has a single concept in mind but does not know for certain that an object is an instance of the concept? In such a context, the person is simultaneously categorizing the object and valuing it. This might occur, for example, when an academic department conducts a job search for a specific disciplinary research position but is willing to consider all applicants regardless of the discipline in which they were trained. In this case, valuation will be affected by the target discipline (the single concept) even if evaluators are not certain that every applicant is actually a specialist in that discipline.

Our treatment of this case (and the parallel case with multiple concepts) builds on the research on feature inference under uncertain categorization mentioned above. Experimental evidence shows that information about a position is used to infer the category of the object, which in turn informs inferences about the feature position on the unobserved dimension (Murphy and Ross, 1994; Konovalova and Le Mens, 2016, 2018). Similarly, we propose here that information about the position is used to infer the category of the object, which in turn informs its valuation by invoking the concept valence. We conjecture that how this is done depends on whether cognition is automatic or deliberate. As indicated in the introduction to this section, we propose that, under automatic cognition, agents categorize or not the object in the concept and then apply the associated valuation. By contrast, under deliberate cognition, agents integrate the valuations in a way that is sensitive to the categorization probability of the object in the focal concept.[2] We formalize these intuitions in the following two postulates.

Postulate 12.4 (Automatic cognition) *Under automatic cognition and uncertainty about applicability of a concept, there is no integration of information in the sense that the valuation is either what is obtained if the object is seen as an instance of the focal concept, c, or what is obtained if the object is seen as not an instance of the focal concept and thus as an instance of the root concept, r. We provide first the formula for the case where position is unknown and then* *for the cases where position is known.*

$$\mathcal{V}^a(o \mid \mathcal{I}^s) = \begin{cases} \mathcal{V}(o \mid c) & \text{with probability } P(c \mid \mathcal{I}^s); \\ \mathcal{V}(o \mid \emptyset) & \text{with probability } P(\emptyset \mid \mathcal{I}^s) = 1 - P(c \mid \mathcal{I}^s). \end{cases}$$
(12.8)

$$\mathcal{V}^a(o \mid \mathcal{I}^s, x) = \begin{cases} \mathcal{V}(o \mid c, x) & \text{with probability } P(c \mid \mathcal{I}^s, x); \\ \mathcal{V}(o \mid \emptyset, x) & \text{with probability } P(\emptyset \mid \mathcal{I}^s, x) = 1 - P(c \mid \mathcal{I}^s, x). \end{cases}$$
(12.9)

Postulate 12.5 (Deliberate cognition) *Suppose that cognition is deliberate and categorization is uncertain. The valuation of the object equals the weighted average of the valuations that is obtained if the object is seen as an instance of the focal concept, c, and the one that is obtained if the object is seen as a non-member of the focal concept. The weight of the first term is the categorization probability in c.*

$$\mathcal{V}^d(o \mid \mathcal{I}^s) = \mathcal{V}(o \mid c) P(c \mid \mathcal{I}^s) + \mathcal{V}(o \mid \emptyset) \cdot (1 - P(c \mid \mathcal{I}^s)).$$
(12.10)
$$\mathcal{V}^d(o \mid \mathcal{I}^s, x) = \mathcal{V}(o \mid c, x) P(c \mid \mathcal{I}^s, x) + \mathcal{V}(o \mid \emptyset, x) \cdot (1 - P(c \mid \mathcal{I}^s, x)).$$
(12.11)

Postulates 12.2 and 12.4 jointly imply that, under automatic cognition, the valuation of an object is either the typicality weighted valence of the focal concept or the typicality weighted valence of the root.

Proposition 12.2 (Automatic cognition) *Under automatic cognition and uncertain categorization, the valuation is either the typicality weighted concept valence, or the typicality weighted valence of the root.*

$$\mathcal{V}^a(o \mid \mathcal{I}^s) = \begin{cases} \mathfrak{v}_c T_c & \text{with probability } P(c \mid \mathcal{I}^s); \\ \mathfrak{v}_r T_r & \text{with probability } 1 - P(c \mid \mathcal{I}^s). \end{cases}$$
(12.12)

$$\mathcal{V}^a(o \mid \mathcal{I}^s, x) = \begin{cases} \mathfrak{v}_c \tau_c(x) & \text{with probability } P(c \mid \mathcal{I}^s, x); \\ \mathfrak{v}_r \tau_r(x) & \text{with probability } 1 - P(c \mid \mathcal{I}^s, x). \end{cases}$$
(12.13)

Under deliberate cognition, postulates 12.2 and 12.5 jointly imply the following explicit formulations.

Proposition 12.3 (Deliberate cognition) *Under deliberate cognition and uncertain categorization, the valuation of the object equals the sum of (1) the valuation that would be obtained if it were seen as an instance of the root concept and (2) an additional term that depends on the categorization probability and* *the difference between the typicality weighted valuations of the focal concept and the root.*

$$\mathcal{V}^d(o \mid \mathcal{I}^s) = \mathfrak{v}_r \, T_r + P(c \mid \mathcal{I}^s)(\mathfrak{v}_c \, T_c - \mathfrak{v}_r \, T_r). \tag{12.14}$$

$$\mathcal{V}^d(o \mid \mathcal{I}^s, x) = \mathfrak{v}_r \, \tau_r(x) + P(c \mid \mathcal{I}^s, x)(\mathfrak{v}_c \, \tau_c(x) - \mathfrak{v}_r \, \tau_r(x)). \tag{12.15}$$

The proposition makes clear that the expressions for valuation in the known categorization cases are special cases of those in the uncertain categorization setting. Eliminating the uncertainty about categorization reduces the result in proposition 12.3 to that in postulate 12.2 if the object is known to be an instance of the focal concept. It reduces the result in proposition 12.3 to that in postulate 12.3 if the object is known *not* to be an instance of the focal concept. The main implication of this analysis is that uncertainty about categorization lowers valuation. In other words, the probability of categorization can be seen as an *uncertainty adjustment* to the corresponding known-categorization case.

In the special case where the valence of the root is zero ($\mathfrak{v}_r = 0$), we can re-express proposition 12.3B as follows, using explicit formulas for the typicality function and the probability of categorization.

Lemma 12.1 *If the valence of the root is equal to 0, we have:*

$$\mathcal{V}^d(o \mid \mathcal{I}^s, x) = \mathfrak{v}_c \, \pi_{\mathbb{F}_c}(x \mid c)^2 \left(\frac{P(c \mid \mathcal{I}^s)}{P_{\mathbb{F}_c}(x \mid \mathcal{I}^s)} \sum_{x' \in \mathbb{F}_c} \tau_c(x') \right). \tag{12.16}$$

The point of showing this complicated formula is that it indicates a main tendency. Due to the multiplication by the square of the concept likelihood, valuation tends to decline sharply with distance of the object's position in the semantic space from the concept (because distance decreases with $\pi_{\mathbb{F}_c}(x \mid c)$ according to proposition 4.1). We cannot state this as a general result because it could be counteracted by the shape of the prior on the position, $P_{\mathbb{F}_c}(x \mid \mathcal{I}^s)$; if the prior increases sharply as $\pi_{\mathbb{F}_c}(x \mid c)$ decreases. In the special case in which the prior is uninformative, that is, has a uniform distribution, it is easy to show that valuation declines monotonically with the distance from the concept.

12.5   Valuation in an Uncertain, Exclusive Categorization Context

In this subsection and the next, we consider settings with multiple candidate concepts—a cohort of several concepts. Here, we consider valuation in contexts of viewing objects as instances of one and only one concept in a cohort. We introduced such exclusive categorization (sometimes called contrastive categorization) in §8.8.

Because this kind of context forces a categorization in one concept, the root and its valuation do not enter the picture for valuation under exclusive categorization. For simplicity of exposition, we assume there are two candidate concepts c_1 and c_2, that the set of possible concept assignments is $\mathfrak{C} = \{\{c_1\}, \{c_2\}\}$.

We will denote the information state for uncertain and exclusive categorization as $\mathcal{I}^e$.

As in the single-concept case, we propose that how concepts affect valuation depends on the cognitive mode. Under automatic cognition, agents first categorize the object in one of the candidate concepts and then apply the associated valuation. By contrast, under deliberate cognition, object valuation depends on the valences of multiple candidate concepts—agents integrate the across possible categorization possibilities. We formalize these proposals in two postulates.

Postulate 12.6 (Automatic cognition) *Under automatic cognition and uncertain categorization in an exclusive-categorization context, there is no integration of information in the sense that the valuation is the valuation as an instance of one of the candidate concepts.*

$$\mathcal{V}^a(o \mid \mathcal{I}^e) = \begin{cases} \mathcal{V}(o \mid c_1) & \text{with probability } P(c_1 \mid \mathcal{I}^e); \\ \mathcal{V}(o \mid c_2) & \text{with probability } P(c_2 \mid \mathcal{I}^e). \end{cases} \tag{12.17}$$

$$\mathcal{V}^a(o \mid \mathcal{I}^e, x) = \begin{cases} \mathcal{V}(o \mid c_1, x) & \text{with probability } P(c_1 \mid \mathcal{I}^e, x); \\ \mathcal{V}(o \mid c_2, x) & \text{with probability } P(c_2 \mid \mathcal{I}^e, x). \end{cases} \tag{12.18}$$

Postulate 12.7 (Deliberate cognition) *Suppose that cognition is deliberate and there is uncertain categorization in an exclusive-categorization context. The valuation of an object equals the weighted average of the valuations obtained if the object is seen as an instance of the candidate concepts; and the weights are the categorization probabilities.*

$$\mathcal{V}^d(o \mid \mathcal{I}^e) = \mathcal{V}(o \mid c_1) P(c_1 \mid \mathcal{I}^e) + \mathcal{V}(o \mid c_2) P(c_2 \mid \mathcal{I}^e). \tag{12.19}$$

$$\mathcal{V}^d(o \mid \mathcal{I}^e, x) = \mathcal{V}(o \mid c_1, x) P(c_1 \mid \mathcal{I}^e, x) + \mathcal{V}(o \mid c_2, x) P(c_2 \mid \mathcal{I}^e, x). \tag{12.20}$$

We can write more explicit formulas by relying on postulate 12.2.

Proposition 12.4 (Automatic Cognition) *Under automatic cognition and uncertain categorization in an exclusive-categorization context, there is no integration of information in the sense that the valuation is the typicality-weighted valence of one of the candidate concepts.*

$$\mathcal{V}^{a}(o \,|\, \mathcal{I}^{e}) = \begin{cases} \mathfrak{v}_{c_1} T_{c_1} & \text{with probability } P(c_1 \,|\, \mathcal{I}^{e}); \\ \mathfrak{v}_{c_2} T_{c_2} & \text{with probability } P(c_2 \,|\, \mathcal{I}^{e}). \end{cases} \tag{12.21}$$

$$\mathcal{V}^{a}(o \,|\, \mathcal{I}^{e}, x) = \begin{cases} \mathfrak{v}_{c_1} \tau_{c_1}(x) & \text{with probability } P(c_1 \,|\, \mathcal{I}^{e}, x); \\ \mathfrak{v}_{c_2} \tau_{c_2}(x) & \text{with probability } P(c_2 \,|\, \mathcal{I}^{e}, x). \end{cases} \tag{12.22}$$

Proposition 12.5 (Deliberate Cognition) *Under deliberate cognition and uncertain categorization in an exclusive-categorization context, valuation of an object is the weighted average of the typicality weighted concept valences.*

$$\mathcal{V}^{d}(o \,|\, \mathcal{I}^{e}) = \mathfrak{v}_{c_1} T_{c_1} P(c_1 \,|\, \mathcal{I}^{e}) + \mathfrak{v}_{c_2} T_{c_2} P(c_2 \,|\, \mathcal{I}^{e}). \tag{12.23}$$

$$\mathcal{V}^{d}(o \,|\, \mathcal{I}^{e}, x) = \mathfrak{v}_{c_1} \tau_{c_1}(x) P(c_1 \,|\, \mathcal{I}^{e}, x) + \mathfrak{v}_{c_2} \tau_{c_2}(x) P(c_2 \,|\, \mathcal{I}^{e}, x). \tag{12.24}$$

We illustrate the implications of the foregoing results in figure 12.1. The setup is the same as in figure 11.1 with two concepts with normal pdfs, concept valences equal to 1 and 0.8, and the valence of the root equal

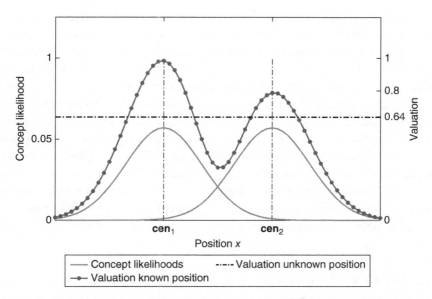

Figure 12.1 Exclusive categorization: valuation as a function of position for the setting of figure 11.1, as implied by proposition 12.5

to 0 ($\mathfrak{v}_{c_1} = 1$, $\mathfrak{v}_{c_2} = .8$, $\mathfrak{v}_r = 0$). The figure shows that valuation falls with distance from the closest concept when position is known: valuation declines with falling typicality. But if position is not known, then valuation is constant at the level indicated by the dashed horizontal line.

12.6   Valuation in a Multiple-Concept Context

Now we must consider a different set of information states that involve known multiple categorization or free categorization over the concepts in the cohort associated with the focal domain. Remember that free categorization was the topic of chapter 9. As in the previous chapter, the cohort of concepts in the domain is denoted by κ, the set of concepts assigned to the object is denoted by $\ell_\kappa(o)$, and the set of candidate concept assignments is denoted by $\mathfrak{C}$. In the free categorization case, it is equal to the powerset of the cohort $\mathfrak{C} = \wp(\kappa)$; all combinations of concepts are allowed. To refer to the background knowledge and the fact that categorization is free, we use $\mathcal{I}^f$.

Known Multiple Categorization

The multiple categorization setting raises a challenge: how do the valuations under the different single-concept assignments combine? In our view, valuations of objects categorized in multiple concepts will not be automatic. As we explained in section 9.2, we distinguish between compound concepts, which are conceptualized, and concept sets, which are not. It is the latter that require cognitive effort. So we restrict attention here to strings of concepts in a cohort. In other words, we assume that an evaluator with a given cohort of concepts does not recognize prototypes for strings of concepts in a cohort. (If they did, this would mean that a combination is itself a concept, counter to the assumption.) Conceptual combinations are not concepts as we see it. Therefore, there is no available structured mental representation that provides the basis for automatic inferences. In other words, when an object has been categorized in multiple concepts, cognition is not automatic but deliberate.

Postulate 12.8 (Multiple categorization and cognitive mode) *When an evaluator has categorized an object in multiple concepts in a cohort, valuation operates in deliberate mode.*

The building block for this part of the model is a simple average of single-concept valuations, as described in the following box.

Notation

We introduce a notation for a baseline for valuation in free categorization environments. The idea is to construct a representation of what happens if the evaluator's judgment is unaffected by concept combination. We propose that a reasonable notion is that the baseline valuation is a weighted average of the corresponding single-concept valuations (for the concepts involved in the combination), where the weights are the rescaled categorization probabilities (equation 11.2).

We start with the single-concept valuations from postulate 12.2. If the individual knows the object's position, then the average of the single-concept valuations can be written (using equation 12.4) as

$$\mathbf{V}(o \,|\, \mathcal{I}^f, \mathbf{C}, x) = \sum_{c \in \mathbf{C}} P^*(\text{IS-A}(c, o) \,|\, \mathcal{I}^f, x, \mathbf{C}) \, \mathfrak{v}_c \tau_c(x). \qquad (12.25)$$

If the individual does not know the object's position, it is written (using equation 12.3) as

$$\mathbf{V}(o \,|\, \mathcal{I}^f, \mathbf{C}) = \sum_{c \in \mathbf{C}} P^*(\text{IS-A}(c, o) \,|\, \mathcal{I}^f, \mathbf{C}) \, \mathfrak{v}_c \, T_c. \qquad (12.26)$$

We will treat as a baseline that valuations in multiple-categorization settings are given by these averages. Clearly, the mechanical and counterfactual nature of the construction of such average total valuations means that they almost certainly mistake the nature of an actual valuation. So, in the next step, we introduce a parameter, θ, and a function, $\zeta(o \,|\, \mathcal{I})$, that reflect the operation of cognitive processes that modify the average of single-concept valuations in producing the overall valuation of an object.

We propose that conceptual ambiguity implies that the cognitive processes lower valuations below what would be expected given the average of the single-concept valuations. As we discussed extensively in the previous chapter, some positions in the semantic space are more ambiguous than others. We argued that conceptual ambiguity reduces fluency and thereby depresses valuation. In the more complicated structure that we have built, we express this intuition in terms of the ζ function. Because conceptual ambiguity is not defined in the absence of known position in the semantic space, we concentrate on the situation in which the evaluator's information state contains information on the position of the object.

Postulate 12.9 (Aggregation) *If an evaluator has categorized an object in multiple concepts in a cohort, then*
[A.] valuation can be characterized as a linear function of the typicality-weighted average of the valences of the concepts.

$$\mathcal{V}^d(o \mid \mathcal{I}) = \theta \mathbf{V}(o \mid \mathcal{I}) + \zeta(o \mid \mathcal{I}) \quad \theta \leq 1; \tag{12.27}$$

and
[B.] $\zeta(o \mid \mathcal{I})$ is a decreasing function of the conceptual ambiguity of the object.

$$\zeta(o \mid \mathcal{I}) = \lambda A(o \mid \mathcal{I}) + \epsilon_3, \quad \lambda \leq 0, \tag{12.28}$$

where $\mathcal{I}$ is equal to $\{\mathcal{I}^f, \mathbf{C}\}$ or $\{\mathcal{I}^f, \mathbf{C}, x\}$ and ϵ_3 is an error term.

We readily recognize the possibility that some contexts and some persons might differ from the general tendency. Goldberg et al. (2016) found that a subset of the reviewers of films and restaurants appreciated films and restaurants that appear to fall between concepts (genres in these cases) and have high conceptual ambiguity.[3] In our terms these people have positive values of λ. It is thus best to think of λ as an individual and context-specific parameter that is non-positive for most people but could be positive for a particular subset of people who like ambiguous items.

Uncertain and Free Categorization

Next we come to situations of great substantive interest: the evaluator knows from the context that multiple concepts potentially apply to objects but is uncertain exactly which concepts apply to a focal object. This is the valuation parallel of what we called free categorization. This can occur, for example, when a website allows films to be categorized in multiple genres. Consider, for example, a prospective diner who is choosing among restaurants and has access to the restaurants' menus and descriptions. In this situation, the diner can read the menus and descriptions with their genre memberships in mind and can reach an assessment of weighted average valuation accordingly. This kind of situation raises a new issue: the difficulty of making sense of objects whose positions in semantic space make them potential instances of multiple concepts in a cohort.

AUTOMATIC COGNITION: In the case of uncertain, free categorization, the mode of cognition need not be deliberate as we assumed for known multiple categorization. We thus consider in turn the automatic cognition and deliberate cognition cases.

What are the implications of automatic cognition for valuation when categorization is free and uncertain? Automaticity presumably requires existing concepts: some property of a concept—such as the features of its prototypes—can get used with minimal cognitive effort. Specifically, we conjecture that under automatic cognition, people categorize the object in just one concept and apply the typicality-weighted valence of the prototype, consistent with what we proposed in the single-concept case. As we will explain in more details below, we believe that simultaneous assignment in multiple concepts reveals doubt from the agent about the nature of the object. Yet, automatic cognition does not recognize doubt. Thus, multiple concept assignments are unlikely to happen under automatic cognition.

Postulate 12.10 *Suppose that an evaluator who relies on automatic cognition in a context that allows free concept assignment confronts an object with uncertain categorization. Then, the set of candidate concept assignments reduces to single concepts or the empty set; it does not contain any concept combinations:* $\mathfrak{C} = \{\{c_1\}, ..., \{c_N\}, \emptyset\}$.

Postulate 12.11 (Automatic cognition) *Under automatic cognition and uncertain categorization, there is no integration of information in the sense that the valuation is the typicality-weighted valence of one of the candidate concepts or of the root.*

$$
\mathcal{V}^a(o \mid \mathcal{I}^f) = \begin{cases} \mathfrak{v}_{c_1} T_{c_1} & \text{with probability } P(c_1 \mid \mathcal{I}^f); \\ \vdots \\ \mathfrak{v}_{c_N} T_{c_N} & \text{with probability } P(c_N \mid \mathcal{I}^f); \\ \mathfrak{v}_r T_r & \text{with probability } P(\emptyset \mid \mathcal{I}^f). \end{cases} \tag{12.29}
$$

$$
\mathcal{V}^a(o \mid \mathcal{I}^f, x) = \begin{cases} \mathfrak{v}_{c_1} \tau_{c_1}(x) & \text{with probability } P(c_1 \mid \mathcal{I}^f, x); \\ \vdots \\ \mathfrak{v}_{c_N} \tau_{c_N}(x) & \text{with probability } P(c_N \mid \mathcal{I}^f, x); \\ \mathfrak{v}_r \tau_r(x) & \text{with probability } P(\emptyset \mid \mathcal{I}^f, x). \end{cases} \tag{12.30}
$$

DELIBERATE COGNITION: For the case of deliberate cognition, we conjecture that people integrate over the various categorization possibilities, consistent with the assumptions made earlier in this section. We propose a simple characterization: an overall valuation is the sum of the valuations of each set of candidate concepts weighted by the probability of the particular concept assignment.

Postulate 12.12 (Deliberate cognition) *Under deliberate cognition and uncertain categorization, the valuation of the object is the weighted average of the valuations that would be obtained if the object were seen as an instance of each candidate concept assignment,* $\mathbf{C} \in \mathfrak{C}$, *where the weights are the categorization probabilities.*

$$\mathcal{V}^d(o \mid \mathcal{I}) = \sum_{\mathbf{C} \in \mathfrak{C}} \mathcal{V}^d(o \mid \mathcal{I}, \mathbf{C}) P(\mathbf{C} \mid \mathcal{I}), \qquad (12.31)$$

where $\mathcal{I}$ equals $\mathcal{I}^f$ or $\{\mathcal{I}^f, x\}$.

As will be shown in the next section, it is important to recognize that the aggregation structure still plays a role. We emphasize this relation in the following lemma.

Lemma 12.2 *The adjustment parameter, θ, and the function ζ control valuation even when categorizations are uncertain.*

$$\mathcal{V}^d(o \mid \mathcal{I}^f) = \sum_{\substack{\mathbf{C} \in \mathfrak{C} \\ |\mathbf{C}| > 1}} (\theta \mathbf{V}(o \mid \mathcal{I}^f, \mathbf{C}) + \zeta(o \mid \mathcal{I}^f, \mathbf{C})) P(\mathbf{C} \mid \mathcal{I}^f)$$

$$+ \sum_{\{c\} \in \mathfrak{C}} \mathfrak{v}_c \, T_c \, P(\{c\} \mid \mathcal{I}^f). \quad (12.32)$$

$$\mathcal{V}^d(o \mid \mathcal{I}^f, x) = \sum_{\substack{\mathbf{C} \in \mathfrak{C} \\ |\mathbf{C}| > 1}} (\theta \mathbf{V}(o \mid \mathcal{I}^f, \mathbf{C}, x) + \zeta(o \mid \mathcal{I}^f, \mathbf{C}, x)) P(\mathbf{C} \mid \mathcal{I}^f, x)$$

$$+ \sum_{\{c\} \in \mathfrak{C}} \mathfrak{v}_c \, \tau_c(x) \, P(\{c\} \mid \mathcal{I}^f, x). \quad (12.33)$$

In the special case where all the concept valences are all equal to one and $\theta = 1$, the valuation implied by lemma 12.2 reduces to that implied by proposition 12.1—it depends on conceptual ambiguity and in particular on average typicality. In the general case, there is no direct dependence of valuation on average typicality. The foregoing lemma provides more refined predictions, because it is sensitive to differences in concept valence. Each concept valence is weighted by the relevant typicality.

In the single-concept case, we could provide an explicit formulation of the valuation by decomposing the probability of categorization in terms of the concept likelihood, and priors on positions and concepts (lemma 12.1). Here, we unfortunately cannot provide such an explicit formulation because we do not know how to form a concept likelihood when the combination of concepts is not itself conceptualized. Despite this, we can formulate a proposition that ties conceptual ambiguity and valuation.

Proposition 12.6 *In the case of free, uncertain categorization, the valuation of an object declines with its conceptual ambiguity.*

As an illustration, consider the setting of figures 11.1 and 12.1 with two concepts with normal pdfs, concept valences equal to 1 and 0.8, and the valence of the root equal to 0 ($\mathfrak{v}_{c_1} = 1$, $\mathfrak{v}_{c_2} = .8$, $\mathfrak{v}_r = 0$). In this case, the average valuation of a concept assignment is no longer (proportional to) the average typicality (equation 12.25). This is because the two concept valences are not the same. The definition of conceptual ambiguity as the entropy of the vector of categorization probabilities suggests that positions of high ambiguity tend to be far from concept centers—that they do not have very high typicality in any concept unless the concepts are very close in semantic space. This, in turn, suggests that the average typicality of high-ambiguity positions is fairly low. Examination of figure 12.2 confirms this intuition. This figure is based on figure 11.1 but adds several plots. It displays how the overall valuation of the object varies with the position under two scenarios. The first scenario excludes fluency effects by computing valuation according to lemma 12.2, assuming $\theta = 1$ and $\lambda = 0$. The result is given by the line with the solid circles.

The second scenario incorporates a fluency effect by setting $\theta = 1$ and $\lambda = -0.7$. The valuations for this scenario are given by the hollow circles. The figure shows that positions in the middle—those that lie between the two concepts—are doubly penalized. Their valuations are depressed by low typicality and high conceptual ambiguity.

In summary, this analysis illustrates that two mechanisms explain associations between conceptual ambiguity and valuation. One mechanism invokes the causal effect of conceptual ambiguity on the aggregation function ζ. The other mechanism relies on the fact that conceptual ambiguity and valuation are both affected by position typicality.

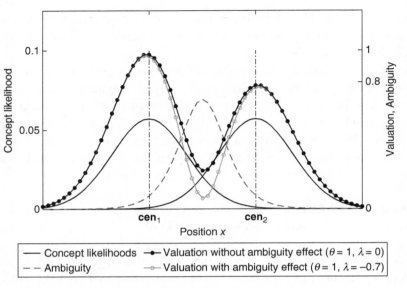

Figure 12.2 Valuation with free uncertain categorization: valuation (as implied by postulate 12.12) and conceptual ambiguity as a function of position for the setting of figure 11.1

12.7   Empirical Evidence

Film Genres

We can see the predicted negative association between conceptual ambiguity and valuations using data on audience valuation of Hollywood feature films. To do this, we use an ordinary least squares (OLS) regression model to estimate a film's valuation to audiences according to two measures: its average user-submitted ratings on Internet Movie Database (IMDb) and its percentage of top critic reviews listed on RottenTomatoes.com that are positive. We estimate the effect of a film's genre ambiguity and release year. The data cover 458 feature films listed on IMDb that were released in the United States during 2001–2003. Using IMDb's genre assignments, we calculate each film's genre ambiguity (according to equations 11.12, 11.15, and 11.19). Values for genre ambiguity range from 0 (for films assigned to a single genre) to 1.94 (the film *Signs* had been assigned seven genres: drama, family, fantasy, horror, mystery, science fiction, and thriller).

Figure 12.3 shows the estimated association between a film's genre ambiguity and its average IMDb user ratings and its percentage of positive top

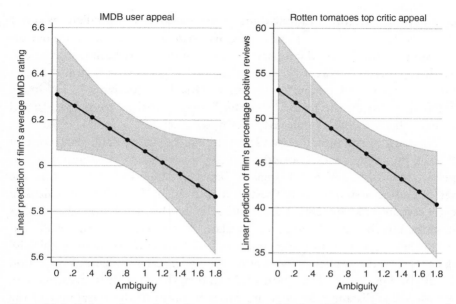

Figure 12.3 Estimated association between genre ambiguity of films and on average valuation to critics and the mass audience

critic reviews. For both, the association between ambiguity and valuation is significantly negative.

This purely label-based approach to specifying conceptual ambiguity is likely to produce results similar to earlier label-based approaches to specifying niche width (Hsu et al., 2009). Among the feature films examined here, for example, the correlation between conceptual ambiguity and niche width is 0.95 for multiple-genre films (single-genre films are treated equivalently according to both measures).

Restaurant Genres

In order to demonstrate in more detail how conceptual ambiguity affects valuation, we next turn to a setting in which we can assess the micro-level consequences of ambiguity. Specifically, we coded the texts of online restaurant reviews and explored whether there are systematic differences in the content of the reviews between low- and high-ambiguity restaurants. To code the text, we relied on the 2015 version of the commonly used text analysis program *Linguistic Inquiry and Word Count* (LIWC) (Pennebaker, Boyd, Jordan, and Blackburn (2015)). This tool provides a coding of words along multiple dimensions. Based on our predictions about the consequences of conceptual ambiguity on valuation, we focus on five dimensions of the LIWC dictionary: Positive emotion (including words such as "love," "nice," "sweet," "dear," "divine"); Negative emotion ("hurt," "ugly," "nasty," "degraded"); Tentative ("maybe," "perhaps," "anytime," "almost"); Anxiety ("worried," "fearful," "apprehensive," "confused"); and Anger ("hate," "kill," "annoyed," "critical," "crude").

We analyze restaurant reviews posted on Yelp.com. The data contain 8,667,760 online reviews posted on 54,492 restaurants in Chicago, Los Angeles, New York, and San Francisco, between 2004 and 2016. Using the set of cuisine assignments for restaurants given by Yelp.com, we calculate each restaurant's conceptual ambiguity. To do this, we follow the process described in chapter 11. First, we calculate the pairwise similarity of all genres in the Yelp data, and using equation 11.21 we convert them to pairwise distances. In the results shown below, we use Jaccard similarities (equation 11.20) and use $s = 2$ in equation 11.21 to turn them into distances. Second, we use these distances to calculate the typicalities of the restaurant in the categories they claim, using equation 11.19. Third, we calculate the baseline probabilities (priors) for each genre by dividing the count of restaurants with the given genre by the total count of restaurants. For example, of the 54,492 restaurants in the dataset, Yelp.com categorizes 343 as French, so the baseline probability for a French restaurant is 0.03. We then plug these probabilities and typicalities into equations 11.15 and 11.17 to calculate the ambiguities.

Next, we run regressions to predict whether conceptual ambiguity influences peoples' affective reactions, as evidenced by what they write in their reviews. Table 12.1 shows the results of OLS regressions in which the

TABLE 12.1
The effect of conceptual ambiguity on the number of words indicating positive emotion, negative emotion, tentativeness, anxiety, and anger in restaurant reviews on Yelp.com

	Dependent variable: number of words indicating					
Indep. var.	positive emotion (1)	negative emotion (2)	tentativeness (3)	anxiety (4)	anger (5)	certainty (6)
Ambiguity	0.082***	0.036***	0.039***	0.009***	0.016***	−0.044***

*** $p<0.01$, ** $p<0.05$, * $p<0.1$

TABLE 12.2

Mediation models: How the negative effect of conceptual ambiguity on ratings is mediated by the number of words indicating positive emotion, negative emotion, tentativeness, anxiety, anger, and certainty in restaurant reviews on Yelp.com

	(1)	(2)	(3)
Ambiguity	−0.038***		−0.035***
	(0.001)		(0.001)
Positive emotion		0.101***	0.101***
		(0.000)	(0.000)
Negative emotion		−0.241***	−0.241***
		(0.001)	(0.001)
Tentativeness		−0.036***	−0.036***
		(0.000)	(0.000)
Anxiety		0.125***	0.125***
		(0.001)	(0.001)
Anger		0.064***	0.065***
		(0.001)	(0.001)
Certainty		0.077***	0.077***
		(0.000)	(0.000)
Constant	3.89***	3.79***	3.81***
	(0.069)	(0.066)	(0.066)
Observations	8,652,749	8,652,964	8,652,749
R-squared	0.398	0.504	0.504

Robust standard errors are in parentheses.
*** $p<0.01$, ** $p<0.05$, * $p<0.1$
The models include fixed effects for years, reviewers, and the price level of the restaurant.

outcome variables are the word counts of the respective LIWC dimensions. The main predictor variable is the conceptual ambiguity of the restaurant.[4] The results show that ambiguity is associated with more negative emotion, more tentativeness, more anxiety, more anger, more uncertainty, but more positive emotion.

Then we examine directly whether conceptual ambiguity is associated with lower ratings as predicted by that proposition. In the models of table 12.2, we estimate linear regressions predicting restaurant ratings.[5] Model 1 shows that higher conceptual ambiguity is associated with lower ratings, as predicted.

Finally, we explore whether affective reactions set off by conceptual ambiguity moderate the effect of conceptual ambiguity on ratings. Model 3 shows that, when controlling for positive and negative emotions, tentativeness, anxiety, and anger, the effect size of conceptual ambiguity decreases by about 10%. This pattern of estimates demonstrates partial mediation. In future research one can explore other mechanisms that contribute to the negative effect of conceptual ambiguity on ratings.

Discussion

In this chapter, we have made the simplifying assumption that the evaluator either perfectly knows the position of the object in semantic space or does not know anything about it. Yet, in many naturally occurring situations, people have partial information about the position of the object they are evaluating because they have observed some but not all of its features. We refrained from explicitly addressing such cases to avoid complicating an already dense chapter. But they could be easily accommodated by building on the claims and results we delineated about the known position case. For example, partial or noisy information could be used to intuitively estimate the probabilities that the object belongs to the candidate concepts. These probabilities could substitute for the categorization probabilities that invoke information about the position in all postulates and propositions.

In closing this chapter, we wish to relate our work to broader themes involving valuation in cultural sociology. In particular, the question of whether and to what extent values are the central driver of human behavior has garnered sustained interest from cultural sociologists and others over the last several decades. One reason to doubt the primacy of values, some have argued, is that people are remarkably bad at giving consistent justifications for their behaviors; rather, people seem to choose their behaviors on the basis of cultural skills or facilities that they possess and then change their values as needed to justify their behaviors.

This debate seems to foreground the notion of values as abstract conceptualizations of what is ideal and desirable in life. While values certainly encompass such things, we think of "valuation" and "values" in more pragmatic, everyday terms, along the lines of how Patterson (2014) defines them:

> At their most basic, values refer to the way we evaluate objects, the affective weights we attribute to objects, and whether we prefer them or not. [p. 11]

Our model of valuation adds specificity to this definition: the way individuals evaluate objects is by seeing them in light of the concepts they have.

We consider three key ways in which people's affective reaction to an object is shaped by categorization. First, the *valence* of a concept is transferred to objects, such that inherited valence shapes affective reactions to objects in proportion to their typicality. Second, the *conceptual ambiguity* of objects affects valuation. Conceptual ambiguity complicates the process of combining the separate valuations pertaining to the concepts that apply to an object. We thus formulate hypotheses about how we combine typicality-weighted valuations into a valuation of an object. Third, uncertainty about which, if any, relevant concepts actually apply to an object might have an effect on valuation over and above the effect of conceptual ambiguity. When a person does not know which concepts apply to an object, the process of aggregating valuations of the potentially applicable concepts gets more complicated.

In modeling the process of valuation, we have also specified how valuation would proceed differently depending on whether it occurs in an automatic or deliberative fashion. In order to predict how an individual will evaluate a given object, then, it is important to know whether the context fosters automatic or deliberative cognition. This insight should be important to students of inequality, particularly scholars interested in how to reduce the tendency to evaluate based on group stereotypes and instead to consider individuating characteristics. Our approach, which specifies when information about typicality will tend to enter the picture (and when it will not), might prove to be a starting point for addressing these issues.

PART FOUR

Concepts in Social Interaction

ACTIONS UNDERTAKEN IN EVERYDAY LIFE are driven by conceptual understandings. Wide sharing of understandings within social groups enables orderly, patterned interactions to emerge. Yet, while the notion of shared understandings is necessary for comprehending fundamental sociological processes such as institutionalization and legitimation, its specification remains somewhat elusive within sociological theories. In this part, we extend our framework beyond the individual level, to considering the way people influence one another's conceptual understandings and how shared understandings emerge.

We first provide formal definitions of key notions, such as the level of conceptual agreement that exists among a group of individuals as well as the level of extensional agreement—the extent to which two or more individuals categorize the same objects in similar ways. The latter is important when seeking to understand how shared understandings emerge because concepts are often difficult to observe directly. We propose that conceptual similarities and differences typically are revealed through observations of others' actions. This idea is consistent with Berger and Luckmann's (1966) process of typification. To wit, patterns of actions that emerge in interaction often give rise to mutually shared typifications coded by a common language. Typification allows agents to make sense of and anticipate one another's actions; over time, these repeated patterns of action lead to the formation of institutions. Concepts thus play a key role in the reproduction of social order, providing the shared presumptions that guide individuals unthinkingly through habituated sequences of interactions (Berger and Luckmann, 1966; Jepperson, 1991).

A key intuition that we exploit in our modeling is that orderly interactions are more likely when people believe that the concepts each holds privately are shared by others. This perception of sharing of meanings facilitates interactions between group members, who choose actions based on anticipated reactions from others. As an individual experiences increasing extensional agreement through patterned interactions with others, he or she increasingly presumes a concept is held more widely, that it has become a taken for granted social fact. Institutional theorists hold that elements of social structure that are taken for granted are deeply embedded in individuals' practices and understanding and are regarded as widely shared "social facts" that go virtually unquestioned (Suchman, 1995). Concepts are clearly central to this dynamic. As DiMaggio (1997, p. 296) argues, "highly schematic cognition is the realm of institutionalized culture, of typification, of the habitus."

We regard a concept as taken for granted to the extent that individuals presume that unfamiliar others share its meaning. This is revealed through the extent to which the individual automatically accepts an unfamiliar alter's categorization of an object. Using our framework, we depict the interactive process through which this type of taken-for-grantedness emerges. We also consider the role key factors (such as the degree to which members of a group diverge in the meanings they associate with a given concept and how distinctive the concepts' meanings are in conceptual space) play in shaping the expected level of extensional agreement experienced.

In the final chapter, we consider broader connections to important lines of sociological inquiry, including culture, social identity, and innovation. Our intention is to highlight implications of our framework for existing sociological theories and potential paths for future research.

CHAPTER THIRTEEN

The Group Level: Conceptual and Extensional Agreement

WITH THE STRUCTURE of the previous chapters in place, we turn now to developing a representation and understanding of how concepts operate in multi-person processes. This chapter aims to clarify the sociological notion of *shared understandings*. We attempt to specify this notion more precisely in terms of the similarity of concepts. As we have shown in previous chapters, concepts fundamentally shape categorization decisions, and in turn, perception and evaluation of the objects we encounter. That means that variation in how widely shared concepts are within a group determines whether or not the members of the group likely see the world in largely the same terms. Group-level variations in concepts and, correspondingly, in how objects get categorized likely affect other important group-level behavioral outcomes.

In this chapter, we build a notation and a set of definitions that we need for modeling interpersonal cognitive processes and for representing the degree of conceptual agreement within a group. We will build on these foundations in the next chapter as we model how observation of the categorization behaviors of others can change perceptions of objects.

Measuring the extent of conceptual agreement between individuals is complicated by the fact that we are dealing with *sets* of concepts. Consider a concrete example. Suppose that three people have conceptualized the domain of jazz in the following way.

- The first has a cohort with one genre: $\kappa_1(\text{jazz}) = \{\text{trad jazz}\}$;
- the second has: $\kappa_2(\text{jazz}) = \{\text{trad jazz, bebop, cool-jazz}\}$; and
- the third has $\kappa_3(\text{jazz}) = \{\text{trad jazz, funk}\}$.

How should we characterize the level of conceptual similarity between them? They diverge both in terms of the extent to which they have conceptualized the music domain (i.e., the individuals distinguish between one, two, or three types of jazz) and the specific concepts they use (i.e., trad jazz is common to all, other concepts are specific to a person). Even more fundamentally, we wish to be able to capture the idea that one person might conceive of jazz in a semantic space composed of *melody*, *harmony*, *rhythm*, and *improvisation*. For another individual, the semantic space might be composed of *harmony*, *improvisation*, *comping*, and *syncopation*. In this chapter, we expand on the machinery for addressing these issues so that we can characterize agreement among these individuals.

We proceed in several steps. In each step, we specify measures of agreement or its converse, dissensus between individuals, between an individual and a group, and among the members of a group. We build on the definition of the distance between two concepts in semantic space introduced at the end of chapter 6 (definition 6.2). We use this measure to specify dissensus about a concept (§13.1). We see conceptual dissensus as the opposite of conceptual agreement. We focus on dissensus rather than agreement because we our formalism builds on the notion of distance between concepts rather than on similarity.

In the following sections, we introduce a measure of extensional agreement that characterizes the extent to which people's categorization decisions agree (§13.2). Finally, we address situations in which people may use different labels to refer to the "same" concept §13.3. This poses a challenge because we cannot determine *ex ante* whether or not two labels refer to the same concept. We solve this issue by focusing on distances between pairs of concepts within cohorts.

13.1 Conceptual Dissensus about a Concept

This chapter returns to distances involving concepts. When two individuals do not agree about the meaning of a concept, there will be a large distance in semantic space between the concepts that individuals a and b associate with a common label. Based on this distance, we can specify dissensus about the meaning of a label between one individual and a social group, and within a social group. Suppose the context focuses attention on a single concept label c. Without loss of generality, let c^a refer to a concept that person a calls c.[1]

Definition 13.1 (Conceptual dissensus)

   A. The conceptual dissensus between an individual a who belongs to a group G and the group about the meaning of c is

$$\mathcal{D}_{aG}(c) = \frac{1}{|G| - 1} \sum_{b \in G} \vec{D}(c^a, c^b),$$

   where |G| denotes the size of the group and $\vec{D}(c^a, c^b)$ is given by equation 6.4.

   B. The conceptual dissensus within a group G about the meaning of c is

$$\overline{\mathcal{D}}_G(c) = \frac{1}{|G|} \sum_{a \in G} \mathcal{D}_{aG}(c).$$

13.2   Extensional Agreement about a Concept

Empirically, conceptual agreement is difficult to observe directly—both for the individuals in the natural world that we seek to characterize and for the researchers. Although people do sometimes spell out what they mean by a particular concept (e.g., a music critic might detail particular characteristics of the genres he covers), we think that conceptual agreement or dissensus more commonly becomes revealed through observation of individuals' categorization decisions. For example, a person whose concept for barbecue centers around smoked pork with a vinegar-based sauce might learn that his or her concept is not universally shared when he or she ventures into a restaurant that serves beef with a tomato-based sauce and labels it barbecue. As explained in chapter 8, categorization decisions define the *extension* of a concept. Therefore, we will say that in this sort of situation, there is a lack of *extensional agreement*.

We turn to specifying extensional agreement. A complication arises from the possibility that two individuals might not be exposed to the same objects. Then, measuring the overlap in their categorizations would reveal little about the extent to which they share concepts. In an ideal world, which one might simulate in a lab-based experiment, we would assess agreement on categorizations only after presenting individuals with the same set of objects. But a researcher studying categorizations in the natural world only has data on observed categorizations for the objects that individuals have encountered.

We think that it makes sense to focus exclusively on the opportunities that individuals have to categorize the same objects. For example, suppose that individual A has seen the movies *Pulp Fiction, When Harry Met Sally, Titanic,* and *Pretty Woman,* while individual B has seen *Pulp Fiction, When Harry Met Sally, Titanic,* and *Love Actually,* and both have categorized these films as to whether they are romantic comedies. Then only the categorizations of *When Harry Met Sally, Titanic,* and *Pulp Fiction* would be informative for us. More generally, we propose measuring extensional consensus via the correlation between each individual's vector of categorization decisions pertaining to the three movies that both have viewed.

If we cannot ensure that the sets of observed objects are the same, as is common outside the laboratory, then we need to restrict the comparison to objects that both people have observed. We can formalize this consideration as follows. Let $o_{ab}(c)$ denote the set of objects that both a and b have categorized with respect to c (the decisions might have been positive ($\|\text{IS-A}(c,o)\| = 1$) or not ($\|\text{IS-A}(c,o)\| = 0$). Let $\rho_{o_{ab}(c)}$ denote the correlation of the categorization decisions of a and b over the set $o_{ab}(c)$.

Definition 13.2 (Extensional agreement about a concept label)

   A. *The extensional agreement about a concept label of a pair of individuals is*

$$ea_{ab}(c) = \begin{cases} \rho_{o_{ab}}(c) & \textit{if } c \textit{ denotes a concept for both } a \textit{ and } b; \\ 0 & \textit{otherwise.} \end{cases}$$

   B. *The extensional agreement about a concept label of an individual and a group is*

$$ea_{aG}(c) = \frac{1}{|G| - 1} \sum_{\substack{b \in G \\ b \neq a}} ea_{ab}(c).$$

   C. *The extensional agreement about a concept label within a group is*

$$\overline{ea}_G(c) = \frac{1}{|G|} \sum_{a \in G} ea_{aG}(c).$$

Other measures of extensional agreement can be devised, but we chose this correlation-based measure for simplicity. This measure is not directly sensitive to the size of the set of objects that any two individuals have categorized (it is insensitive to "sample size"). One could imagine more sophisticated measures that would take into account the size of this set (by incorporating the error in the distribution of the error on the correlation, for example).

13.3   Conceptual Agreement and Dissensus over a Domain

Having defined distances between concepts, we turn to conceptual agreement and dissensus within a domain. This is the extent to which people agree on the meanings of concepts.

In the previous sections, we assumed that the individuals in a group have a common label for their concepts. Then distances and agreement can be defined with respect to that label. But it is a strong assumption to require that all the individuals within a domain use the same terms to refer to all concepts in order to define dissensus. Some sociological applications require treating situations in which the assumption of a common label does not hold. Consider, for example, four individuals who assign the same meaning to pomme, mela, alma, and apple—they speak French, Italian, Hungarian, and English, respectively. If the meanings are the same, then this part of the conceptual structure is the same, despite the language difference. How could we tell? If we have access to concepts, we could begin with the concept used by one individual and search for the closest one used by the second. In this example, we would find an identical concept. This is the procedure we want to represent.

We continue to assume that the cognitive and social processes of interest are bounded by domains. That is, we and the individuals being characterized do not have to take account of all of an individual's concepts, just those that are members of the same domain. We assume that the individuals being compared share a label for the root of a domain. For instance, two individuals might share the label jazz but have (partially) non-overlapping sets of subgenres—for example {fast jazz, slow jazz} for one individual and {modern jazz, swing} for the other.

In the above example, the first individual's concept of fast jazz might correspond to the second individual's concept for modern jazz. We want to determine whether the probability distributions of position in semantic space of one of a's concepts corresponds to one of b's concepts, even if the concepts are labeled differently.

We first need to extend the notion of distance between concepts given in definition 6.2. Instead of calculating the distance from one concept to another, we calculate the distance from one person's concept to the cohort of concepts of the other. The cohorts are *sets* of concepts.

The standard measure for the distances between sets in a metric space is Hausdorff distance. Let $\mathbf{C}_1$ and $\mathbf{C}_2$ refer to two sets of concepts. The Hausdorff distance between these sets is

$$d_H(\mathbf{C}_1, \mathbf{C}_2) = \max \left\{ \max_{c_1 \in \mathbf{C}_1} \vec{D}(c_1, \mathbf{C}_2), \max_{c_2 \in \mathbf{C}_2} \vec{D}(c_2, \mathbf{C}_1) \right\},$$

where $\vec{D}(c_1, \mathbf{C}_2) = \min_{c_1 \in \mathbf{C}_1} \vec{d}(c_1, \mathbf{C}_2)$. This measure is heavily influenced by a single concept that lies very far from the others. For our purposes, we might want to sacrifice satisfaction of the metric properties and use the modified Hausdorff distance instead.

We use a modified Hausdorff distance, the measure that Dubuison and Jain 1994 label as d_{22} (see also Goldberg et al. (2016)). Construction of the modified Hausdorff distance begins with the average directed distances from elements in one set to the other set:

$$\vec{\mathbf{D}}(\mathbf{C}_1, \mathbf{C}_2) = \frac{1}{|\mathbf{C}_1|} \sum_{c_1 \in \mathbf{C}_1} \vec{D}(c_1, \mathbf{C}_2). \tag{13.1}$$

Definition 13.3 (Distance between sets of concepts) *The modified Hausdorff distance between a pair of sets of concepts is given by*

$$mH(\mathbf{C}_1, \mathbf{C}_2) = \max \left\{ \vec{\mathbf{D}}(\mathbf{C}_1, \mathbf{C}_2), \vec{\mathbf{D}}(\mathbf{C}_2, \mathbf{C}_1) \right\}.$$

With definition 13.3, we can now specify the dissensus about a domain between two individuals, one individual and a social group, and within a social group.

Definition 13.4 (Conceptual dissensus about a domain)

A. *The dissensus between a pair of individuals a and b about the domain $\mathfrak{D}_r$ is*

$$\mathcal{D}_{ab}(r) = mH(\kappa^a(r), \kappa^b(r)),$$

where $\kappa^a(r)$ denotes individual a's cohort of concepts in that domain.

B. *The dissensus between an individual a and a group G about the domain $\mathfrak{D}_r$ is*

$$\mathcal{D}_{aG}(r) = \frac{1}{|G|} \sum_{b \in G} \mathcal{D}_{ab}(r),$$

where $|G|$ denotes the size of the group.

C. The dissensus within a group G about the domain $\mathcal{D}_r$ is

$$\overline{\mathcal{D}}_G(r) = \frac{1}{|G|} \sum_{a \in G} \mathcal{D}_{aG}(r).$$

The dissensus between two individuals equals zero only when the two individuals have identical cohorts of concepts, with each concept having the same semantic spaces and probability distribution functions.

The individuals making up group G have perfect consensus (identical cohorts for the common root r made of up identical concepts) when $\overline{\mathcal{D}}_G(r) = 0$. As $\overline{\mathcal{D}}_G(r)$ increases, group G's conceptual consensus about the domain with root r decreases. $\overline{\mathcal{D}}_G(r)$ reflects the extent to which a group of individuals conceptualize the part of the world included in the domain using the same set of concepts (which we refer to as a cohort).

Finally, we can use the formalism to express the conceptual distance between two groups, a basic step in characterizing a heterogenous audience. Let G_1 and G_2 be two groups, which might have overlapping membership.

Definition 13.5 (Conceptual dissensus from group G_1 to group G_2) *Let all members of the two groups have domains with the common root r.*

$$\vec{\daleth}_{G_1 G_2}(r) = \frac{1}{|G_1|} \sum_{a \in G_1} \mathcal{D}_{aG_2}(r).$$

We define the distance between the two groups as the maximum between the two average distances.

Definition 13.6 (Conceptual dissensus between two groups) *The conceptual dissensus between two groups, G_1 and G_2, is*

$$\daleth_{G_1 G_2}(r) = \max \left\{ \vec{\daleth}_{G_1 G_2}(r), \vec{\daleth}_{G_2 G_1}(r) \right\},$$

where r is the root of a domain for all members of the groups G_1 and G_2.

EMPIRICAL APPROACHES TO MEASURING EXTENSIONAL AGREEMENT: Empirical measurement of the distances between the concepts held by different groups requires data on classification by multiple audiences. We illustrate this using data on categorizations of Hollywood feature films and of restaurants in seven major United States metropolitan areas. The first dataset consists of films distributed in the U.S. during 2002–2003. We gather genre classifications from five sources: the Internet Movie Database (IMDb), Showbizdata.com (SBD), Rottentomatoes.com (RT), Movies.Go.com (MG), and CinemaReview.com (CR). Earlier, we noted that

TABLE 13.1
Film coverage by five archival sources

| | Total Film Cnt | Pairwise overlap | | | |
		IMDB	SBD	RT	MG
IMDB	1883				
SBD	872	797			
RT	756	716	511		
MG	529	524	524	455	
CR	295	294	281	268	285

film datasets such as AFI list films' key subject matter, which can be treated as feature values. However, this particular dataset information is only about categorization (not feature values) and thus lends itself purely to measures of extensional agreement.

Comparing genre assignments across sources requires consistency in agents' cohorts of concepts and in the objects assigned—a consistency that often does not exist in natural settings. In particular, three complications likely arise: (1) differences in the set of objects the sources cover, (2) differences in the cohorts of genres employed by the sources, and (3) multiple genre assignments to objects. As an example of the first complication, we show the distribution of film coverage for the 2,184 films in the dataset in table 13.1. No single source covers all of the films; the most extensive coverage is by IMDb, which categorizes 1,883 of the 2,184 films. CR covers the fewest (295) films, and nearly all (294) of the films covered by CR are covered by the other four sources.

When seeking to calculate extensional agreement between the five sources, we can assess dissensus only for films that were categorized by all of the sources. To illustrate how we calculate extensional agreement about a concept, consider the genres of comedy and drama. In total, 130 of the 294 films classified by all five sources are categorized as comedy by at least one source. Table 13.2 reports pairwise correlations of observed categorizations by the five sources with regards to which films should be categorized as comedy. The average of these pairwise correlations is 0.77.

As a comparison, table 13.3 shows the correlations of categorization decisions for films categorized as drama; the average pairwise correlation is 0.59. This suggests that there is less agreement about the set of films that belong to drama than for comedy.

A second complication is that sources often have somewhat different cohorts of concepts. Some genres are not shared across all five sources.

TABLE 13.2
Pairwise correlations of films categorized as comedy

	IMDB	SBD	RT	MG	CR
IMDB	1				
SBD	0.76	1			
RT	0.86	0.75	1		
MG	0.78	0.74	0.80	1	
CR	0.79	0.78	0.74	0.75	1

Sometimes the genres appear to reference subgenres within larger common genres. For example, while all five sources use comedy, a subset listed additional subgenres of comedy such as dark comedy and satire. Similarly, while all sources use action, only a subset had the additional subgenre of martial arts. A simple way to handle the existence of non-shared subconcepts is by grouping the objects assigned to an unshared subconcept under its shared parent concept.

Other times, the genres appear to correspond to unrelated genres that do not fit clearly into any more-inclusive ones. For example, experimental, sequel, and college were not shared across the five sources, and they are not clear subgenres of any shared genre. If it is not clear how to embed a genre into a parent genre, then the researcher is left with the choice of how to treat a film categorized with an idiosyncratic genre. One possibility is to drop the idiosyncratic genre from consideration and retain only the shared genres. This would work in the case of films with multiple categorizations. For example, if one source categorizes a film as both comedy and experimental, then the researcher could simply ignore the experimental assignment if it is not common across sources. Another possibility is to retain experimental as

TABLE 13.3
Pairwise correlations of films categorized as drama

	IMDB	SBD	RT	MG	CR
IMDB	1				
SBD	0.58	1			
RT	0.67	0.54	1		
MG	0.56	0.64	0.62	1	
CR	0.53	0.59	0.57	0.62	1

a distinct genre and regard all films as "not experimental" from the standpoint of sources that do not employ that label. These different approaches will impact measures of extensional consensus.

A final complication is that some films can be classified under multiple genres. The researcher can either assign each film as a full member of each of the genres applied in calculations of extensional similarity or assign a proportionate membership. For example, if a film is categorized as {drama, comedy} by a source, then its membership in each of those genres might be 0.5 in drama and 0.5 in comedy. Weighting films' membership in comedy and drama by the total number of genres assigned by each source very slightly decreases average pairwise correlations for comedy slightly (0.77 to 0.76) but substantially increases average pairwise correlations for drama (from 0.56 to 0.64).

In general, it is important to acknowledge that comparing categorizations across sources almost always requires the researcher to impose some judgments regarding the structure of the overall classification system to facilitate comparison. Any changes to existing classifications should be made cautiously.

Comparing Concepts for Cuisines Across Agents, Locations, and Time

Next, we demonstrate a way to map out whether concepts have different meanings across different agents, communities, or time periods. As we discussed above, our aim here is to quantify "shared understandings." Specifically, we provide an illustration of geographical variation in communities' understandings of certain cuisines. We use the restaurant-menu dataset described earlier, and we compare the menu words most highly associated with cuisines such as Italian, American, and Irish in different metropolitan areas such as Chicago, New York City, and San Francisco. This provides an indication of the most salient features for these cuisines and whether they differ across geographical regions. The same empirical approach could be applied to comparisons across agents or (within agents) across time periods.

To quantify conceptual agreement about restaurant cuisines across cities, we begin by creating a matrix of the co-occurrences of objects (words on the menus) and concepts (genres) for each metropolitan area separately. In order to this, we process all the restaurant menus and count the number of times the menu word appeared in that city for restaurants with a particular categorization. For example, we find that *cheese* appears 775 times in New York City restaurants that are categorized as French; and *tomato* appears 3,517 times in Boston restaurants that are categorized as Italian. Clearly, higher counts in these cells indicate stronger association between the menu word and the cuisine. In order to properly establish the strength of the association, however, one needs to account for the baseline probabilities of the menu words and the cuisines. That is, a higher word count might be due to the popularity of the item for all cuisines or because there are many restaurants in the category or the menus of these restaurants contain more words. One measure that takes these baseline probabilities into account is the approach used in the Chi-square tests for contingency tables, in which the observed count of co-occurrence is compared to the expected count based on independence given the marginal distributions. For example, *cheese* appears 371,106 times on all menus, and French restaurants in New York City contain altogether 39,572 words. Therefore, as the total number of words in the menus is 18,121,439, the expected number of times that *cheese* would appear on French menus in New York City is 810.388 (equal to $(371,106 \times 39,572)/18,121,439$). Comparing this to the observed 775 mentions, we find that *cheese* appears less frequently on French menus than expected by the baseline distribution. This does not mean that French restaurants do not serve cheese, but rather, that they might use more specific words (e.g., *brie*).

Table 13.4 illustrates the results by showing, for a selected set of cuisines and metropolitan areas, the top 10 words with the highest ratio of observed to expected counts. For example, the first two lines show that the words most strongly associated with the New American label in Boston are *vermont, local, brioche, boston, farm, aioli, chick, ale, bitters, puree,* while in Chicago these are *chicago, ale, farm, goose, brussel, maple, brewing, valley, chick, roasted.* Perhaps not surprisingly, in both cities the New American cuisine is related to local produce (boston, vermont, chicago), microbrews, and ingredients that are less mainstream, such as *goose, chicks, aioli,* or *brioche.*

While New American has different meanings across cities, one can also see the connections. In other cases, there is more overlap across geographical regions, such as in the case of Italian. But even in this case, we see interesting variations, such as "veal" and "vitello" [veal in Italian]; these variations are prominent in New York City but not in the other metropolitan areas. One can formally assess this conceptual agreement across cities, for example, by calculating the correlation between the association ratios of word occurrences across cuisines and cities. Table 13.5 shows a few examples. The first line, for example, shows that the closest concept to New York City's New American is Washington, DC's New American with the conceptual agreement of 0.563, followed by South Florida's New American at 0.443, and San Francisco's Californian at 0.397. Note that while these magnitudes of the correlation coefficients clearly indicate that these concepts

TABLE 13.4

Top 10 most typical words, in decreasing order

Cuisine	City	Top 10 most typical words
New American	Boston	vermont, local, brioche, boston, farm, aioli, chick, ale, bitters, puree
New American	Chicago	chicago, ale, farm, goose, brussel, maple, brewing, valley, chick, roasted
New American	Los Angeles	market, heirloom, farm, burrata, santa, organic, valley, kale, fraiche, ale
New American	San Francisco	dungeness, valley, fra, farms, farm, francisco, anchor, blanc, coast, ale
New American	South Florida	florida, heirloom, chick, roll, vin, vinaigrette, truffle, mahi, local, rice
Asian Fusion	Chicago	noodle, thai, stir, pods, carrot, unagi, entr, maki, tofu, spicy
Asian Fusion	Los Angeles	chili, thai, rice, korean, noodle, spicy, tofu, chinese, curry, peanuts
Asian Fusion	San Francisco	jelly, tofu, coconut, prawn, coco, grass, taro, noodle, gras, wok
Italian	Chicago	italian, mostaccioli, pasta, marinara, mozzarella, parm, giardiniera, pizza, bread, ravioli
Italian	Los Angeles	mozzarella, marinara, parm, spaghetti, italian, olive, pasta, insalata, live, ricotta
Italian	New York City	insalata, salata, veal, vitello, griglia, mozzarella, parm, parmigiano, prosciutto, ricotta
Italian	San Francisco	insalata, polenta, pancetta, olive, ros, live, pesto, ravioli, prosciutto, mozzarella
Californian	San Francisco	dungeness, meyer, valley, fra, brut, farm, county, bitters, market, lavender
Californian	South Florida	artichokes, club, aged, pear, bleu, layer, garlic, mac, skin, merlot, plantain
Californian	New York City	asado, carnitas, asada, pinto, carne, burrito, pollo, quesadilla, guacamole, dill

TABLE 13.5
Comparing cuisines across cities: The 10 most similar cuisines–city to the focal cuisine–city

Focal cuisine-city	Most similar to focal (with correlation values)
New American New York City	New American Washington DC 0.563, New American South Florida 0.443, Californian San Francisco 0.397, New American San Francisco 0.384, Mediterranean Boston 0.364, Bistro Los Angeles 0.298, Cocktails Boston 0.290, Pub Food Boston 0.288, French Los Angeles 0.280
Italian New York City	Italian San Francisco 0.674, Italian Washington DC 0.670, Italian South Florida 0.663, Pizza South Florida 0.464, Pizza New York City 0.381, Pizza Los Angeles 0.341, Pasta South Florida 0.324, Pizza Washington DC 0.305, Wild Game New York City 0.289
Deli Food New York City	Sandwiches New York City 0.974, Salads New York City 0.567, Sandwiches San Francisco 0.463, Deli Food Washington DC 0.416, Deli Food San Francisco 0.373, Sandwiches Los Angeles 0.353, Deli Food South Florida 0.341, Sandwiches Washington DC 0.333, Sandwiches South Florida 0.315
Hot Dogs Chicago	Hot Dogs South Florida 0.746, Hot Dogs Los Angeles 0.739, Hot Dogs San Francisco 0.737, Hot Dogs Washington DC 0.718, Hot Dogs New York City 0.663, Sandwiches Chicago 0.420, Polish Los Angeles 0.183, Polish Chicago 0.136, Wings South Florida 0.116

are related, they are far from being perfectly identical, except perhaps the Deli Food and Sandwiches concepts in New York City, at 0.974.

Discussion

In this chapter, we have specified different ways to approach the measurement of conceptual dissensus at both the individual and group level. We developed the following measures, where a and b can indicate either an individual or a group.

1. Conceptual dissensus about a concept: the distance between the meanings of a concept held by a and b, which can be specified through either an asymmetric or symmetric measure.
2. Extensional agreement about a concept label: the correlation between the categorization decisions associated by a and by b with a concept label.
3. Conceptual dissensus about a domain: the distance between the cohorts of concepts held by a and by b about a domain.
4. Conceptual dissensus between groups: the distance between two groups of individuals about a domain.

CHAPTER FOURTEEN

Social Inference and
Taken-for-Grantedness

IN THE PREVIOUS CHAPTER, we began to consider how concepts operate in social interaction. In particular, we developed an approach to measuring the distance between concepts held by different individuals, allowing us to characterize the degree of conceptual agreement at the group level. In this chapter, we turn to consider a common social situation when an individual observes another person applying a concept label to an object. For example, one person tells another that the movie she just watched is a comedy or that her friend is a doctor. This routine type of communicative activity can also occur between individuals when one tries to describe a specific entity with which the other is unfamiliar. This chapter draws out the consequences of such categorization for a focal individual's perceptions and inferences.

An important determinant of how the focal individual responds to observing someone else's categorization of an object is the extent to which the individual presumes that she and others share similar concepts. For example, if a focal individual believes the movie genre comedy has a meaning that is widely shared within a particular social group, she likely will give great credence to another group member's categorization of a particular movie that way. She will begin to make inferences about the particular features of an unseen movie based on the meaning that is implied by her concept for comedy, maybe discussing how the jokes and goofy scenes fit in with the development of the plot. On the other hand, if one individual observes another categorizing a movie with a genre label that the person believes is not widely understood or about whose meaning there is great disagreement, then she will likely disregard the categorization; then the categorization will not affect her inferences about an object much, if at all.

We believe this intuition about the importance of the perception of shared meanings for a concept relates closely to the longstanding sociological notion of taken-for-grantedness. For sociologists, a concept is a social fact—taken for granted—if the people in a system share it and treat it as a natural and inevitable element in the cultural ontology (Meyer and Rowan, 1977). In this chapter, we emphasize the facet of taken-for-grantedness that entails an individual's belief that other group members have very similar conceptualizations. Importantly, when taken-for-grantedness is high, this belief extends to new individuals of whom the focal individual has no direct knowledge or previous experience with respect to their categorization behaviors.

Modeling social interactions of the sort described above provides a basis for developing a formal specification of the causes and consequences of a concept's taken-for-grantedness. We believe, as Berger and Luckmann (1966) argued, that individuals coordinate conceptualizations primarily through interaction. Therefore, we work from the premise that taken-for-grantedness emerges over time as individuals experience extensional agreement with other individuals—when they have seen others categorizing objects in the same way they would. They then generalize from those dyadic interactions and begin to reason presuming their own concepts are similar to those of others in the group with which they lack any direct experience.

Taken together, this leads individuals to believe that a concept is widely shared within the group. We show that taken-for-grantedness then shapes subsequent perception of objects. This means that the categorization behaviors of even unfamiliar others within a group can be influential, as they cause the focal individual to update his or her own beliefs about an object. Though this logic also extends to one's own conceptualization—namely, observing others' extensional behaviors might lead an individual to make inferences about others' concept probability density functions and to update her own probability functions accordingly—we do not extend our model to such second-order interpersonal coordination.

We first develop a model of dyadic social influence in which a person observes the categorization of an object by another individual and updates his or her beliefs about the feature values of the object. We call this process *social inference* because the focal individual *infers* features on the basis of the categorization by the other individual. Second, we build on this dyadic model to offer a definition of the taken-for-grantedness of a concept for an individual with respect to a social group. Third, we discuss how observations of others' behaviors affect taken-for-grantedness. Finally, we move from the individual to the group level of analysis and propose a definition for the taken-of-grantedness of a concept in a social group.

14.1 Social Inference via Categorization by Others

In our analysis of social inference, we assume that the context fixes the domain, which we denote by its root r. This means that the focal person takes as given that the focal object is an instance of r but does not know which of the concepts in the cohort of concepts κ apply to it. For instance, the person knows that the object with not-yet-observed features is a film, say, but does not know anything about its genre-relevant features. This assumption implies that the baseline inference uses background knowledge about the domain. In the example, this background knowledge would encompass prior beliefs on the features of films.

We begin with a pair of individuals in a group. We want to capture what happens when one individual lacks information about the feature values of an object but observes that the other categorizes it as, say, a c. We will refer to the person being influenced as the "focal" individual, a, and to the potential influencer as individual b. We will assume that the categorization of the object as an instance of the concept c converts the context for a to what we have called in previous chapters a single-concept context (denoted by the information state $\mathcal{I}^s$).

Suppose that all that a knows about the focal object is that it is an instance of the domain and that b has categorized it as a c. The main question in this chapter is, to what extent does a accept the implications of b's categorization and update her beliefs about the features of the object (formally, its position in semantic space) based on this knowledge? This propensity is variable. At one end of the spectrum, a might fully accept the implications of b's categorization. In this case, a has great confidence that the label given by b refers to the same concept as her own. In other words the individual behaves as if the categorization by the other is equivalent to her own categorization. At the other end of the spectrum, if a believes that b might assign a very different meaning to the label associated with the concept, she might disregard the other's categorization and not apply her own corresponding concept. Then a's belief about the position of the object will remain unchanged by the knowledge of the other person's categorization. To capture not only these extreme cases, but also the possibility that a has doubts about the use of the concept by b, we take a probabilistic view. We introduce a non-negative real parameter that characterizes the likelihood that a accepts the implications of b's categorization. We denote a's propensity to accept the implications of b's categorization of an arbitrary object as a c by $\omega_{ab}(c)$ in the general case.[1]

As we noted earlier, in the body of this chapter, we specify social inference in the situation in which a person a has no information about the position of an object, aside from knowledge of the relevant domain and the fact that the other person b has categorized it as a c. We address the more realistic case in which a already has some information relevant to the position in the chapter appendix. We also assume that the person has some background or situational knowledge that gives her a set of expectations about the likely features of the object and the likely or surprising categorizations of the object.

We represent these ideas with the formal notion of *information states,* as in previous chapters. We focus on the information state on which a focal person, here called a, relies to make an inference about the feature values of an object or to categorize it. In the current analysis, we will denote a's initial information state, before she learns of b's categorization of the object as a c, as $\mathcal{I}_1$. This information state contains two kinds of information.

First, it contains $\mathcal{I}^s$. This includes a's background knowledge of the focal domain, $\mathcal{I}_0$, the fact that the categorization context is a single-concept context (the focus will be on whether the object is a c or not a c), and the fact that the category of the object is uncertain.

Second, it contains the information that a possesses about b's use of the concept c, denoted $\mathcal{I}^c_{ab}$. The most direct observable information here is b's categorizations of objects as cs. However, learning about categorizations in closely related concepts also provides relevant information. Suppose we are concentrating on a film genre, say action. A person might not have observed another's categorizations of any films as action but might have such information about categorizations as sci fi, comedy, and war. If the focal person agrees with other's categorizations of films in these three categories, she might conclude that her typology for films is close to the other's (set of subconcepts of the root concept film). This might, in turn, positively affect someone's propensity to accept the other's categorization of a film as action, even if she has not observed the other's use of this genre in the past. Conversely, if she has observed some of the categorization history by the other, and she has concluded that they tend to disagree on film genre assignments, then she might be less likely to accept the other's categorization of a film as a member of a specific genre, action in this case.

Because we want to model the possible consequences of such information, we will assume that the information relevant to b's use of concept c, $\mathcal{I}^c_{ab}$, comprises categorizations by b of objects in concepts of the cohort κ of the domain to which c belongs.[2] For each categorization, $\mathcal{I}^c_{ab}$ includes the assigned concept and whatever a observed about the position of the object in semantic space $\mathbb{F}_c$. Note that categorizations of objects as cs for which

a possesses no position information (other than that they are members the focal domain) are included in the information set. Even if no corresponding position information is available, these categorizations are relevant for a to estimate b's baseline propensity to use particular concepts. Finally, if a has not observed any instance of categorization by b in the focal concept c or in any of the other concepts in the cohort κ, then $\mathcal{I}_{ab}^c = \emptyset$.

A crucial assumption of our model is that the information $\mathcal{I}_{ab}^c$ affects a's propensity to accept the consequences of b's categorization, $\omega_{ab}(c)$. To reflect this informational dependence, we will denote this parameter by $\omega_{ab}(c \mid \mathcal{I}_{ab}^c)$, a notation inspired by the usual "conditional probability" notation.

With the two information sets, $\mathcal{I}^s$ and $\mathcal{I}_{ab}^c$, we can characterize a's initial information state, $\mathcal{I}_1$:

$$\mathcal{I}^s \cup \mathcal{I}_{ab}^c \subseteq \mathcal{I}_1 \tag{14.1}$$

We do not use an "equal" sign because the information a possesses need not be restricted to the union of $\mathcal{I}^s$ and $\mathcal{I}_{ab}^c$. But a needs to possess *at least* this information in order to perform the inferences our model will describe. When a learns of b's categorization of the object as a c, the information state is updated and becomes

$$\mathcal{I}_2 = \mathcal{I}_1 \cup \{(\text{IS-A}_b(c, o) = 1) \in \mathcal{I}_{ab}^c\}. \tag{14.2}$$

We operationalize social influence as a transition of a's information state from $\mathcal{I}_1$ to $\mathcal{I}_2$. That is, we examine changes in a's beliefs about the position of the object when she learns that b has categorized the object as an instance of concept c. Person a's initial belief about the position of the object in the semantic space associated with her concept c is a probability density function over semantic space $\mathbb{F}_c$. It is denoted $P_{\mathbb{F}_c}^a(x \mid \mathcal{I}_1)$. The updated belief is denoted $P_{\mathbb{F}_c}^a(x \mid \mathcal{I}_2)$.

To facilitate the exposition of this complicated model, we start with the two "extreme cases" discussed above: a fully accepts the implications of b's categorization or she disregards it completely. In this chapter, we index the subjective probabilities by the individual in order to clarify whose beliefs the expressions refer to.

In the first case, a is completely confident that the object is a c, based on b's categorization. Person a's belief about the position of the object under the new information state thus comes from the concept likelihood:

$$P_{\mathbb{F}_c}^a(x \mid \mathcal{I}_2) = \pi_{\mathbb{F}_c}^a(x \mid c). \tag{14.3}$$

In the second case, a ignores the categorization by b. In other words, a treats b's categorization as completely uninformative. Therefore, a's belief does not change; it is the same as under the initial information state:

$$P^a_{\mathbb{F}_c}(x \mid \mathcal{I}_2) = P^a_{\mathbb{F}_c}(x \mid \mathcal{I}_1). \tag{14.4}$$

This scenario also applies if b has categorized the object using a concept that a lacks, which we discuss in more detail below.

We now turn to the general specification, which allows for the extreme cases as well as for the possibility that a has some doubt about the validity or relevance of the categorization by b.

Postulate 14.1 (Updating belief about position based on a categorization by another person) *Consider a person a facing an inference task about an object o that is believed to belong to a domain $\mathfrak{D}_r$. We assume that*

1. $[\![c]\!]^a = \pi^a_{\mathbb{F}_c}(x \mid c)$—*that is, c is one of a's concepts;*
2. *a's initial information state is given by $\mathcal{I}_1$;*
3. *a learns that b has categorized the object as a c. Her new information state is $\mathcal{I}_2 = \mathcal{I}_1 \cup \{\text{IS-A}_b(c, o) = 1\}$.*

In this new information state, a's belief about the position of the object in semantic space $\mathbb{F}_c$ is expressed as a mixture distribution that depends on two terms:[3]

1. *a's prior belief that the object is at position x: $P^a_{\mathbb{F}_c}(x \mid \mathcal{I}_1)$, where $P^a_{\mathbb{F}_c}$ is the uniform extension of $P^a_{\mathbb{F}_r}$ to the semantic space $\mathbb{F}_c$;*
2. *a's concept likelihood for c: $\pi^a_{\mathbb{F}_c}(x \mid c)$.*

An individual's belief about the position of the object in the semantic space associated with the concept c, $\mathbb{F}_c$, is given by the following subjective probability distribution:

$$P^a_{\mathbb{F}_c}(x \mid \mathcal{I}_2) = (1 - \vartheta^s_{ab}) P^a_{\mathbb{F}_c}(x \mid \mathcal{I}_1) + \vartheta^s_{ab} \pi^a_{\mathbb{F}_c}(x \mid c), \tag{14.5}$$

where[4,5]

$$\vartheta^s_{ab} = P^a(c \mid \mathcal{I}_1)^{1/\omega_{ab}(c \mid \mathcal{I}^c_{ab})}. \tag{14.6}$$

To understand the intuition behind this general specification, it is useful to relate it to the extreme cases discussed before the formulation of the postulate. If knowledge of b's categorization makes a believe that the unseen object must be a c, then we are in the first case described before the postulate: all of the weight in the mixture distribution should be given to a's concept likelihood $\pi^a_{\mathbb{F}_c}(x \mid c)$. This is because this function characterizes a's belief about the position of the object, when she believes that it is a c. In this case, the influence of b on a is maximal, and $\vartheta^s_{ab} = 1$. On the other hand, if knowledge of b's categorization is treated as uninformative, then we are in the second case described before the postulate: all of the weight should be given to a's prior belief about the position of the object (her belief under the initial information state $\mathcal{I}_1$: $P^a_{\mathbb{F}_c}(x \mid \mathcal{I}_1)$. In this case, the influence of b on a is nonexistent, and $\vartheta^s_{ab} = 0$.

It results from this analysis that ϑ^s_{ab} can be interpreted as a *social influence coefficient*. When it is high (close to 1), the influence of b on a is maximal. When it is low (close to 0), influence is minimal.

When person a has some doubt about whether she should accept the categorization by person b, a's belief is represented by a mixture distribution of these to extreme cases. In other words, the new probability density function about the position is a weighted average of the two "elemental probabilities": the prior on the position $P^a_{\mathbb{F}_c}(x \mid \mathcal{I}_1)$ and the concept likelihood $\pi^a_{\mathbb{F}_c}(x \mid c)$.

The social influence coefficient, ϑ^s_{ab}, depends on a's propensity to accept the categorization by b, $\omega_{ab}(c \mid \mathcal{I}^c_{ab})$. More precisely, ϑ^s_{ab} is defined as the prior on the concept, $P^a(c \mid \mathcal{I}_1)$, raised to the power $1/\omega_{ab}(c \mid \mathcal{I}^c_{ab})$. With this specification, the social influence coefficient increases with $\omega_{ab}(c \mid \mathcal{I}^c_{ab})$, consistent with our objective to make the weight of the concept likelihood increase with the propensity to accept the categorization by b. We used this specific functional form to capture the idea that when the categorization by b is unsurprising, then a is more likely to accept the categorization by b than when this categorization is surprising. To understand this intuition, note that an "unsurprising" categorization as a c by b occurs when a would also have been likely to categorize the object as a c—when $P^a(c \mid \mathcal{I}_1)$ is *high*; and a "surprising" categorization occurs when $P^a(c \mid \mathcal{I}_1)$ is *low*.

As the propensity to accept b's categorization, $\omega_{ab}(c \mid \mathcal{I}^c_{ab})$, falls to zero, the social influence coefficient, ϑ^s_{ab}, declines toward zero (assuming the prior on concept c, $P^a(c \mid \mathcal{I}_1)$, is less than one, which should be the case most of the time). In this case, nearly all of the weight in inference goes to the prior on position as given by the focal person's information state, $P^a_{\mathbb{F}_c}(x \mid \mathcal{I}_1)$. A similar analysis shows that as the propensity to accept becomes large, then the social influence coefficient is large. The weight given to the prior on position $P^a_{\mathbb{F}_c}(x \mid \mathcal{I}_1)$ falls to zero, and all of the weight goes to the concept likelihood, $\pi^a_{\mathbb{F}_c}(x \mid c)$.

The analysis so far assumes that person b referred to a concept with a label that a possessed. But what if b calls the object a c, but a has no concept for c? Then a cannot interpret this information, and a's belief about the position of the object remains unchanged. In that case we have:

$$P^a_{\mathbb{F}_r}(x \mid \mathcal{I}_2) = P^a_{\mathbb{F}_r}(x \mid \mathcal{I}_1), \tag{14.7}$$

where $P^a_{\mathbb{F}_r}$ denotes the probability distribution over the semantic space of the root concept of the domain. This amounts to assuming that $\omega_{ab}(c \mid \mathcal{I}^c_{ab})$ equals zero. We formalize this reasoning in the following postulate:

Postulate 14.2 *The propensity to accept the categorization by another individual equals zero when the focal individual does not hold the concept. If all of the statements listed in the preamble of postulate 14.1 hold with the exception that the focal person does not have a concept c, then $\omega_{ab}(c \mid \mathcal{I}^c_{ab}) = 0$.*

We assume that, if a accepts the categorization done by b, then she applies her *own* concept in making inferences about the object. Because the concepts of others are generally not accessible, individuals do not have any other simple option. In particular, we do *not* assume that a has beliefs about the nature of feature space and concept probability density functions used by b.

An interesting question pertains to what happens when a accepts the categorization by b but later learns additional information about the object which would have made her unlikely to positively categorize it. For example, suppose that b tells a that a certain restaurant is a Thai restaurant, but when a encounters the restaurant, it fits her concept of a Vietnamese restaurant in a better way. We envision a few possibilities in such situations: a might (1) update her priors about the concept Thai restaurant, (2) update the extent to which she relies on information by b about restaurant genres, that is, by decreasing ω_{ab}, or (3) doubt her own perception (Griffiths, 2004). Addressing these questions would require a model of concept learning and updating, which goes beyond the scope of this book.

When Is Social Influence Strong?

What are the likely determinants of the propensity to accept categorizations by others, $\omega_{ab}(c \mid \mathcal{I}^c_{ab})$, assuming that a possesses concept c? Some depend on the identity of b. While providing a full characterization of the antecedents of $\omega_{ab}(c \mid \mathcal{I}^c_{ab})$ is beyond the scope of this chapter, here we discuss a few major determinants and refer readers to the rich literatures on social influence in social psychology and communication studies (Wood, 2000). We believe that the extent to which one person accepts b's categorization might depend on the characteristics of the influencer, the influenced person, and their relationship to each other. One major factor shaping $\omega_{ab}(c \mid \mathcal{I}^c_{ab})$ is the (perceived) difference in expertise between the influencer and the influenced. Specifically, we conjecture that the higher the relative expertise of the influencer is to the person being influenced, and the more this is acknowledged by the influenced person, the higher this propensity will be. The perceived expertise of the influencer might come from her qualifications, status, or reputation. In addition, it probably depends on the nature of the social relationship between the influencer and the person being influenced. Shared social background, such as common language, ethnicity, race, age, or sex, likely magnifies the social influence. Shared social ties, such as friendship, are likely also to increase $\omega_{ab}(c \mid \mathcal{I}^c_{ab})$.

14.2   Taken-for-Grantedness: Individual Level

We now build on our specification of the social inference process between individuals to examine the causes and consequences of variation in the extent to which a concept is taken for granted. In this chapter, we develop an approach to defining concept taken-for-grantedness that can be used to model the emergence of taken-for-grantedness in the next section of this chapter. According to prior work, when concepts have low taken-for-grantedness, an individual seeking to communicate with others about an object she associates with the concept must expend considerable effort explicating not only the object's perceived features, but also the concept and its perceived relationship to others (Colyvas and Powell, 2006). Hsu and Grodal (2015), for example, find that cigarette manufacturers seeking to communicate with consumers about a particular light cigarette brand before the concept became taken for granted produced advertisements filled with explanations about the central features of light cigarettes. This included information about key components within cigarettes (e.g., tar, nicotine, and carbon monoxide) as well as the technologies, methods, and materials used to produce the lower tar and nicotine deliveries that distinguished light cigarettes from other types of cigarette offerings. As the membership of the category proliferated and consumers became increasingly familiar with the concept, explicit explanations of the concept disappeared from advertisements of light cigarette brands. Presumably, by that point the category had become highly taken for granted, and the simple act of labeling a brand as light was enough for consumers to construct clear expectations about feature values.

Our central intuition is that a concept is more taken for granted when the person accepts the categorizations of objects by "unfamiliar" group members. We mean something narrow by the qualifier "unfamiliar": that a has no knowledge of how b uses the labels associated with the concepts in the cohort. We focus on this kind of ignorance so that we can distinguish this stark situation from others that involve the acceptance of another's categorization due to relationship-specific factors between the two individuals such as power dynamics, to differences in expertise, or from learning about the other's concept due to previous exposure. We want to take these important issues out of the picture so that we can narrow down on acceptance due to the mere perception that the concept is widely shared.

No Information about the Other's Categorizations

We propose that taken-for-grantedness is the propensity to accept the implications of categorizations of members of the group whose relevant previous categorization histories are not observed. Consider a person a and a social group G (a set of people). Person a is facing a feature inference task like that characterized by postulate 14.1. Namely, a is trying to infer the position of an object in the feature space, $\mathbb{F}_c$, on the basis of the categorization of the object as a c by b, a member of G. In that postulate, the parameter that characterized a's propensity to accept b's characterization was denoted $\omega_{ab}(c \mid \mathcal{I}_{ab}^c)$. Here, the assumption that a has no information about any of b's relevant categorization histories translates into $\mathcal{I}_{ab}^c = \emptyset$.

Our assumption about a's inference about the object is given by the following meaning postulate.

Meaning Postulate 14.1 (Taken-for-grantedness) *The taken-for-grantedness for individual a of concept c, from a domain $\mathfrak{D}_r$ in the context of group G, in notation $\Omega_{aG}(c)$, is the strength of the propensity to accept the implications of the categorizations of any group member for whom they lack observations of prior categorizations in concepts of the domain's cohort $\kappa(r)$.*

Consider a person a, a concept c from domain $\mathfrak{D}_r (c \in \kappa(r))$, and a group G. There exists a level of taken-for-grantedness of concept c for person a with respect to group G, which we denote by $\Omega_{aG}(c)$:

$$\exists \, \Omega_{aG}(c) \, \forall \, b \left[(b \in G) \wedge \left(\mathcal{I}_{ab}^c = \emptyset \right) \rightarrow \Omega_{aG}(c) = \omega_{ab}\left(c \mid \mathcal{I}_{ab}^c \right) \right].$$

Notice that this meaning postulate simultaneously "defines" taken-for-grantedness and group membership, stating that agents (in the absence of more specific information) do not discriminate between members of a group with respect to the propensity to accept the consequences of their categorizations.

Although this meaning postulate holds that $\Omega_{aG}(c)$ exists, it does not say anything about its level. At one extreme, an individual might not trust at all the categorizations by members of a group, in which case $\Omega_{aG}(c) = 0$. Recall that we impose that $\omega_{ab}(c \mid \mathcal{I}_{ab}^c) = 0$ if c is not one of a's concepts (postulate 14.2). This in turn means that $\Omega_{aG}(c) = 0$ under the same condition. At the other extreme, high levels of $\Omega_{aG}(c)$ correspond to high levels of confidence that group members share a concept similar to a's.

How does incorporating taken-for-grantedness into the social-inference process change things? Taken-for-grantedness most directly affects inferences when a has no particular tie to the influencer, b. More precisely, the social inference mechanism we posited above (formulated in postulate 14.1) can work even if the two individuals a and b have no common experience—that is, even if the only thing that a knows about b is that b is a member of group G and a has never observed b's categorizations with respect to c or the other concepts in the cohort of the domain. In this case, $\mathcal{I}_{ab}^c = \emptyset$ and the initial information state is reduced to $\mathcal{I}^s$. The inference process is formalized in the following lemma.

Lemma 14.1 (Inference under taken-for-grantedness) *Consider an individual, a, and another, b, who is a member of group G. Assume that a has not observed any of b's categorizations for any of the concepts in c's cohort ($\mathcal{I}_{ab}^c = \emptyset$). Moreover, let the conditions stated in the preamble of postulate 14.1 hold.*

Person a's belief about the position of the object after learning that b categorizes the object as a c is given by

$$P_{\mathbb{F}_c}^a(x \mid \mathcal{I}_2) = (1 - \Theta_{aG}(c)) P_{\mathbb{F}_c}^a(x \mid \mathcal{I}_1) + \Theta_{aG}(c) \pi_{\mathbb{F}_c}^a(x \mid c), \qquad (14.8)$$

where

$$\Theta_{aG}(c) = P^a(c \mid \mathcal{I}_1)^{1/\Omega_{aG}(c)}. \qquad (14.9)$$

Note that the only difference between the equations of postulate 14.1 and lemma 14.1 is the substitution of the propensity to accept b's categorization, $\omega_{ab}(c \mid \mathcal{I}_{ab}^c)$, by taken-for-grantedness $\Omega_{aG}(c)$. When a has not observed relevant categorizations by individual b, what matters is the taken-for-grantedness of the concept.

We have tried to keep the model relatively simple by assuming that the focal person does not know anything about the feature values of the object in question. The appendix to this chapter relaxes this assumption and generalizes the model to cases in which the person has a partial observation of the relevant feature values.

Information about Another's Prior Categorizations

Does the assumption that a has not observed any of b's categorization of objects in concepts in c's cohort, $\mathcal{I}_{ab}^c = \emptyset$, imply that taken-for-grantedness plays no role when the focal person *has* information about relevant past categorizations by b? On the contrary, taken-for-grantedness likely affects a's propensity to accept categorization by b, $\omega_{ab}(c \mid \mathcal{I}_{ab}^c)$, even when a has observed some relevant categorizations by b, $\mathcal{I}_{ab}^c \neq \emptyset$. In such settings, the higher the taken-for-grantedness of concept c, the more likely is a to accept the categorization by any member of the group, *all else equal*. We formalize this intuition in the following postulate.[6]

Postulate 14.3 *The propensity to accept the implications of categorizations by members of a social group increases with taken-for-grantedness when the focal person has observed relevant categorizations of objects by the group member.*

Consider an individual a and another b who is a member of group G. Assume that a has observed at least some of b's relevant categorizations: $\mathcal{I}_{ab}^c \neq \emptyset$. *If the conditions stated in the preamble of postulate 14.1 hold, then*

$$\frac{\partial \omega_{ab}(c \mid \mathcal{I}_{ab}^c)}{\partial \Omega_{aG}(c)} > 0.$$

Postulates 14.3 and 14.1 about belief updating jointly imply that taken-for-grantedness has a positive effect on the weight of the concept likelihood in social inference situations:

Proposition 14.1 *The social influence coefficient, in notation* ϑ_{ab}^s, *increases with the taken-for-grantedness of the concept.*

Consider an individual a and another b who is a member of group G. Assume that a has observed at least some of b's relevant categorizations, $\mathcal{I}_{ab}^c \neq \emptyset$. *When the conditions stated in the preamble of postulate 14.1 hold and the prior on the concept is less than one* $(P(c) < 1)$, *then*

$$\frac{\partial \vartheta_{ab}^s}{\partial \Omega_{aG}(c)} > 0.$$

14.3   How Does Taken-for-Grantedness Arise?

As we have specified, taken-for-grantedness refers to a person's beliefs about other people's concepts and, in particular, his or her conviction that unfamiliar others intend the concept to mean the same thing as they do. In this section, we describe two mechanisms to enable people to make this assessment.

The first invokes the extensional agreement between the focal individual and group members. The second focuses on the focal person's perception of the level of dissensus prevailing among pairs of agents in the group, or in other words, the variability in meaning of what the focal person calls a c.

Extensional Agreement with Members of the Group

People can rarely observe another person's concept directly; they much more frequently witness others' categorization *behaviors*. Here, we model the emergence of taken-for-grantedness as a process by which a person's beliefs about others' concepts change with observation of their categorizations.

In chapter 13, we defined the extensional agreement about a concept between individuals as the correlation of their categorization decisions, $ea_{ab}(c)$ in definition 13.2A. In small groups, one can observe categorization decisions by each member. Then extensional agreement in the group is some aggregation over pairs of members of the pairwise correlations between categorization vectors. Often, however, we have access to the categorization decisions of only a subgroup.

Next we consider two cases for the extensional agreement a person likely experiences with a subgroup. In the first, the person has direct experience with the categorizations of objects with respect to the focal concept by the members of the subgroup. In particular, she can assess the degree to which her extension of the concept overlaps with the extensions of the members of the subgroup. We call this *experienced extensional agreement* on the focal concept. In the second case, a person lacks such experience but has instead experienced extensional agreement about others' concepts in the cohort that contains the focal concept, as we discussed above.

Let us first denote the relevant subgroups for such cases:

$$\mathbf{j} = \left\{ b \,|\, (b \in G) \wedge \exists\, o\, [\{\text{IS-A}_b(c,o)\} \in \mathcal{I}^c_{ab})] \right\}; \tag{14.10}$$

$$\mathbf{J} = \left\{ b \,|\, (b \in G) \wedge (\mathcal{I}^c_{ab} \neq \emptyset) \right\}. \tag{14.11}$$

The form of experienced extensional agreement comes from experience with the subgroup denoted by $\mathbf{j}$, specifically the correlation between the categorization decisions of a focal person (a) and those by the members of this group: $ea_{a\mathbf{j}}(c)$ (see definition 13.2C). Consistent with the discussion about the nature of $\mathcal{I}^c_{ab}$, we also consider the experienced extensional agreement with subgroup $\mathbf{J}$, with respect to the cohort of concepts κ, which we denote as $ea_{a\mathbf{J}}(\kappa)$.

We focus on these two cases because either having experience with the subgroup on a focal concept or, alternatively, lacking evidence of agreement on a focal concept but having experience with related concepts can affect the emergence of taken-for-grantedness.

This account relies on two forms of generalization. In the simpler case in which the observable behavior is experienced extensional agreement with respect to the focal concept, the generalization goes from a subgroup to the group. A good reason for the assumption that people generalize their experience with a subgroup to the group is what Klaus Fiedler (2012) calls meta-cognitive myopia. This term refers to the well-documented tendency for people to remember the inferences and decisions that they made in the past but to forget the context and information on which these inferences and decisions were based. In particular, this tendency leads people to treat information from highly atypical samples as though it were representative. Such myopia in the present analysis means that people treat information from nonrandom samples of groups as representative of the groups.

When the experienced agreement concerns concepts in the focal concept's cohort (but not the focal concept), there is a second generalization: from the cohort to the concept. In this case, the metacognitive myopia involves treating observations on subsets of a cohort of concepts as representative of *all* the concepts in the cohort. In other words, people recall that they agreed with others in categorizations on genres within the film domain, but they forgot or overlooked which of the genres was the focus of this agreement.

The experience of extensional agreement with a subsample affects taken-for-grantedness through an intermediary step—by shaping perceptions of how distant one's conceptualizations are from those of the group. In chapter 13, we referred to such distance as *conceptual dissensus* (definition 13.1). This perception of dissensus is shaped by experience with either the focal concept or other concepts in its cohort. Because here we do not invoke actual dissensus, but rather the subjective perception of dissensus by the focal agent, we will denote this perceived dissensus with a "hat." More precisely, individual a's perceived conceptual dissensus about the meaning of concept c between her and group G is denoted as $\widehat{\mathcal{D}}_{aG}(c)$.

Postulate 14.4 *An individual's perceived dissensus from a group regarding a concept is a decreasing function of experienced extensional agreement with members of the group about that concept*

$$\frac{\partial \widehat{\mathcal{D}}_{aG}(c)}{\partial \, ea_{aj}(c)} < 0;$$

and is a decreasing function of experienced extensional agreement about the concepts in the domain of the focal concept (the cohort) with members of the group

$$\frac{\partial \widehat{\mathcal{D}}_{aG}(c)}{\partial e\, a_{aJ}(\kappa)} < 0.$$

Then a person's perception of dissensus with a group, which is based on the group members she has observed, affects her willingness to assume or trust that the categorizations by unfamiliar group members are similar to what her own would be.

Postulate 14.5 *The level of taken-for-grantedness of a concept for an individual in the context of a social group declines with the dissensus with the group in the semantic space for that concept.*

$$\frac{\partial \Omega_{aG}(c)}{\partial \widehat{\mathcal{D}}_{aG}(c)} < 0.$$

The relation between extensional agreement and taken-for-grantedness implied by these two postulates is formalized in the following proposition:

Proposition 14.2 *The taken-for-grantedness of a concept for an individual in the context of a social group is an increasing function of experienced extensional agreement with members of the group about that concept:*

$$[A.] \quad \frac{\partial \Omega_{aG}(c)}{\partial e\, a_{aj}(c)} > 0;$$

and it is an increasing function of experienced extensional agreement about the concepts in the domain of the focal concept (the cohort) with members of the group:

$$[B.] \quad \frac{\partial \Omega_{aG}(c)}{\partial e\, a_{aJ}(\kappa)} > 0.$$

On the general grounds that more specific information overrides the implications of less specific information, we believe that information about agreement on the focal concept has a stronger impact on perceived dissensus with the group, and in turn, on taken-for-grantedness than does experienced agreement about other concepts in the cohort. Investigating this issue empirically is an interesting avenue for further research.

Perceived Prevailing Group Dissensus

So far, we have assumed that the taken-for-grantedness of a concept for the focal person depends on her perception of dissensus between *her* meaning of a concept and the meaning held by other members of the social group. The more the person's own categorizations diverge from the categorizations of others in the group, the more dissensus she perceives and the less likely the person is to treat a concept as taken-for-granted in the sense of making inferences on the basis of unfamiliar others using the concept.

We believe that taken-for-grantedness is also affected by her perception of the dissensus *among other* members of the group. If person a perceives that group members tend to disagree on the meaning of the concept, then if a member of this group uses a concept, she will be uncertain as to what this means. A high level of dissensus among group members implies that, although some members might have a meaning similar to a's, others might mean something very different when they use c. Therefore, we conjecture that a is unlikely to accept the consequences of the categorization by an unfamiliar group member, if she perceives that a high level of dissensus prevails in this group. We will formulate this idea in a postulate, but before doing so, we need to introduce some notations.

Let $G \backslash \{a\}$ refer group G without person a.[7] Building on the notation introduced in definition 13.4C, we denote person a's *perceived* dissensus about concept c in group $G \backslash \{a\}$ by $\widehat{\mathcal{D}}_{G \backslash \{a\}}(c)$. As earlier in this section, we use a "hat" to denote the fact that this is not actual dissensus, since the concepts of others are not observable to a, but *perceived* dissensus. This quantity is a measure of the perceived variability, among group members, in meanings associated with what a calls a c. A close reading of the formal definition indicates that this can be interpreted as the average pairwise dissensus about c among all pairs of individuals in group G, excluding a.

Postulate 14.6 *Consider a person a, a social group G, and a concept c. The taken-for-grantedness of concept c for a in the context of a group G is decreasing with the perceived dissensus about the concept among other members of the group about that concept.*

$$\frac{\partial \Omega_{aG}(c)}{\partial \widehat{\mathcal{D}}_{G \backslash \{a\}}(c)} < 0.$$

We are not aware of existing empirical studies testing this claim. But investigating how perceived group dissensus affects taken-for-grantedness experimentally is an interesting avenue for future research.

14.4   Taken-for-Grantedness of a Concept in a Social Group

To this point, we have developed our model from the perspective of a particular individual's beliefs about the extent to which his or her understanding of a concept is similar to that of the members of a given group. But we also wish to characterize concepts in terms of the extent to which members of the group generally take them for granted—a task to which we now turn.

As we indicated in the introduction to the chapter, sociologists generally assume that something has fact-like, taken-for-granted status in a social group when all of the members assume that they use the concept in the same way. This requires that they share the label for the concept. This presents a complication in aggregating from individuals to the group level. In the simplest case in which all members share the label, then it is meaningful to define the taken-for-grantedness of a concept in a group as the average level of the individual $\Omega_{aG}(c)$. But if some do not use the common label, their contribution to the group taken-for-grantedness should be zero. The following definition makes such an adjustment implicitly.

Definition 14.1 (Group-level taken-for-grantedness) *The taken-for-grantedness of a concept in a social group is the average over the group members of the taken-for-grantedness of the concept with respect to the group.*

$$\overline{\Omega}_G(c) = \frac{1}{|G|}\sum\nolimits_{a\in G}\Omega_{aG}(c).$$

Recall that postulate 14.2 holds that $\omega_{ab}(c\,|\,\mathcal{I}_{ab}^c)=0$ if c is not a concept for a; by the construction this implies that $\Omega_{aG}(c)=0$ if c is not a concept for a (see meaning postulate 14.1). So the contributions to the sum in definition 14.1 are zero for all group members for whom c is not a concept. The prevalence of a concept in a group shapes taken-for-grantedness. Taken-for-grantedness of a concept in a group can be high only if most of the members possess that concept and take it for granted.

Of course, the structure of a group can affect the level of taken-for-grantedness. For example, one can imagine a large group that consists of relatively homogeneous subgroups (e.g., a college with different departments or a class with different friendship cliques). Over time, each subgroup might develop its own language, and certain of their concepts might become taken-for-granted. But the meaning of these concepts can differ across subgroups. In such cases, taken-for-granted would be high if G refers to a subgroup but low/medium when it refers to the group in its entirety. If the subgroups are really heterogeneous, then taken-for-grantedness at the level of the group is probably not a useful construct. It seems that in this kind of situation, the analyst should change the level of analysis and focus on the subgroups instead of focusing on the overarching group.

In the previous section, we established that taken-for-grantedness of a concept for an individual increases with extensional agreement about the concept between that individual and members of the group (proposition 14.2). Here, we want to address the question of how experienced extensional agreement of group members affects group-level taken-for-grantedness.

To connect the individual level and the group level, we need to further specify the relation between extensional agreement and individual level taken-for-grantedness of proposition 14.2A. We assume that a linear relationship exists between the two quantities. We formulate this in the following auxiliary assumption:

Auxiliary assumption 14.1 *There exists a positive linear relationship between extensional agreement and taken-for-grantedness at the individual level (across group members).*

$$\forall c, G \,\exists \alpha, \beta \,\forall a \,[(\beta > 0) \wedge (a \in G) \rightarrow \Omega_{aG}(c) = \alpha + \beta \, ea_{aj}(c)]. \quad (14.12)$$

With this additional assumption, we can show that group level taken-for-grantedness, $\overline{\Omega}_G(c)$ is increasing in the group-level experienced extensional agreement, $\overline{ea}_G(c)$ (see definition 13.2C.).

Proposition 14.3 (Group-level taken-for-grantedness and extensional agreement) *The taken-for-grantedness of a concept in group is increasing with experienced extensional agreement about that concept.*

$$\frac{\partial \overline{\Omega}_G(c)}{\partial \overline{ea}_G(c)} > 0.$$

Discussion

We defined taken-for-grantedness in terms of a person's propensity to accept the consequences of categorizations by others. This depends on the person's belief about the similarity of his or her own concepts to the concepts held by others. Because concepts are rarely observable directly, people typically assess the similarity of their concepts to others' concepts by observing the past categorization decisions of others. In this approach, the emergence of taken-for-grantedness is a process by which a person's beliefs about others' concepts change with observation of their categorizations.

What does it mean to be a widely shared presumption within the probabilistic framework we develop? We propose that the answer lies in the strength of expectations an individual is able to form when communicating with other individuals about a given concept. A concept is taken for granted to the extent that knowledge that another individual attaches a label to an object provides reliable information about the position of the object in semantic space. This occurs because the focal actor presumes that belief is widely shared. The strength and automaticity of information updates enable smooth and effortless interaction among individuals and promote the replication of activities and interaction sequences.

By translating taken-for-grantedness to our framework, we open opportunities to develop understanding of antecedents to its development as well as to its decline. When studying the emergence and cognitive legitimation of categories in markets, researchers often focus analytical attention on the composition of the organizations or market offerings being categorized. For example, McKendrick et al. (2003) find that the entry of de-alio producers involved in a broad set of other activities does not promote the cognitive legitimation of a new market category as much as does the entry of producers with more focused activities.

Our framework highlights that taken-for-grantedness is a group-level phenomenon. This recognition would seem to be fundamental to the idea that taken-for-grantedness entails a sense that something is exterior and objective—beyond any one person. However, this group-level aspect has, in our opinion, been underemphasized. And it follows that, in studying the early legitimation of a category, one must also attend to the composition of the market audience. Information conveyed by sources that are socially homophilous, trusted, consistent, and perceived as experts or authoritative is more likely to influence an individual's understanding of a concept than information conveyed by others. Thus, the extent to which the early audience members for a category are homogeneous in background or role, relationally connected, or occupy positions of authority or expertise likely shape the dynamics of taken-for-grantedness. For example, whether the set of market analysts who first study a category are similar in their industry expertise might shape the speed at which they develop a new shared concept.

Our framework also emphasizes the role of social interaction (or lack thereof) in shaping taken-for-grantedness. Concepts that are taken for granted can develop quickly among a small set of individuals who are sharply bounded in social space. They might also persist despite disagreement with others' concepts as long as those boundaries persist, implying that individuals do not encounter others who have a different conceptualization. Sociologists who are interested in contestation of meanings might find it productive to consider when in the stage of concept development individuals with diverging concepts interact and how this shapes the ways that differences in understandings are voiced or negotiated as well as their outcomes. One possibility is that interaction with others who have divergent conceptualizations stalls the growth in taken-for-grantedness or leads to the development of alternative terminology to point to each group's distinct concept. On the other hand, it is possible that group-level disagreement forces individuals to be explicit about their meanings and that surfacing divergence might lead strategic actors to work to promote their favored meaning. Future work should examine contextual factors that influence which trajectory ensues.

Chapter Appendix:
Social Inference via Categorization by Others with *Partial* Information about the Focal Object

In the body of the chapter, we assumed that a does not know anything about the feature values of the object under consideration. What happens in the more general case in which a does have such information? We now generalize the model to allow us to answer this question.

Consider individual a who tries to infer the feature values of an object o on the basis of the knowledge that b has categorized the object as a c, just as in §14.1. In that section, we had assumed that the individual knew nothing about the object, aside from the inference context. Here we consider a more general setup in which the individual might have some knowledge about the feature values of the object. We will refer to this knowledge as a "signal" about the position of the object, and we will denote it as z_o. This signal is a realization of a random variable, Z_o. It is informative in the sense that the beliefs about the position of the object in a semantic space $\mathbb{F}_c$ is affected by z_o. Formally, the following is true:

$$\exists x_0 \left[(x_0 \in \mathbb{F}_c) \wedge \left(P^a_{\mathbb{F}_c}(x_0 \,|\, c \cup z_o) \neq \pi^a_{\mathbb{F}_c}(x_0 \,|\, c) \right) \right].$$

As before, we use the term *information state* to refer to the information the individual possesses initially about the object and to the information she possesses once she has learned that b, categorized the object as a c. We consider two states.

- $\mathcal{I}_{1z_0}$ denotes the information state that contains person a's background knowledge about the situation and a signal about the object, z_0, that is,

$$\mathcal{I}_{1z_0} \equiv \mathcal{I}_1 \cup \{z_0\}.$$

- $\mathcal{I}_{2z_0}$ denotes the information state that is an update on $\mathcal{I}_{1z_0}$ with the information that b has categorized the object as a c, that is,

$$\mathcal{I}_{2z_0} \equiv \mathcal{I}_{1z_0} \cup \{\text{IS-A}_b(c,o) = 1\}.$$

Suppose that a's information state is initially $\mathcal{I}_{1z_0}$. Her belief about the position of the object in the semantic space associated with her concept c given this information is captured by $P^a_{\mathbb{F}_c}(x \mid \mathcal{I}_{1z_0})$. This quantity is given by postulate 10.2.

Now suppose that a learns that b has categorized the object as a c. Her information state gets updated to $\mathcal{I}_{2z_0}$ (defined above). As in §14.1, two things can happen: a can accept the implications of b's categorization or not. We express this in the following postulate, which parallels postulate 14.1. The main difference between that postulate and the one presented below is the conditioning of some expressions on information state $\mathcal{I}_{1z_0}$ instead of $\mathcal{I}_1$ and information state $\mathcal{I}_{2z_0}$ instead of $\mathcal{I}_2$.

Postulate 14.7 (Updating belief about position on the basis of a categorization by another individual when the focal individual has a signal about the position of the object) *Consider an individual a facing an inference task about an object o that is believed to belong to a domain $\mathfrak{D}_r$. We assume that*

1. *c is the label of one of a's concepts:* $[\![\,c\,]\!] = \pi^a_{\mathbb{F}_c}(x \mid c)$;
2. *a's initial information state, $\mathcal{I}_{1z_0}$, is given by her background knowledge about the context, and her signal about the position of the object (z_0):* $\mathcal{I}_{1z_0} = \mathcal{I}_1 \cup \{z_0\}$; *and*
3. *a learns that b has categorized the object as a c. Her new information state is $\mathcal{I}_{2z_0} = \mathcal{I}_{1z_0} \cup \{\text{IS-A}_b(c,o) = 1\}$.*

In the new information state given by the update from $\mathcal{I}_{1z_0}$ to $\mathcal{I}_{2z_0}$, the subjective probability, for a, that the object is at position x in semantic space $\mathbb{F}_c$ is expressed as a mixture distribution that depends on two terms:[8]

1. *a's prior belief that the object is at position x: $P^a_{\mathbb{F}_c}(x \mid \mathcal{I}_{1z_0})$, where $P^a_{\mathbb{F}_c}$ is the uniform extension of $P^a_{\mathbb{F}_r}$ to the semantic space $\mathbb{F}_c$; and*
2. *a's belief about the position given $\mathcal{I}_{1z_0} \cup c$: $P^a_{\mathbb{F}_c}(x \mid \mathcal{I}_{1z_0} \cup c)$.*

The belief of the individual a about the position of the object in the semantic space associated with concept c, $\mathbb{F}_c$, is given by the following subjective probability distribution:

$$P^a_{\mathbb{F}_c}(x \mid \mathcal{I}_{2z_0}) = \left(1 - \vartheta^s_{ab}\right) P^a_{\mathbb{F}_c}(x \mid \mathcal{I}_{1z_0}) + \vartheta^s_{ab}\, P^a_{\mathbb{F}_c}(x \mid \mathcal{I}_{1z_0} \cup c), \quad (14.13)$$

where

$$\vartheta^s_{ab} = P^a(c \mid \mathcal{I}_{1z_0})^{1/\omega_{ab}(c \mid \mathcal{I}^c_{ab})}.$$

This postulate is a more general version of postulate 14.1. To see this, note that if the signal is *not* informative ($\mathcal{I}_{1z_0} = \mathcal{I}_1 \cup \{z_0\} = \mathcal{I}_1$), then the new postulate reads exactly like the original because one can substitute $\mathcal{I}_1$ for $\mathcal{I}_{1z_0}$.[9] So this postulate adds something new only in the case of *informative* signals. A signal is informative if

1. there exists, $x_0 \in \mathbb{F}_c$ such that $P^a_{\mathbb{F}_c}(x_0 \mid \mathcal{I}_{1z_0} \cup c) \neq \pi^a_{\mathbb{F}_c}(x_0 \mid c)$, and
2. $P^a(c \mid \mathcal{I}_{1z_0}) \neq P^a(c \mid \mathcal{I}_1)$.

The first term $P^a_{\mathbb{F}_c}(x \mid \mathcal{I}_{1z_0} \cup c)$ is given by equation 10.1 when the concept likelihood and the signal are normally distributed random variables.

CHAPTER FIFTEEN

Broadening the Scope
of Application

OUR GENERAL AIM IN THIS BOOK was to develop a formal language with the expressive power needed for diverse forms of sociological analysis. Throughout, we used short experiments and empirical examples to help illustrate relevant processes. In this final chapter, we explore connections to broader sociological lines of inquiry. More specifically, we consider the implications of this modeling approach for sociological research on organizations, the economy, and cultural domains.

15.1   Valuation in Markets

Extensive empirical research supports the basic relationship between categorization processes and evaluation that we analyzed in chapter 11 and chapter 12 (Leahey, 2007; Hsu et al., 2009; Negro et al., 2010; Negro and Leung, 2013; Leung and Sharkey, 2014; Heaney and Rojas, 2014; Negro et al., 2015). More specifically, a negative association between membership in multiple categories and market appeal has been documented in many and diverse settings, including experience goods such as feature films and wine, but also search goods such as financial stocks, software products, and free-lance services. Measurement of appeal varies according to the setting under study, ranging from ratings of likability of products to career success of individuals to survival rates of firms that make or release market goods.

Thus far, argumentation linking an object's membership in multiple categories and lowered evaluation has focused mainly on its lack of clear fit with any one category. This literature starts with the basic assumption that nonconformity is generally something that people dislike and prefer to avoid (Zuckerman, 1999). Psychological research on cognitive processing fluency sharpens this argument by demonstrating through experimental research how objects that are more difficult to process create negative emotional reactions which, in turn, influence their valuation. Our framework incorporates both lack-of-fit and disfluency by positing two independent effects underlying the penalty associated with multiple categorization: (1) lowered typicality of an object in the concepts in which it is categorized and (2) greater conceptual ambiguity associated with processing information about an object that is located in a position in semantic space that lies between concepts.

In empirical research, an object's profile of categorizations provides information about its ambiguity. Early research took simple counts of assigned category labels or indices of dispersion of category labels or features as measures of "categorical niche width." While this provided a rough proxy for lowered typicality of objects (assuming that objects that are members of multiple categories are, on average, less typical of each), it did not explicitly address conceptual ambiguity. Some recent studies have used measures of category spanning that take account of distances between concepts to measure conceptual ambiguity (Kovács and Hannan, 2015; Olzak, 2016).

Our framework suggests future directions that this general line of research might take. Relatively few studies, for example, have focused explicitly on how evaluations of objects vary by audience member. Research generally assumes that people might differ in terms of which objects they prefer, but everyone prefers prototypical objects. But preference for typicality might not be universal. In one study, appeal for category spanning is found to depend on the role performed by an individual in the market (Pontikes, 2012). In particular, for final consumers who operate under low uncertainty and value more technical efficiency or price, products that span multiple categories (and the firms that make them) are less appealing. For investors who commit resources when uncertainty about the success of the product is higher, products that span categories can be more appealing because they guarantee some flexibility in future market uses. A second study suggests that a tolerance for category spanning is the result of culture-based taste differences among groups of individuals (Goldberg et al., 2016). Some people have a marked preference for typical objects, and they are also narrow in what they choose to consume; other people have the same preference for typical objects but sample across a variety of categories; yet other people have appreciation for atypical objects that explicitly defy cultural boundaries; and another group chooses anything and everything and do not seem to be concerned with cultural boundaries in general.

Chapter 13's treatment of conceptual agreement and dissensus suggests a potential alternative mechanism that might be driving the results in

Pontikes (2012) and Goldberg et al. (2016). There might exist conceptual dissensus between the different agents in these accounts, which in turn drives differences in evaluations. For example, people who appear to have a preference for atypical objects might simply hold different concepts than the rest of the audience. In the restaurant example, an agent might view a food truck serving Korean tacos as an atypical Asian, Mexican hybrid or a typical "after-club" street-food vendor. Venture capitalists might classify prospective investments as "disruptive" or "me-too" companies. Since most empirical studies do not collect information on different agents' conceptual systems (but rather focus on a shared set of concepts that define a domain), this is an open question.

The series of evaluative scenarios outlined in chapter 12 suggests that, beyond variation in preferences for typicality, there might be systematic context-based differences that shape perceptions of appeal. For example, one key difference is whether an object's category membership is known versus unknown at the start of evaluation. Lower confidence that an object is an instance of a concept decreases an object's expected appeal. This suggests the possibility that evaluations might be generally more muted in contexts where the evaluator encounters unlabeled objects relative to one where objects are already assigned labels. Another key distinction is whether the context restricts evaluation to a single relevant concept versus allowing evaluation relative to several concepts. It is likely that greater penalties might be applied to objects resting in the intersection of multiple concepts in the latter scenario, when the effect of categorization uncertainty is combined with ambiguity about aggregation. Finally, there might be cases where only an object's label is observed as an audience member is forming beliefs about its appeal (versus others where positions can be directly observed). In this instance, the audience members' prior experiences with objects categorized as members of that concept will directly shape perceived appeal, leaving object typicality out of the picture. Audience members' subsequent evaluations of the object might shift more, as greater knowledge of the object's position is gained. By outlining the parameters that shape the relationship between the object and its perceived appeal, our framework provides a systematic way to approach thinking about the different context-based differences that might systematically impact how audiences evaluate objects.

An open question recent studies have aimed to address is why, in some cases, objects that combine elements from multiple categories appear to be rewarded rather than penalized. Potential explanations include the possibility that a person's needs or motivations might lead him or her to evaluate multiply-categorized objects differently (Smith, 2011; Durand and Paolella,

2012) or that the perceived novelty or innovativeness of multiple-category objects overrides the disfluency discount (Hsu et al., 2012). Connecting the multiple-category discount literature to theory on cognitive processing fluency suggests that emotions might play a key role. For example, novel stimuli might provoke stronger emotional reactions than more familiar stimuli. If so, novelty and fluency may interact in ways that produce strong valence in evaluations, creating both stronger penalties and larger rewards for multiple-concept objects. Tying category-related explanations that have largely relied on intuition to insights within cognitive science is important for a structured, informed development of this thriving literature.

15.2   Innovation

In a related vein, we believe that the framework developed in this book can also provide insights into the study of innovations and patenting. A main point of connection between the conceptual spaces approach developed in this book and the innovation literature is that the technological space that inventors navigate is itself a conceptual space, covering the set of past, current, and future ideas and solutions. Inventors and organizations search this idea space to assess whether their ideas are novel, and they also search for prior innovations to learn from and to build on. Patent examiners and patent attorneys search the knowledge space in order to differentiate the patent application they handle from other existing innovations.

Similarly to how concepts and categories dissect the conceptual space, the technological space is often divided into categories and classes. Users of technological space attach labels to technological concepts and categories, calling them fields, technologies, or, in the specific case of the United States Patent Office (USPTO), primary and secondary technology classes. Such classification systems often encompass a large portion of the technology space.

For example, the USPTO's classification system consists of roughly 500 primary classes and 100,000+ secondary classes, and is aimed at providing a comprehensive classification system into which any possible patent application could be sorted. These classes help users of the patent system to navigate the otherwise vast technological space. Examiners, for example, rely heavily on the patent classification system when they engage in a search for relevant prior art: as the Patent Examination Manual (2015) details, "the class and subclass must be recorded in the Search Notes page along with the date that the search was performed (or updated)."

Our theory suggests that the classification of patents into technology classes will influence the way in which inventors, examiners, and attorneys use the technological space; and that this, in turn, can influence the fate of innovations. Patent classes aid information processing, increase social visibility, and reduce the cognitive load of inventors, examiners, and attorneys. So, for example, patents that are misclassified or classified into vague categories are at risk of not being found by relevant audiences. The theoretical framework developed in this book would suggest that, for example, the contrast and distinctiveness of the technology classes influence the extent to which these technological domains are used. This is because distinctive, internally coherent, and high-contrast classes facilitate information processing and the search for relevant patents. Indeed, Kovács, Carnabuci, and Wezel (2017) find that patents classified in a high-contrast patent class are more likely to be cited than the same patents classified in a lower-contrast patent class.

Further connections between the conceptual spaces approach and innovation studies involve their interest in the consequences of recombination and in exploring the structure of distances between concepts. Since the beginning of innovation research, innovativeness and creativity have been equated with "the carrying out of new combinations." This approach can be found as early as Adam Smith (1776, p. 329), extending to Schumpeter (1934, p. 66) and Nelson and Winter (1982, p. 130). To assess patent recombinativeness, researchers measure the extent to which an innovation spans distant patent classes. On the one hand, some researchers have documented the advantages of recombination: recombining diverse and unrelated technological domains has been found to positively affect a patent's impact (Rosenkopf and Nerkar, 2001; Fleming, 2001; Fleming and Sorenson, 2004; Nerkar, 2003). On the other hand, another stream of work has illustrated the benefits to innovations from fitting into an established technological trajectory. Dosi (1982) argued that novel technologies develop from belonging to existing technological trajectories: as progress proceeds cumulatively, an innovation's impact is affected by its marginal contribution to a trajectory of reference. As innovations are developed through a continuous process of interactive learning, relevant actors can become blind to alternative technological opportunities after a technological trajectory gains momentum because "paradigms entail specific heuristics and visions on how to do things" (Cimoli and Dosi, 1995, p. 246). As a consequence, innovations can be harmed if they fall outside of an established technological trajectory.

The approach outlined in this book might spur further conjectures for future research in the innovation domain. For example, innovation research has not yet examined the role of prototypicality. We have argued that prototypical objects would enjoy multiple benefits, such as higher recognition and valuation. Innovation researchers could test whether this conjecture holds in the domain of patents. Another avenue for future research could be an investigation into how other properties of categories (beside contrast), such as informativeness, distinctiveness, or the perceptual-magnet effect, might affect the ways in which audiences use the patent system. Conceptual ambiguity of patents/innovation can also affect their fate: highly ambiguous patents are likely to be misclassified and therefore ignored by future audience members who use classification as a basis for search. Finally, the innovation domain and the setting of a patent classification system (due to ambiguity) might provide a fruitful empirical focus for studying the change of conceptual spaces: as science and technology evolves, so does technological space, bringing with it new categories, labels, and meanings.

15.3   Social Identity

Our framework also provides insights into psychological and sociological research on social identity. In psychology, a core aspect of social identity theory is that a person's self-concept is partly derived from how she categorizes herself (Tajfel and Turner, 1986). The social categories she belongs to are her "ingroup," and other categories are the "outgroup." Whether others are members of the ingroup or outgroup has far-reaching implications: people favor ingroup members; exaggerate differences between themselves and outgroup members; minimize differences between ingroup members; and are more disposed to remember positive things about ingroup members and negative things about outgroup members.

Intergroup discrimination relies on stereotypes that are based in social concepts and categories (Oldmeadow and Fiske, 2010). In sociological research, Goffman (1959) emphasizes that social interactions are performances in which people play roles for an audience, based on an agreed upon definition of the situation. The types of "roles" available to the "actor" and the definition of the situation are based on the social concepts claimed and assigned, similar to what is described in psychological research on social identity.

In these research streams, the concepts that people use to assign others to social categories are central. But this work typically does not explore the basis for these social concepts. Our framework explicitly models the relationship between people's concepts and social categories, and might be able to shed light on which social categories (and associated concepts) are most relevant to social identities in certain situations. Whether concepts are distinctive and informative and whether social categories have high contrast can affect social cognition, stereotyping, and thus social identity. Specifically, we surmise that concepts are used as a basis of cognition to the extent that they are highly informative and distinctive. The lower the contrast of a social category, the less likely are people to make concept-based decisions based on membership in the category. This can be a good thing or a bad thing, depending on the point of view of the actor and the nature of the concept/category. For example, high-contrast job categories might help students meaningfully choose careers, while lowering the category contrast of a racial/ethnic group might decrease racial hostility.

In chapter 11, we argued that the conceptual ambiguity of objects would affect how they are approached, used, and valued. Applying these insights to social identity, we expect that people whose social categorization is ambiguous might be less subject to stereotyping. One aspect of, or origin of, conceptual ambiguity can be "intersectionality," that is, the tendency for people to belong to multiple social groups and categories along many dimensions (race, gender, occupation, wealth, etc.). Our formulation implies that a person's intersectionality would be most confusing to others if the spanned identities are rarely combined or occur together, which would make it difficult for a person to capitalize on the benefits of ingroup status or suffer harm from outgroup status. In this way, our model can provide a coherent basis for understanding multiplicities in social identities.

Another insight relevant to social identity concerns feature value inheritance across levels of hierarchies of social categories. The stereotypes people use are not always at the same conceptual level. For example, one might have a stereotype about men and a different stereotype about old men who own red sports cars. While research in social cognition acknowledges this fact and explores when these different levels of categories will be activated (Fiske and Taylor, 2017), we know of no prior work that studies the relationship between the content of social stereotypes at different levels. Our analysis of feature inheritance can help in understanding such questions.

15.4   Culture

In the first chapters of the book, we emphasized how our interest in mental structures brings our analysis close to the study of culture in sociology and other disciplines. In cultural anthropology, some scholars focus on objects and public practices as the center of a pattern of meanings (Geertz, 1983), while others are more attentive to interpreting human behavior not as a "thing" but as a relation between human minds and context (D'Andrade, 1995; Strauss and Quinn, 1997). Our work is closer to this second type of cultural analysis that seeks to comprehend meaning systems by focusing on shared understandings between individuals, groups, and other entities in a social context.

We hope that by now some connections with the study of culture can be seen more clearly. The theoretical approach we have developed in the foregoing chapters has two main components: concepts and contexts. Contexts are central in our model because they orient a person's cognitive focus to sets of concepts to use when interpreting objects. A context focuses attention on a domain and a cohort of concepts.

In our approach, concepts are just as important and perhaps more so. The cultural theories with which our framework intersects stress that meanings are created through the interaction of the intrapersonal (what we think) and the contextual (objects and events in the public social world). Strauss and Quinn (1997, p. 20) argue explicitly that culture exists in the mind, not outside of it:

> True, these ideas, feelings, and motivations can only be observed from things people say and do publicly; they are probably held in common with many other people; they are learned through participation in social institutions and reinforced by being associated with symbols of various sorts; and they are enacted with concrete objects in everyday settings and can be improvised in these settings. But the point remains that these meanings are the actor's meanings. ...As others have insisted before us, meanings can only be evoked in a person.

Several sociological accounts highlight cognition as central to the processes through which people understand their life experience and use what they have learned from it. In Vaisey's dual-process model of culture, the difference between moral commitments and behavior is based on the relationship between explicitly articulated values and underlying cognitive schemas (Vaisey, 2009). Here decisions such as drinking alcohol or cutting class are better explained by the moral dispositions that people internalize cognitively than by explicit statements provided in interviews. Lizardo (2017) also proposed a cognitively grounded conception of enculturation. In this conception, culture involves the internalization of experience (in terms of modification of neural encoding and storing of knowledge in memory systems) via a developmental learning process. Our approach agrees with these accounts in the sense that we see cognition and culture as essentially interlaced. Meanings arise in response to the outer world that people encounter. But concepts and, therefore, culture exist in people's brains.

Take the IS-A relation, introduced in chapter 5, which tells whether one mental representation (of a person, event, etc.) is or is not an instance of another. From this relationship, the judgments and decisions that people make are based on perceived relationships between one concept and another, which in turn entails property inheritance. Similarly, we proposed that the appeal of an object, such as a market product, for an individual depends on the valence of the concept that the object instantiates and the ambiguity of the position of the object vis-à-vis concepts.

Reasoning about culture and cultural meanings reminds us of the importance of sharedness (Strauss and Quinn, 1997). In our model, agreement among people depends on one making and observing similar categorization decisions by others. In this way, emotional responses and judgments in individuals and collective processes in groups all depend on the structure of the underlying mental representations that we develop. People have individual mental representations, but cultural meaning defines the interpretation of some type of object or event evoked in people as a result of their similar life experience. Having similar life experiences does not mean having the same experience. Rather, it means developing similar mental representations from observing similar patterns. For instance, any one of us grows up in a different version of family, but we can relate to the common experience of cohabitation and nurturing environment (or lack thereof).

This argument has two distinct implications. On the one hand, cultures are not strictly bounded, coherent, timeless systems of meanings (Swidler, 1986, 2001). In fact, conceptual understandings, and therefore cultural meanings, can and do vary. Our probabilistic approach builds on this idea. We model one of our key constructs, the categorization probability, that is the probability of categorizing an object as an instance of a concept, as a function of three factors. Two are prior probabilities, namely, the subjective probability that a randomly encountered object in the context belongs to the category and the subjective probability that a randomly encountered object in the context has a particular combination of feature values (a particular position in the semantic space). People estimate base rates from the objects that they have encountered in a domain. These encounters differ among people and influence their categorization decisions, which helps explain part of the variation in cultural meaning. In a dynamic framework, people's interactions with others and their distinct conceptual understandings and their priors can explain how culture evolves. For example, making color classifications based on categorizations by others results in convergence of color partitions (Xu, Dowman, and Griffiths, 2013).

In our approach, the variation for encounters can be linked to multiple sources. Psychological factors are one such source. Sociologists bring attention to another: dimensions of the social structure (age, gender, race, income) that provide individuals with similarly patterned opportunities and resources. These social factors can help explain distributions of cultural meanings through categorization behaviors. Finally, not only base rates but also concept likelihoods can be a source of cultural variation. Typicality is defined in terms of probability distributions over a semantic space, and the semantic space depends on the cohorts of concepts invoked by the context.

Social action rests on stable, pervasive, and motivating understandings that are shared within social groups. We develop two ways in which cultural meanings move beyond the individual level. One is the social inference process in which others can influence our own beliefs about an object by categorizing it. In this basic way, we recognize that our categorization decisions, and therefore the meanings that we infer, do not arise in a social vacuum. Influential social factors range from the perceived expertise and status of the other individual to the nature of the social relationship between us, to similarity in social background. The other way in which we address sharedness of meaning is by linking social inference with taken-for-grantedness. We propose that the propensity to accept another unfamiliar individual's categorizations defines taken-for-grantedness. But we connect beliefs about what is accepted in general by unfamiliar members of a group to shared agreement about categorizations of a familiar group of individuals.

All in all, our approach shows important affinities with cultural analysis for its focus on the cognitive foundations of meaning in a social context, and for examining some forces that increase and reduce the degree to which meanings are shared among people–what Strauss and Quinn refer to as centripetal and centrifugal tendencies of sharedness.

Researchers of culture argue that meanings are a combination of ideas (concepts), feelings, and motivations. In our probabilistic Bayesian model, treatment of concepts has a prominent role, for example, in explaining categorization decisions. The model also incorporates emotions in the analysis of appeal. We acknowledge that motivations are important for learning and developing cognitive schemas. And we know that one property of motivation is that we can share the same schemas but not all act on them. This property is important, for example, in explaining why our moral decision making does not necessarily reflect our moral consciousness (Vaisey, 2009). In our model, we see how motivations associated with social relationships can enter as distinct predictors of social inference in categorization, or how material interests can help explain certain patterns of appeal and evaluation (e.g., critics seeking to differentiate from one another in creative markets). Although motivations are not addressed directly, they can be incorporated as additional parameters in the model. This is one clear advantage of the formal construction of our approach.

In general, motivations are critical in explaining how certain schemas become "tools" in strategies of social action, as described in Swidler (1986). Our model refocuses the culture-as-toolkit metaphor in one important way. The central distinction we make between concepts and categories suggests that categorization decisions depend on our semantic and conceptual spaces. Other, more complex behaviors, or strategies of action, as Swidler put it, depend on cognition as well. Much use of the toolkit idea is made to explain that social action is strategic but not necessarily coherent and unified. This is an important observation, and social action can indeed be strategic. At the same time, this does not mean that incoherent action follows from incoherence between concepts and values. In our model, some incoherence in behavior can also result from incoherence among different concepts we learn or because different contexts retrieve distinct meanings of the same concepts. Our model points to the importance of distinguishing between cognitive and strategic determinants in patterns of social action.

PART FIVE

Appendixes

APPENDIX A

Glossary of Technical Terms

TABLE A.1
Key Predicates and Sets

	Meaning
Predicates:	
IS-A(c, c')	"the focal person judges that c' is a c"
EXCLUSIVE$(\mathbf{C})$	"the task demands choice of one concept from $\mathbf{C}$"
FIRST-LEVEL SUBCONCEPT(c, c')	"c' is a first-level subconcept of c"
FREE(r)	"the task does not limit categorizations within $\mathcal{D}_r$"
IND(κ)	"conditional independence holds for the cohort κ"
ROOT(c, Λ)	"c is a root of the set of concepts Λ"
SINGLE(c)	"the categorization task concerns a single concept c"
Sets:	
$\mathfrak{C}$	the allowed categorization alternatives
$\mathbf{cat}(\cdot)$	category for a concept
$\mathbf{cen}(\cdot)$	the center of concept
$\mathcal{D}_r$	domain consisting of root r and its subconcepts
$\mathcal{I}$	an information state
$\mathcal{I}^e$	context is "exclusive categorization"
$\mathcal{I}^f$	context is "free categorization"
$\mathcal{I}^s$	context is "single-concept categorization"
κ	a cohort of concepts
$\wp(\cdot)$	power-set

TABLE A.2
Key Functions

Function	Meaning
$A(o)$	conceptual ambiguity of an object
$cohort(r, \Lambda)$	cohort of concepts in domain r of inventory Λ
$\Gamma(\cdot)$	contrast of a category
$\vec{d}_{\mathbb{F}_c}(x, c)$	distance in semantic space of position x from concept c
$\vec{D}_{\mathbb{G}}(c_1, c_2)$	distance in semantic space from concept c_1 to c_2
$d_{ab}(\cdot)$	dissensus between a and b about a domain
$\vec{d}_{aG}(\cdot)$	dissensus between a and group G about a concept
$\mathcal{D}_G(\cdot)$	dissensus within G about the meaning of a concept
D_{KL}	Kullbach–Leibler divergence
$\Delta_{\boldsymbol{\kappa}}(c)$	distinctiveness of c wrt the cohort $\boldsymbol{\kappa}$
$\daleth_{G_1, G_2}(\cdot)$	conceptual dissensus between two groups, G_1 and G_2
$ea_{ab}(c)$	extensional agreement of a and b about the concept c
$ea_{aj}(c)$	extensional agreement of a with a subset of the group G about c
$ea_{a\mathbf{J}}(\boldsymbol{\kappa})$	extensional agreement of a with a subset of the group Gs about a cohort of concepts
$H(c)$	entropy of the concept c
$I(c, \mathcal{D}_r)$	informativeness of c relative to $\mathcal{D}_r$
$\ell(\cdot)$	the set of concepts applied to the object
$mH(c_1, c_2)$	modified Hausdorff distance between the concepts c_1 and c_2
$\phi(\cdot)$	fluency of an object
$P^*(c, o)$	scaled probability that object o is (at least) a c
$P(\text{IS-A}(c, o) \mid x_o)$	categorization probability of o as a c
$P_{\mathbb{F}_c}(\cdot)$	prior probability
$P_{\mathcal{D}_r}$	background conceptual knowledge of domain with root r
$\pi_{\mathbb{F}}(\cdot)$	concept likelihood
$R_{\mathbb{F}}(\cdot)$	mental representation of an object in the space $\mathbb{F}$
$\vec{s}_{\mathbb{F}}(x, y)$	similarity of y to x in the space $\mathbb{F}$
$t_c(\cdot)$	typicality of an object as an instance of the concept c
$\tau_c(\cdot)$	typicality of position x for an instance of the concept c
$\tau_c^*(\cdot)$	scaled typicality of position x for an instance of the concept c
$uni(P_{\mathbb{F}}, \mathbb{G})$	uniform extension of probability function $P_{\mathbb{F}}$ to space $\mathbb{G}$
$\mathcal{V}(\cdot)$	valuation of an object
$\mathfrak{v}_c$	valence of concept c
$\omega_{ab}(\cdot)$	a's propensity to accept categorizations by b
$\Omega_{aG}(\cdot)$	a's propensity to accept categorizations by any member of G (taken-for-grantedness)

Some Elemental First-Order Logic

IN THIS BOOK, we present a formal theory of (some aspects of) social cognition, and we derive some of its consequences that explain various cultural phenomena. Even though the book presents our views on social cognition, we believe some of the readers might find it beneficial to have some details on what we mean by formal theory. It is specifically so as in the social sciences there is little consensus about a simpler question, the meaning of the term "theory." As it is not possible to build on an existing consensus, we can only offer clarification of our own position. We adopt Alfred Tarski's (1956) somewhat laconic definition of a theory as a *deductively closed set of sentences.* This definition sounds good, but it obviously requires further explanation of the key terms. What is a sentence? What is a set? What does it mean to be deductively closed?

Considerations concerning all three of these questions offer valuable insights, but we assume that elementary mathematics sheds sufficient light on the middle question, so that we can take the concept of a set taken for granted. In this appendix, we focus on answering the remaining two questions. There are several reasonable answers to these questions. One can opt for a simple language and a simple answer to the question concerning the deductive closure. But this option has to face the difficulty stemming from the lack of expressive power of the language. Someone else might prefer a more expressive language. The price for the increased expressive power is a considerably more complicated answer to the question: What does the deductive closure look like?

As no canonical answer is available, practical choices are required. This means trying to balance the intricacy of the language with the expressive power required for the theory we present. It is also important to minimize the idiosyncrasy of the language to make it broadly accessible.

The first question can only be answered if it is asked more precisely: "What is a sentence of a given language?" To make it simple we offer a particular language, that of classical first-order logic, the formal language of most mathematics.

The Language of First-Order Logic

The language of first-order logic (FOL) is defined by its (linguistic) categories. Some of these categories contain expressions that are linguistically not decomposable, atomic expressions; others are composed from simpler expressions following a set of well-defined composition rules. We start with the atomic expressions.

Atomic Expressions

The set of atomic expressions contain two subsets: the variables and the constants. The variables of FOL (similarly to natural language pronouns) refer to the elements of the universe of discourse. For a variable, context matters. The context of the variables is that of quantifications such as *exists*, or *for all*.

In this book, we use sorted variables for easier readability that allow us to differentiate between variables referring to agents, objects, concepts, natural or real numbers, and so on, without being forced to declare every time what they refer to.[1]

The constants are either logical constants or nonlogical constants. The meaning, or interpretation, of the logical constants is fixed. For nonlogical constants it is a matter of interpretation reflecting the fact that green can refer to a primary color or to part of a golf course).

The logical constants belong to exactly one of the following subsets:

- logical connectives: $\{\neg, \wedge, \vee \rightarrow, \leftrightarrow\}$,
- the symbol of identity: $\{=\}$, and
- quantifiers: $\{\forall, \exists\}$.

The logical constants having the following interpretations: $\neg$ reads as "it is not the case that..."; $\wedge$ can be read as "and" $\vee$ as "or". $\rightarrow$ reads as "if...then...", and $\leftrightarrow$ as "if and only if." $\forall$ reads as "for all", and $\exists$ reads as "there is a ...". For disambiguation purposes, two pairs of brackets are useful $\{(,), [,]\}$.

There are three subsets of nonlogical constants: individual constants, predicates, and functions. Any one of these subsets might be empty, and in this book we do not use individual constants. Terms are a superset of variables, and in what follows we will spell out what else is a term.

Both predicates and functions come with a number of argument slots, and they can take terms into their argument slots. For example, Chapter 5 introduces the predicate IS-A(m, m'), which predicates the "instance of" relationship between two mental representations m and m'. It also introduces the two-place function $cohort(r, \Lambda)$ that maps a root and conceptual inventory to a set of concepts.

Molecular Expressions

1. If P is a predicate with n argument slots and $t_1, t_2, \ldots t_n$ are terms, then $P(t_1, t_2, \ldots t_n)$ is an atomic sentence of the language of FOL.
2. If P is a function with n argument slots and $t_1, t_2, \ldots t_n$ are terms, then $P(t_1, t_2, \ldots t_n)$ is a term of the language of FOL.
3. If t_1 and t_2 are terms in the language, then $t_1 = t_2$ is a sentence of the same language.
4. If S is a sentence of the language, then $\neg S$ is also sentence of the same language.
5. If S_1 and S_2 are sentences in the language, then the following are sentences in the same language:

   (a) $(S_1 \wedge S_2)$;
   (b) $(S_1 \vee S_2)$;
   (c) $(S_1 \rightarrow S_2)$ and $(S_1 \leftrightarrow S_2)$.

6. If x is a variable in the language of FOL and S is a sentence of the same language, then $\forall x[S]$ and $\exists x[S]$ are sentences of the same language.

Deductive Closure

A set of sentences is deductively closed if and only if all of the implications of any subset of the sentences also belong to the set. In the distant past, when the notion of the logical implication appeared to be clear and unambiguous, so was the deductive closure. The development of logic, especially in the last century, showed that there are several, nonequivalent ways to define the logical consequence relation. (The first dramatically disturbing example of this possibility was Brouwer's intuitionist logic in the 1920s.) From this multiplicity it is immediately clear that the notion of logical implication needs to be developed in order to make the definition operational. Logic offers alternative approaches to defining the logical consequence relation, and the alternatives give different results outside of classical FOL. The situation is simpler for classical FOL for which the alternative definitions of the logical consequence relation, specifically proof-theoretical (axiomatic) and semantic definitions, yield the same results. (So choice between them is purely a matter of taste in exposition.)

An Axiomatization of Classical First-Order Logic

The logical implication relation of classical FOL can be axiomatized by a set of axiom schemata:

1. $(A \rightarrow (\rightarrow A))$
2. $((A \rightarrow (B \rightarrow C)) \rightarrow ((A \rightarrow B) \rightarrow (A \rightarrow C)))$
3. $(\neg A \rightarrow \neg B) \rightarrow (B \rightarrow A))$
4. $\forall x[A] \rightarrow A_x^t$ where A_x^t is the same as A except the free occurrences of x are substituted by t
5. $\forall x[(A \rightarrow B)] \rightarrow (\forall x[A] \rightarrow \forall x[B])$
6. $\forall x[(A \rightarrow B_x^t)] \rightarrow (A \rightarrow \forall x[B_x^t])$
7. $t = t$
8. $t = t' \rightarrow (A_a^{t'} \rightarrow A_a^t)$

The foregoing are called axiom schemata, meaning that any substitution of A, B, or C with a sentence of the language of FOL in any schema results in an axiom. So, too, do substitutions of x with any variable, and the exchange of t and (any suitable) t' term.

One simple derivation rule is required:

the cut rule: $(A \rightarrow C)$ is derivable from $(A \rightarrow B)$ and $(B \rightarrow C)$.

A set of sentences Φ syntactically implies a sentence ϕ if there is a proof of ϕ from the axioms and the elements of Φ. Any element of such a proof is either an axiom or an element of Φ, or is derivable from them using the above derivation rule, and the last element of the proof is ϕ. Note that this is an idealization of a proof; mathematical proofs are often less detailed, though they provide sufficient evidence that such an idealized proof exists.

A Semantics of Classical First-Order Logic

To give the meanings of the sentences of classical FOL, one has to interpret the nonlogical constants and assign value to the variables. Once that is done, the structure of the language allows us to evidently calculate the truth (or falsity) of any sentence of the language.

We call a set of first-order sentences *satisfiable* if and only if there is an interpretation of the nonlogical constants and a valuation of the variables that make all sentences in the set true simultaneously.

A set of sentences Φ semantically implies a sentence ϕ if $\Phi \cup \neg\phi$ is not satisfiable; in other words it is impossible that all elements of Φ are true but ϕ is not.

As we mentioned earlier, the syntactic/axiomatic approach and the semantic approach match. The axiom system is sound and complete: Φ semantically implies ϕ if and only if Φ syntactically implies ϕ.

(Meta-)terminology

Throughout this book, we applied certain labels to different sentences of the language of FOL, signaling their epistemological status. Even though Tarski's definition of theory considers theories as sets of sentences without any hierarchy, the development and application of theories signal some differences.

Assumptions

Theories are dealing with constructs created by those who developed the theory, and such constructions are revealed by *definitions*. It is immediately clear that such definitions have to build on already established concepts. To avoid infinite regression, any theory must rely on a number of concepts that are not defined. But these concepts have to be characterized in one way or another.

In this book, we distinguish between three different ways of characterizations. Mathematical objects are defined axiomatically, relative to each other. Postulates play a similar role as axioms but in an empirical domain. They can be interpreted as restrictions on the models the (empirical) theory pictures. For example, postulate 5.1 holds that the semantic space over which a concept is defined includes the features that define the semantic space of the root concept.

Meaning postulates are similar to definitions but offer only a partial characterization of mental constructs. They are especially useful to derive some implications of the theory even when the complete characterization is not possible.

Propositions and Lemmas, the Consequences of Assumptions

The sentences we described above are all assumptions, and they do not require any proofs (technically speaking, their proofs involve only one step). To turn them into a theory, we expand the set of these assumptions so that the result is deductively closed. In this book, we use the term *proposition* for those consequences of the assumptions that express substantively relevant insights.

In this respect, we follow Imre Lakatos's (1976) vision in *Proofs and Refutations, The Logic of Mathematical Discovery*. This seminal book showed that even in mathematics the persistent parts of theory development are the theorems. They communicate key insights. If analysis of a "proof" reveals that the "proof" is not a proof, then it is common practice to change the definitions and sometimes other assumptions too, to repair the proof. Propositions and theorems are the claims that we intend to make persistent.

Formal mathematical proofs of these claims depict lines of argumentation. The culmination points of these lines of argumentation do not necessarily show an immediate empirical/substantive relevance, but here they are useful to note separately, so that complex arguments can be decomposed to more comprehensible parts. In this book, we follow the mathematical practice of calling these culmination points *lemmas*. This practice is particularly helpful when a lemma can be used in proofs of several substantively relevant theorems. In short, lemmas are culmination points of (potentially) recyclable parts of formal proofs.

Sometimes a proof is a practically trivial augmentation of an already presented line of argumentation. Whatever these augmentations prove might be substantively significant, so technically they are propositions or theorems, but their derivations are so simple, almost trivial that we felt they do not deserve the theorem status. So we call them corollaries.

APPENDIX C

Proofs

THIS APPENDIX PROVIDES THE PROOFS of the propositions and lemmas.

Proposition 4.1 *The concept likelihood of a position and its typicality decline with distance from the concept.*

Let $[\![\, c \,]\!] = \pi_{\mathbb{F}_c}(x \mid c)$, and let x and x' be any two positions in $\mathbb{F}_c$. We have

$$\vec{d}_{\mathbb{F}_c}(x, c) > \vec{d}_{\mathbb{F}_c}(x', c) \rightarrow \pi_{\mathbb{F}_c}(x \mid c) < \pi_{\mathbb{F}_c}(x' \mid c) \wedge \tau_c(x) < \tau_c(x').$$

Proof. For any fixed x and x', let q and q' denote the positions in the center for which $\vec{d}_{\mathbb{F}_c}(x, c)$ and $\vec{d}_{\mathbb{F}_c}(x', c)$ are minimum, respectively. We have $\vec{d}_{\mathbb{F}_c}(x, c) = d(q, x)$ and $\vec{d}_{\mathbb{F}_c}(x', c) = d(q', x')$. According to postulate 4.2, $d(q, x) > d(q', x') \rightarrow \vec{s}_{\mathbb{F}_c}(q, x) < \vec{s}_{\mathbb{F}_c}(q', x')$. By construction and using meaning postulate 4.1, we have $\vec{s}_{\mathbb{F}_c}(q, x) = \tau_c(x)$ and $\vec{s}_{\mathbb{F}_c}(q', x') = \tau_c(x')$. Therefore, $\tau_c(x) < \tau_c(x')$. Postulate 4.1 yields $\pi_{\mathbb{F}_c}(x \mid c) < \pi_{\mathbb{F}_c}(x' \mid c)$. $\qquad\square$

Proposition 8.1 *The categorization probability can be expressed as a product of the concept likelihood and terms that depend on information about the inference context. Under the specification of the categorization task given in the preamble of postulate 8.1,*

$$P(c \mid \mathcal{I}_0, x) = \pi_{\mathbb{F}_c}(x \mid c) \frac{P(c \mid \mathcal{I}_0)}{P_{\mathbb{F}_c}(x \mid \mathcal{I}_0)}.$$

Proof. Substitution of $\pi_{\mathbb{F}_c}(x \mid c)$ for $P_{\mathbb{F}_c}(x \mid \mathcal{I}_0, c)$, warranted by postulate 8.2, into equation 8.3 in postulate 8.1 yields the result. $\qquad\square$

Lemma 8.1 *The probability that an object will be categorized as an instance of a concept is an increasing function of its typicality in that concept in the single-concept case.*

Let the categorization task be as described in the preamble to postulate 8.1.

$$P_{\mathbb{F}_c}(c \mid \mathcal{I}_0, x) = q_c(\mathcal{I}_0) \frac{\tau_c(x)}{P_{\mathbb{F}_c}(x \mid \mathcal{I}_0)}.$$

where

$$q_c(\mathcal{I}_0) = \frac{P_{\mathbb{F}_c}(c \mid \mathcal{I}_0)}{\sum_{x' \in \mathbb{F}_c} \tau_c(x')}.$$

Proof. Replacing $\pi_{\mathbb{F}_c}(x \mid c)$ in proposition 8.1 with $\tau_c(x)$ as warranted by postulate 4.1 gives the result. $\qquad\square$

Proposition 8.2 *The probability of categorizing an object as an instance of a concept declines with the distance of (the mental representation of) the object from the center of the concept (conditional on the prior on the position remaining the same).*

Suppose the specification of the categorization task given in the preamble of postulate 8.1 holds and x and x' are two positions in $\mathbb{F}_c$. We have

$$\vec{d}_{\mathbb{F}_c}(x, c) > \vec{d}_{\mathbb{F}_c}(x', c) \wedge P_{\mathbb{F}_c}(x \mid \mathcal{I}_0) = P_{\mathbb{F}_c}(x' \mid \mathcal{I}_0)$$
$$\rightarrow P(c \mid \mathcal{I}_0, x) < P(c \mid \mathcal{I}_0, x').$$

Proof. Consider two positions x and x' such that $\vec{d}_{\mathbb{F}_c}(x, c) > \vec{d}_{\mathbb{F}_c}(x', c)$. Proposition 4.1 implies $\pi_{\mathbb{F}_c}(x \mid c) < \pi_{\mathbb{F}_c}(x' \mid c)$. The proposition then follows by application of proposition 8.1. $\qquad\square$

Proposition 8.3 *Under the specification of the categorization task given in the preamble of postulate 8.3, it follows that*

$$P(c_k \mid \mathcal{I}_0, x) = \pi_{\mathbb{G}}(x \mid c_k) \left(\frac{P(c_k \mid \mathcal{I}_0)}{\sum_{j=1}^K \pi_{\mathbb{G}}(x \mid c_j) P(c_j \mid \mathcal{I}_0)} \right).$$

Proof. The result follows from postulate 8.3 and two substitutions. The first one consists in replacing $P_{\mathbb{G}}(x \mid \mathcal{I}_0, c_k)$ with $\pi_{\mathbb{G}}(x \mid c_j)$, as warranted by postulate 8.2. The second one consists in using the law of total probability and applying postulate 8.2 again. $\qquad\square$

Proposition 9.1 *Suppose an object o has received a set of categorizations $c_1, ..., c_J$ ($J < K$). The probability that the individual also categorizes object o as a c_{J+1} has the following form, provided that conditional independence holds:*

$$\text{IND}(\kappa) \rightarrow P_{\mathbb{G}}(c \in \mathbf{c}(o) | \mathcal{I}_0, x, \mathbf{c}_1 \in \mathbf{c}(o)) = P_{\mathbb{G}}(c \in \mathbf{c}(o) | \mathcal{I}_0, x).$$

Proof. Suppose $\text{IND}(\kappa)$ holds. We have

$$P_{\mathbb{G}}(c \in \mathbf{c}(o) | \mathcal{I}_0, x, \mathbf{c}_1 \in \mathbf{c}(o)) = \frac{P_{\mathbb{G}}(\{c, \mathbf{c}_1\} \in \mathbf{c}(o) | \mathcal{I}_0, x)}{P_{\mathbb{G}}(\mathbf{c}_1 \in \mathbf{c}(o) | \mathcal{I}_0, x)},$$

$$= \frac{P_{\mathbb{G}}(c \in \mathbf{c}(o) | \mathcal{I}_0, x) \prod_{c' \in \mathbf{c}_1} P_{\mathbb{G}}(c' \in \mathbf{c}(o) | \mathcal{I}_0, x)}{\prod_{c' \in \mathbf{c}_1} P_{\mathbb{G}}(c' \in \mathbf{c}(o) | \mathcal{I}_0, x)},$$

$$= P_{\mathbb{G}}(c \in \mathbf{c}(o) | \mathcal{I}_0, x).$$

The first equality is just an application of the standard formula for writing conditional probabilities. The second equality is implied by the definition of conditional independence. □

Proposition 12.1 There exist $\beta_A < 0$ and $\beta_T > 0$ such that

$$V(o_1 | \mathcal{I}) = \beta_A A(o | \mathcal{I}) + \beta_T \mathbf{T}(o | \mathcal{I}) + \epsilon_2, \tag{C.1}$$

where ϵ_2 is an error term, and $\mathcal{I}$ equals $\mathcal{I}^f$, $\{\mathcal{I}^f, x\}$, $\{\mathcal{I}^f, \mathbf{C}\}$ or $\{\mathcal{I}^f, \mathbf{C}, x\}$.

Proof. Postulate 12.1 holds that

$$V(o | \mathcal{I}) = \beta \phi(o | \mathcal{I}) + \epsilon_1.$$

The proposition follows immediately from substitution from postulate 11.2 which holds that

$$\phi(o | \mathcal{I}) = a A(o_1 | \mathcal{I}) + b \mathbf{T}_{\mathbf{C}}(o | \mathcal{I}) + \epsilon.$$

□

Proposition 12.2 Under automatic cognition and uncertain categorization, the valuation is either the typicality weighted concept valence, or the typicality weighted valence of the root.

$$V^a(o | \mathcal{I}^s) = \begin{cases} \mathfrak{v}_c T_c & \text{with probability } P(c | \mathcal{I}^s); \\ \mathfrak{v}_r T_r & \text{with probability } 1 - P(c | \mathcal{I}^s). \end{cases} \tag{C.2}$$

$$V^a(o | \mathcal{I}^s, x) = \begin{cases} \mathfrak{v}_c \tau_c(x) & \text{with probability } P(c | \mathcal{I}^s, x); \\ \mathfrak{v}_r \tau_r(x) & \text{with probability } 1 - P(c | \mathcal{I}^s, x). \end{cases} \tag{C.3}$$

Proof. Simple substitution of the values of $\mathcal{V}(o|c)$ and $\mathcal{V}(o|\emptyset)$ from postulate 12.2 and of $\mathcal{V}(o|c,x)$ and $\mathcal{V}(o|\emptyset,x)$ from postulate 12.3 into postulate 12.4 gives the result.   □

Proposition 12.3 *Under deliberate cognition and uncertainty about membership, then the valuation of the object equals the sum of (1) the valuation that would be obtained if it were seen as a member of the root concept and (2) an additional term that depends on the categorization probability and the difference between the typicality weighted valuations of the focal concept and the root.*

$$\mathcal{V}^d(o\,|\,\mathcal{I}) = \mathfrak{v}_r\,T_r + P(c\,|\,\mathcal{I}^s)(\mathfrak{v}_c\,T_c - \mathfrak{v}_r\,T_r). \tag{C.4}$$

$$\mathcal{V}^d(o\,|\,\mathcal{I},x) = \mathfrak{v}_r\,\tau_r(x) + P(c\,|\,\mathcal{I}^s,x)(\mathfrak{v}_c\,\tau_c(x) - \mathfrak{v}_r\,\tau_r(x)). \tag{C.5}$$

Proof. Simple substitution of the values of $\mathcal{V}(o|c)$ and $\mathcal{V}(o|\emptyset)$ from postulate 12.2 and of $\mathcal{V}(o|c,x)$ and $\mathcal{V}(o|\emptyset,x)$ from postulate 12.3 into postulate 12.5 and rearranging terms gives the result.   □

Lemma 12.1 *If the valence of the root is equal to 0,*

$$\mathcal{V}^d(o\,|\,\mathcal{I},x) = \mathfrak{v}_c\,\pi_{\mathbb{F}_c}(x\,|\,c)^2\left(\frac{P(c\,|\,\mathcal{I}^s)}{P_{\mathbb{F}_c}(x\,|\,\mathcal{I}^s)}\sum_{x'\in\mathbb{F}_c}\tau_c(x')\right). \tag{C.6}$$

Proof. The lemma is a reformulation of the second equation in proposition 12.3 (with $\mathfrak{v}_r = 0$) in terms of explicit formulæ for the typicality function and for categorization probability. For the typicality, we have, according to postulate 4.1 and equation 4.1,

$$\tau_c(x) = \pi_{\mathbb{F}_c}(x\,|\,c)\sum_{x'\in\mathbb{F}_c}\tau_c(x').$$

For the categorization probability, according to proposition 8.1, we have

$$P(c\,|\,\mathcal{I}_u^c) = \pi_{\mathbb{F}_c}(x\,|\,c)\frac{P(c\,|\,\mathcal{I}^c)}{P_{\mathbb{F}_c}(x\,|\,\mathcal{I}^c)}.$$

    □

Proposition 12.4 *Under automatic cognition and uncertain categorization in an exclusive-categorization context, there is no integration of information in* *the sense that the valuation is the valuation as a member of one of the candidate concepts.*

$$\mathcal{V}^a(o) = \begin{cases} \mathfrak{v}_{c_1} T_{c_1} & \text{with probability } P(c_1 \mid \mathcal{I}^e); \\ \mathfrak{v}_{c_2} T_{c_2} & \text{with probability } P(c_2 \mid \mathcal{I}^e). \end{cases} \tag{C.7}$$

$$\mathcal{V}^a(o \mid x) = \begin{cases} \mathfrak{v}_{c_1} \tau_{c_1}(x) & \text{with probability } P(c_1 \mid \mathcal{I}^e, x); \\ \mathfrak{v}_{c_2} \tau_{c_2}(x) & \text{with probability } P(c_2 \mid \mathcal{I}^e, x). \end{cases} \tag{C.8}$$

Proof. Simple substitution of the values of $\mathcal{V}(o \mid c)$ and $\mathcal{V}(o \mid \emptyset)$ from postulate 12.2 and of $\mathcal{V}(o \mid c, x)$ and $\mathcal{V}(o \mid \emptyset, x)$ from postulate 12.3 into postulate 12.6 gives the result. □

Proposition 12.5 *Under deliberate cognition and uncertainty about membership in an exclusive-categorization context, evaluation of the object is the weighted average of the typicality weighted concept valences.*

$$\mathcal{V}^d(o \mid \mathcal{I}^e) = \mathfrak{v}_{c_1} T_{c_1} P(c_1 \mid \mathcal{I}^e) + \mathfrak{v}_{c_2} T_{c_2} P(c_2 \mid \mathcal{I}^e). \tag{C.9}$$

$$\mathcal{V}^d(o \mid \mathcal{I}^e, x) = \mathfrak{v}_{c_1} \tau_{c_1}(x) P(c_1 \mid \mathcal{I}^e, x) + \mathfrak{v}_{c_2} \tau_{c_2}(x) P(c_2 \mid \mathcal{I}^e, x). \tag{C.10}$$

Proof. Simple substitution of the values of $\mathcal{V}(o \mid c)$ and $\mathcal{V}(o \mid \emptyset)$ from postulate 12.2 and of $\mathcal{V}(o \mid c, x)$ and $\mathcal{V}(o \mid \emptyset, x)$ from postulate 12.3 into postulate 12.7 gives the result. □

Lemma 12.2 *The adjustment parameter, θ, and the function, ζ, control valuation even when categorizations are uncertain.*

$$\mathcal{V}^d(o \mid \mathcal{I}^f) = \sum_{\substack{\mathbf{C} \in \mathfrak{C} \\ |\mathbf{C}| > 1}} (\theta \mathbf{V}(o \mid \mathcal{I}^f, \mathbf{C}) + \zeta(o \mid \mathcal{I}^f, \mathbf{C})) P(\mathbf{C} \mid \mathcal{I}^f)$$

$$+ \sum_{\{c\} \in \mathfrak{C}} \mathfrak{v}_c T_c P(\{c\} \mid \mathcal{I}^f). \tag{C.11}$$

$$\mathcal{V}^d(o \mid \mathcal{I}^f, x) = \sum_{\substack{\mathbf{C} \in \mathfrak{C} \\ |\mathbf{C}| > 1}} (\theta \mathbf{V}(o \mid \mathcal{I}^f, \mathbf{C}, x) + \zeta(o \mid \mathcal{I}^f, \mathbf{C}, x)) P(\mathbf{C} \mid \mathcal{I}^f, x)$$

$$+ \sum_{\{c\} \in \mathfrak{C}} \mathfrak{v}_c \tau_c(x) P(\{c\} \mid \mathcal{I}^f, x). \tag{C.12}$$

Proof. We provide the details only for the case where position is unknown since both formulas have the same structure. The reasoning for the second case is the same *mutatis mutandis*. First, we write the sum over $\mathbf{C} \in \mathfrak{C}$ from postulate 12.12 as two separate sums depending on the cardinal of $\mathbf{C}$. Then, we use substitutions afforded by postulates 12.2 and 12.9.

$$\mathcal{V}^d(o) = \sum_{\mathbf{C} \in \mathfrak{C}} \mathcal{V}(o \mid \mathbf{C}) P(\mathbf{C} \mid \mathcal{I}^f); \tag{C.13}$$

$$= \sum_{\substack{\mathbf{C} \in \mathfrak{C} \\ |\mathbf{C}| > 1}} \mathcal{V}(o \mid \mathbf{C}) P(\mathbf{C} \mid \mathcal{I}^f) + \sum_{\substack{\mathbf{C} \in \mathfrak{C} \\ |\mathbf{C}| = 1}} \mathcal{V}(o \mid \mathbf{C}) P(\mathbf{C} \mid \mathcal{I}^f); \tag{C.14}$$

$$= \sum_{\substack{\mathbf{C} \in \mathfrak{C} \\ |\mathbf{C}| > 1}} (\theta \mathbf{V}(o \mid x) + \zeta(o \mid \mathcal{I}^f, \mathbf{C}) P(\mathbf{C} \mid \mathcal{I}^f) + \sum_{\{c\} \in \mathfrak{C}} \mathfrak{v}_c \tau_c(x) P(\{c\} \mid \mathcal{I}^f).$$
$$\tag{C.15}$$

□

Proposition 12.6 *In the case of free, uncertain categorization, the valuation of an object declines with the ambiguity of the object.*

Proof. Again we give the proof for the case in which the position of the object is not observed; the case with known position follows *mutatis mutandis*. We have from lemma 12.2,

$$\mathcal{V}^d(o \mid \mathcal{I}^f) = \sum_{\substack{\mathbf{C} \in \mathfrak{C} \\ |\mathbf{C}| > 1}} (\theta \mathbf{V}(o \mid \mathcal{I}^f, \mathbf{C}) + \zeta(o \mid \mathcal{I}^f, \mathbf{C})) P(\mathbf{C} \mid \mathcal{I}^f)$$

$$+ \sum_{\{c\} \in \mathfrak{C}} \mathfrak{v}_c \, T_c \, P(\{c\} \mid \mathcal{I}^f).$$

Substitution from the aggregation postulate, postulate 12.9B

$$\zeta(o \mid \mathcal{I}^f, \mathbf{C}) = \lambda A(o \mid \mathcal{I}^f, \mathbf{C}) + \epsilon_3, \quad \lambda \leq 0$$

completes the proof. □

Lemma 14.1 *Consider an individual, a, and another, b, who is a member of group G. Assume that a has not observed any of b's categorizations for c ($\mathcal{I}_{ab}^c \neq \emptyset$). Moreover, let the conditions stated in the preamble of postulate 14.1 hold.*

Individual a's belief about the position of the object after an update is given by

$$P_{\mathbb{F}_c}^a(x \mid \mathcal{I}_2) = (1 - \Theta_{aG}(c)) P_{\mathbb{F}_c}^a(x \mid \mathcal{I}_1) + \Theta_{aG}(c) \pi_{\mathbb{F}_c}^a(x \mid c),$$

where

$$\Theta_{aG}(c) = P_{\mathbb{F}_c}^a(c \mid \mathcal{I}_1)^{1/\Omega_{aG}(c)}.$$

Proof. The lemma follows immediately from postulate 14.1 and meaning postulate 14.1: replace $\omega_{ab}(c)$ by $\Omega_{aG}(c)$ in equation 14.6. $\qquad\square$

Proposition 14.1 *The social influence coefficient, in notation ϑ_{ab}^c, increases with the taken-for-grantedness of the concept.*

Consider an individual a and another b who is a member of group G. Assume that a has observed at least some of b's categorizations for c, $\mathcal{I}_{ab}^c \neq \emptyset$. When the conditions stated in the preamble of postulate 14.1 hold and the prior on the concept is less than one $(P(c) < 1)$, then

$$\frac{\partial \vartheta_{ab}^c}{\partial \Omega_{aG}(c)} > 0.$$

Proof. The condition stated in the preamble brings postulate 14.1 into the picture. The proposition follows from equation 14.6 and postulate 14.3. $\qquad\square$

Proposition 14.2 *The taken-for-grantedness of a concept for an individual in the context of a social group is an increasing function of experienced extensional agreement with members of the group about that concept:*

$$[\text{A.}] \quad \frac{\partial \Omega_{aG}(c)}{\partial ea_{aj}(c)} > 0;$$

and it is an increasing function of experienced extensional agreement about the concepts in the domain of the focal concept (the cohort) with members of the group:

$$[\text{B.}] \quad \frac{\partial \Omega_{aG}(c)}{\partial ea_{aj}(\kappa)} > 0.$$

Proof. The two parts of the conclusion follow by an application of the cut rule to postulate 14.4 and to postulate 14.5. $\qquad\square$

Proposition 14.3 The taken-for-grantedness of a concept in group is increasing with experienced extensional agreement about that concept.

$$\frac{\partial \Omega_{aG}(c)}{\partial \overline{ea}_G(c)} > 0.$$

Proof. Definition 14.1 and Auxiliary Assumption 14.1 imply:

$$\overline{\Omega}_G(c) = \alpha + \beta \frac{1}{|G|} \sum_{a \in G} e a_{aj}(c). \tag{C.16}$$

Note that the definition of **j** (equation 14.10) implies that $e a_{aj}(c) = e a_{aG}(c)$. This, and definition 13.2C imply

$$\frac{1}{|G|} \sum_{a \in G} e a_{aj}(c) = \overline{e a}_G(c).$$

Using this relation in equation C.16, we get:

$$\overline{\Omega}_G(c) = \alpha + \beta \, \overline{e a}_G(c).$$

The proposition follows from this equation and the fact that $\beta > 0$.   □

Notes

Preface

1. In social contexts like markets, individuals can and do use concepts strategically, for example, when top managers categorize their firms as belonging to a certain industry in order to facilitate the selection of a more favorable comparison group for use in determining their compensation. For us, however, the broader and more general issue is that concepts generally affect how individuals interpret information, especially in settings where they are not using them in an active, conscious, and strategic manner.

2. We have relegated some technical details to the appendix, which provides a glossary of technical terms, brief discussion of the most relevant tools from first-order logic, and the proofs of all propositions and lemmas.

1. Concepts in Sociological Analysis

1. Wuthnow and Witten (1987), DiMaggio (1997), and Patterson (2014) provide detailed critiques.

2. Preliminaries

1. For linguists, a "speech community" refers to a group of people who share a set of norms and expectations regarding how their language should be used (Gumperz, 1968; Holmes, 2013).

2. This claim refers to concepts in natural settings. The example of prime number is characteristic of the desired crispness of concepts in formal languages such as mathematics. In this book, we consider only concepts that are used in so-called natural languages.

3. Wittgenstein's analysis presupposes a consensual labeling of the objects that belong in some sense to the focal concept: members of a family show family resemblances, objects that are called games resemble each other, and so on. On the other hand, he keeps open the question of whether such resemblances cause objects to share a label.

4. We find this language confusing. We prefer to distinguish features (functions) and feature values (the output of the functions applied to objects).

5. This research finds that the size of the transformation step entailed in deleting a component from an object is smaller than that of adding one.

6. Extensive research shows that people are subject to metacognitive myopia (Fiedler, 2012). This means that we can often recall the decisions and inferences that we made but cannot recall well the contexts and information sets that shaped the inferences and decisions.

7. The class of Bayesian rational models on which we build in subsequent chapters increasingly finds ways to build bridges between the computational and algorithmic levels (Griffiths, Lieder, and Goodman, 2015). A more nuanced statement of our position is that we think sociological work should exploit such developments, beginning at the computational level.

3. Semantic Space

1. Throughout we assume that the label c is part of the language of the focal person, not of the researcher. That is, it is part of the object language.

2. Impressionist painting is a subconcept (or subgenre) of painting. As we discuss in chapter 7, subconcepts inherit properties of their "parents." In characterizing the subconcept, people usually do not need to make reference to the inherited properties.

3. Albums can be assigned to more than one style.

4. Concepts as Probability Densities in Semantic Space

1. It might seem to be overkill to index the semantic space by the concept. However, in subsequent chapters, we will analyze concepts over

expanded feature spaces, and it will prove helpful to change the index on the semantic space as the context of the analysis changes.

2. The question of how the mind performs the computations is addressed by another class of models referred to as algorithmic models. These models, such as Medin and Schaffer's (1978) exemplar model, specify the sequence of basic operations that the mind performs to complete a complicated task, such as categorizing an object representation.

3. Note that this representation of similarity pins it down to a given set of features, those entailed by meaning of the focal concept. This narrowing eliminates the glaring problems of the ill-defined character of similarity discussed in chapter 3.

4. To be true to the threshold model, we should add that there is a bound on this claim. In the interest of generality, we keep things simple.

5. Here we follow Pontikes and Hannan (2014), whose postulate 1 specifies this same relationship in a parametric form: a negative exponential. Our proposition builds on weaker assumptions about the underlying relationships.

6. Twenty-one participants were recruited via Amazon Mechanical Turk and completed the experiments as Qualtrics online surveys. Five participants failed to pass our attention checks. The data analyzed below includes 16 participants.

7. For simplicity, we focus only on the Akka style at this stage. Similar results hold for the other style.

8. Suppose that y is the position of the Akka prototype and x is the position of a stimulus. We assume that the Euclidean distance, $|x - y|$, is proportional to the psychological distance, $d(x, y)$.

9. The parameters were obtained by MLE.

10. We run topic models using tracks (songs) as documents. We average over tracks to locate albums in feature space. Alternatively, we could have used albums as documents. But using tracks as documents allows us to employ more complex metrics in the future, such as the variance of an album's tracks in feature space.

11. Specifically we multiply the normalized album matrix by the transpose of the normalized style matrix.

5. Conceptual Spaces: Domains and Cohorts

1. Here we adapt a modified version of the formulation of Collins and Quillian (1969) and Brachman (1983).

2. Obvious counterexamples arise when a term for a subconcept appears in a number of domains and the higher-level concept needs reference for disambiguation. For instance, we generally speak of folk music and folk dance because folk can refer to either.

3. We face this issue in modeling the assignment of multiple concepts in chapter 9, the effect of conceptual structure on perception (the perceptual-magnet effect) in chapter 10, the definition of categorical ambiguity in chapter 11, and modeling of social inference and the emergence of taken for grantedness in chapter 14.

4. Here the distance notion is neither the distance in the semantic space nor the distance between the concepts as probability-density functions; in this context, the distance is the graph distance measured within a domain, along the IS-A relation.

7. Informativeness and Distinctiveness

1. In the next chapter, which makes heavy use of Bayes' theorem, we will refer to $P_{\mathbb{G}}(\cdot \mid r)$ as the "prior" on positions in the domain.

2. Murphy (2002) acknowledges this kind of context dependence.

8. Categories and Categorization

1. There might be a complicated time structure that depends on memory, but we do not address this issue here.

2. For example, in §8.8 we consider a standard model that treats a person as applying the "best" or "most appropriate" of a set of candidate concepts to an object; and in chapter 9 we generalize the judgment situation to one in which a person might apply several concepts in the same cohort to an object.

3. The subject can decline to categorize the object. We do not need to represent the option "decline" explicitly because the probability of declining to categorize simply equals one minus the probability of categorization.

4. In some subsequent chapters we express the information update on learning the position of the object as a change in the person's information state from $\mathcal{I}_0$ to $\mathcal{I}_1 \equiv \mathcal{I}_0 \wedge (R_{\mathbb{F}_c}(o) = x)$. Those who find this kind of expression more congenial can, in reading the formulas here, globally replace $f(\cdot \mid \mathcal{I}_0, x)$ with $f(\cdot \mid \mathcal{I}_1)$.

5. This assumption is most credible over short time spans. We do not complicate the analysis by bringing such issues into the picture.

6. Research on decision making suggests that the context can affect the nature of the semantic space associated with the focal concept: thinking about a feature dimension might increase the weight of values on this dimension in the categorization decision. For simplicity, we do not incorporate this kind of effect in our model. Interested readers can build on our model to provide new ways of thinking about such effects.

7. Pontikes and Hannan (2014) derived this relationship from slightly different premises.

8. Fiske and Taylor (2017) provide a useful review.

9. In exclusive categorization settings, to avoid overly complicated notation, we will write $\{c \in \mathfrak{C}\}$ to refer to the set of single categorizations (formally, this should be written $\{c : \{c\} \in \mathfrak{C}\}$).

10. We use this basic result of probability theory repeatedly. In the relevant discrete probability case, suppose that $\mathbf{B}$ consists of a set of mutually exclusive events (the set of events partitions the sample space). The law of total probability holds that

$$\Pr(A) = \sum_{B \in \mathbf{B}} \Pr(A \mid B) \cdot \Pr(B).$$

11. These applications have sparked considerable controversy. Hahn (2014) provides sketches of the influential critiques of Bayesian work in cognitive psychology as well as convincing counterarguments.

9. Free Categorization

1. Descriptive content includes basic information on artists and their released recordings such as names, titles, year of release, and production credits, indicating the personnel involved in the recording of an album.

2. Classical recordings are also reviewed by Allmusic.com, but we excluded them from this descriptive analysis because recordings map less clearly to music compositions. For example, the same symphony has been recorded multiple times, and not all movements of the same symphony are recorded together.

3. This publication that provides detailed information on all feature films released in the United States, including the names of the production and distribution companies, release date, cast, and genre. Experts generally consider the AFI Catalog the most complete and comprehensive source on the film industry (Mezias and Mezias, 2000; Cattani et al., 2008; Hsu et al., 2012).

4. Sometimes firms claim multiple memberships that correspond to an array of products, but frequently producers have one product or one suite of products that they view as fitting more than one category.

5. These data differ from the others just described in that objects are not directly assigned to categories by one individual. Instead, the firm's analysts produce lists of firms that participate in the subindustries, from which firm categorization can be obtained.

6. Research on machine learning calls this multiple classification (Tsoumakis and Katakis, 2007).

7. In machine learning this is called the binary relevance method: binary classifiers are created for each label and the label assignment to an object is the result of the set of binary classifications (Read, Pfahringer, Holmes, and Frank, 2011).

8. In this example, we do not index the probabilities by the semantic space because the space is the same for the two concepts.

9. Specifically, there is a sharp decrease from the fourth to the fifth dimension, and plots of the stimuli in a four-dimensional space comes very close to reproducing what is expected if the designed dimensions are the perceived dimensions.

10. A t-statistic computed for the two stimuli that lie inside the span of the prototypes comparing the probability of the choice "both style" relative to the prediction under conditional independence is 7.26 ($p = 0.01$); the test statistic for the response "neither style" equals -3.78 ($p = 0.03$).

11. Parallel tests statistics to those noted in the previous footnote for the two stimuli that lie outside the span equal 1.35 ($p = 0.15$) and -1.72 ($p = 0.11$).

10. Concepts, Perception, and Inference

1. The stimulus sounds were generated using a standard psychophysical scale; this procedure gives a measurement of distances among the stimuli.

2. Lupyan (2012) proposes a label-feedback hypothesis and suggests that language produces a transient modulation of perceptual and cognitive processing that is rapid and automatic and that changes the structure and content of thought. For example, labeling enhances search (Lupyan, 2008a) and distorts memory—specifically along dimensions associated with the category label (Lupyan, 2008b). As a result, invoking a category label activates perceptual representations of the label, resulting in a "temporary warping of the perceptual space," similar to how Kuhl defined the magnet effect. For example, when the label green is activated, "greens [are] pushed together and/or greens are dragged further from non-greens" (Lupyan, 2012, p. 4).

3. To this point in the book, we have not considered position to be stochastic. Treating position as deterministic made sense given that we were not considering noise in perception.

4. Like elsewhere in the book, we use capital letters to refer to random variables and lower-case letters to refer to realizations of random variables.

5. The first two sets of stimuli are drawn from Landau and Shipley (2001), and the third set of stimuli contains the stylized arrowheads employed in the experiments described in chapter 4.

6. For the first two pairs, the two anchor images are standards that lie at the opposite ends of a space defined by changes in object shape. The first two sets are, respectively, objects 2 and 6 of Landau and Shipley's set. The image at the top corresponds to their object 4, and it has an intermediate shape equidistant in shape from the two standards that was created using a morph distance from a commercially available morphing package. The third set uses arrow widths of 4 and 20, and the image at the top has a width of 12.

7. We recruited subjects on Amazon Mechanical Turk (mturk.com). A total of 848 adults who responded to the announcement and passed the attention checks in the survey are included in the analysis. Each subject was assigned to one of the three object sets.

8. The order of the standard objects at the bottom was randomized, as was which image was assigned which label. We verified that order did not change results using the first two sets of images, and we did not randomize the left/right order or which image was assigned the label for the Akka/Boko object set that was run after.

9. ANOVA tests are significant at $p = 0.01$.

10. In an ANOVA test, there is a significant difference between the no-label and different-label conditions for the Blicket/Steb objects $(F(1,311) = 4.53, p = 0.03)$, but the difference between the no-label and same-label conditions is not significantly different from zero. For the Fendel/Stad and Akka/Boko objects, there is a significant difference between no-label and same-label conditions $(F(1,327) = 3.60, p = 0.06$ for Fendel/Stad; $F(1,1,055) = 9.43, p < 0.01$ for Akka/Boko) but the difference between the no-label and different-label conditions is not significant.

11. A total of 196 adults were recruited on Mechanical Turk using the same procedure described for Study 1. An additional ten subjects did not pass the attention check and were excluded from this analysis.

12. Participants rate similarities to both prototypes on each trial.

13. We define this as the entire range on the outside of each prototype, and within sixteen units toward the other prototype.

14. Mean difference close to the prototype (16 units or less) equals 0.93 (std. err. $= 0.37$), and mean difference distant from the prototype (more than 16 units) equals -0.21. A t-test shows that the difference in differences is significant at $p = 0.02$.

15. Mean difference for outside space (width thinner than Akka or larger than Boko) equals 1.40 (std. err. $= 0.52$), and mean difference for inside space (width between the prototypes) equals 0.02. A t-test shows that the difference in differences is significant at $p = 0.02$.

16. Our empirical estimates of typicality functions from the arrowhead experiments (figure 4.2b) do not show this pattern, however.

11. Conceptual Ambiguity and Contrast

1. In these data, albums can be assigned to more than one style. We therefore divide by the total number of album-style pairs.

2. Ambiguity is binned by rounding to the nearest whole number.

3. The dataset that Kovács and Hannan (2015) analyze actually contains a restaurant with this dual categorization.

4. Different functional forms might be used. This choice has the advantage of simplicity and, as we will show below, of easy generalization to inclusion of distances among categories.

5. For a detailed discussion of alternative similarity and dissimilarity measures, see Batagelj and Bren (1995).

6. The reason we add one to average conceptual ambiguity in the denominator is purely technical. This ensures that contrast is mathematically defined when average conceptual ambiguity is equal to zero.

12. Valuation

1. We are well aware that a number of cognitive psychologists see this distinction as too coarse and underspecified. Yet, we feel that given our audience and the state of development of the theory, this level of theoretical specificity is the most appropriate at this stage.

2. The central, and still unresolved, debate in the literature on feature inference under uncertain categorization concerns whether and when people rely on just one category (presumably the most likely one) to infer the unobserved feature value, or integrate across candidate categories. We do not directly address this issue here because the setting of this chapter is valuation, not feature inference. Yet, our proposal that the propensity to integrate

information across categories depends on the mode of cognition could apply to feature inference under uncertain categorization. Investigating this conjecture empirically both in the setting of valuation and in the setting of feature inference is an exciting avenue for future research. See Murphy, Chen, and Ross (2012a).

3. A note of caution is needed in evaluating this finding. This study, like all non-experimental studies of the subject, infers the locations of concepts and measures typicality using data on all of the evaluators. Our model applies to individuals. It is possible that the people who appear to like ambiguous items have unusual conceptual spaces and that the items that they like have low conceptual ambiguity when viewed in their spaces.

4. In all regressions, we include year and reviewer fixed effects. We also control for the restaurant's price, as well as the total count of words in the focal review. Table 12.1 presents results with robust standard errors, but we note that the results are robust to other model specification (e.g., Poisson) and standard error calculations as well (e.g., clustered S.E.).

5. The pattern of results is robust to choice of stochastic specifications, such as Poisson and ordered logit. In all regressions, we include year fixed effects and reviewer fixed effects, and the restaurant's price, as well as the total count of words in the review.

13. The Group Level: Conceptual and Extensional Agreement

1. The meaning of c for the individual a, denoted by $[\![c]\!]^a$, is given by a probability-density function over the semantic space that a associates with c, namely $\mathbb{F}_c^a$: $[\![c]\!]^a = \pi_{\mathbb{F}_c^a}(x \mid c)$. Equivalently, and to achieve consistency with the notation used in the definition of distance, we write: $[\![c]\!]^a = \pi_{\mathbb{F}_{c_a}}(x \mid c^a)$, where $\mathbb{F}_{c_a} \equiv \mathbb{F}_c^a$ denotes the semantic space that a associates with concept label c and $\pi_{\mathbb{F}_c^a}(\cdot \mid c) \equiv \pi_{\mathbb{F}_{c_a}}(\cdot \mid c^a)$ denotes the concept likelihood of concept c for individual a.

14. Social Inference and Taken-for-Grantedness

1. Below we introduce a more complicated notation that reflects the fact that $\omega_{ab}(c)$ depends on the information a possesses about b's past categorization behavior. Additional model elements need to be introduced for this notation to be understandable by the reader, so for now we use $\omega_{ab}(c)$, to be understood as a simplified notation.

2. The relevant cohort comes from a's mental representation of the domain $\mathfrak{D}_r$.

3. Because $\mathbb{G} = \mathbb{F}_c$ for this case, we can write all of these expressions in terms of $\mathbb{F}_c$ the (unexpanded) semantic space for the concept c.

4. This expression is not strictly defined for $\omega_{ab}(c \mid \mathcal{I}_{ab}^c) = 0$, but it is possible to extend it to this case (by continuity) by looking at the limiting behavior of the expression as $\omega_{ab}(c \mid \mathcal{I}_{ab}^c)$ goes to 0. In this case, the exponent becomes infinitely large. If the prior on concept c, $P^a(c \mid \mathcal{I}_1)$, is lower than 1, then $\vartheta_{ab}^s = 0$. Otherwise, $\vartheta_{ab}^s = 1$.

5. Note that $\omega_{ab}(c \mid \mathcal{I}_{ab}^c) = \omega_{ab}(c \mid \mathcal{I}_1)$. We could have used $\omega_{ab}(c \mid \mathcal{I}_1)$ in equation 14.6, but we believe that the current formulation is more explicit and thus easier for the reader to understand and interpret.

6. We believe it is possible to formulate a specific Bayesian model of how taken-for-grantedness affects a's propensity to accept the categorization by another individual, b. In this model, taken-for-grantedness would be the prior on $\omega_{ab}(c \mid \mathcal{I}_{ab}^c)$ because if $\mathcal{I}_{ab}^c = \emptyset$, then $\omega_{ab}(c \mid \mathcal{I}_{ab}^c) = \Omega_{aG}(c)$. If $\mathcal{I}_{ab}^c \neq \emptyset$, then $\omega_{ab}(c \mid \mathcal{I}_{ab}^c)$ would be the (Bayesian) posterior obtained by updating the prior (taken-for-grantedness) based on the information captured in $\mathcal{I}_{ab}^c$. We leave development of this idea for future work.

7. We do not have to assume that a belongs to G. In this case, $G \backslash \{a\} = G$. The postulates and proposition apply without any change.

8. Because $\mathbb{G} = \mathbb{F}_c$, we can write all of these expressions in terms of $\mathbb{F}_c$, the (unexpanded) semantic space for the concept c.

9. Note that postulate 8.2 implies that $P_{\mathbb{F}_c}^a(x \mid \mathcal{I}_1 \cup c) = \pi_{\mathbb{F}_c}^a(x \mid c)$.

Bibliography

Alter, Adam L. and Daniel M. Oppenheimer. 2008. "Easy on the Mind, Easy on the Wallet: The Roles of Familiarity and Processing Fluency in Valuation Judgments." *Psychonomic Bulletin and Review* 15:985–990.

Altman, Rick. 1999. *Film/Genre*. London: British Film Institute.

Anderson, John R. 1991. "The Adaptive Nature of Human Categorization." *Psychological Review* 98:409–429.

ArtMovements. 2016. "Impressionism." http://www.artmovements.co. uk/impressionism.htm/nggallery/page/1.

Ashby, F. Gregory and Leola A. Alfonso-Reese. 1995. "Categorization as Probability Density Estimation." *Journal of Mathematical Psychology* 39:216–233.

Bargh, John. 1994. "The Four Horsemen of Automaticity: Awareness, Intention, Efficiency, and Control in Social Cognition." In *Handbook of Social Cognition*, edited by Robert Wyer and Thomas Srull, chapter 4. New York: Psychology Press.

Bargh, John. 1997. "The Automaticity of Everyday Life." In *Advances in Social Cognition*, edited by Robert Wyer, volume 10, pp. 1–61. Mahwah, NJ: Erlbaum.

Batagelj, Vladimir and Matevz Bren. 1995. "Comparing Resemblance Measures." *Journal of Classification* 12:73–90.

Berger, Peter L. and Thomas Luckmann. 1966. *The Social Construction of Reality*. Garden City, N.Y.: Anchor Doubleday.

Bernoulli, Daniel. 1738. "Specimen Theoriae Novae de Mensura Sortis." *Commentarii Academiae Scientiarum Imperialis Petropolitanae* 5.

Blau, Peter M. and Otis Dudley Duncan. 1967. *The American Occupational Structure*. New York: Wiley.

Blei, David M. 2012. "Probabilistic Topic Models." *Communications of the ACM* 55:77–84.

Blei, David M., Andrew Y. Ng, and Michael I. Jordan. 2003. "Latent Dirichlet Allocation." *The Journal of Machine Learning Research* 3:993–1022.

Brachman, Ronald J. 1983. "What IS-A Is and Isn't: An Analysis of Taxonomic Links in Semantic Networks." *IEEE Computer* 16:30–36.

Brooks, Lee R., Geoffrey R. Norman, and Scott W. Allen. 1991. "Role of Specific Similarity in a Medical Diagnosis Task." *Journal of Experimental Psychology: General* 120:1035–1042.

Carnabuci, Gianluca, Elisa Operti, and Balázs Kovács. 2015. "The Categorical Imperative and Structural Reproduction: Dynamics of Technological Entry in the Semiconductor Industry." *Organization Science* 26:1734–1751.

Carroll, Glenn R. and Michael T. Hannan. 2000. *The Demography of Corporations and Industries.* Princeton, N.J.: Princeton University Press.

Carroll, Glenn R. and Anand Swaminathan. 2000. "Why the Microbrewery Movement? Organizational Dynamics of Resource Partitioning in the U.S. Brewing Industry." *American Journal of Sociology* 106:715–762.

Cattani, Gino, Simone Ferriani, Giacomo Negro, and Fabrizio Perretti. 2008. "The Structure of Consensus: Network Ties, Legitimation, and Exit Rates of U.S. Feature Film Producer Organizations." *Administrative Science Quarterly* 53:145–182.

Chater, Nick and George Lowenstein. 2016. "The Under-appreciated Drive for Sense-Making." *Journal of Economic Behavior and Organization* 126 (Part B):137–154.

Chater, Nick and Paul M. B. Vitányi. 2003. "The Generalized Universal Law of Generalization." *Journal of Mathematical Psychology* 47:346–369.

Cimoli, Mario and Giovanni Dosi. 1995. "Technological Paradigms, Patterns of Learning and Development: An Introductory Roadmap." *Journal of Evolutionary Economics* 5:243–268.

Collins, Allan M. and Ross M. Quillian. 1969. "Retrieval Time From Semantic Memory." *Journal of Verbal Learning and Verbal Behavior* 8: 241–248.

Colyvas, Jeannette A. and Walter W. Powell. 2006. "Roads to Institutionalization: The Remaking of Boundaries between Public and Private Science." *Research in Organizational Behavior* 27:315–363.

Dancyger, Ken and Jeff Rush. 2002. *Alternative Scriptwriting: Successfully Breaking the Rules.* Boston: Focal Press, 3rd edition.

D'Andrade, Roy. 1984. "Cultural Meaning Systems." In *Culture Theory: Essays on Mind, Self and Emotion*, edited by R. A. Shweder and R. A. Levine. Cambridge: Cambridge University Press.

D'Andrade, Roy. 1995. *The Development of Cognitive Anthropology*. Cambridge: Cambridge University Press.

Davidoff, Jules, Ian Davies, and Debi Roberson. 1999. "Color Categories in a Stone-age Tribe." *Nature* 398:203–204.

DiMaggio, Paul J. 1987. "Classification in Art." *American Sociological Review* 52:440–455.

DiMaggio, Paul J. 1997. "Culture and Cognition." *Annual Review of Sociology* 23:263–287.

DiMaggio, Paul J., Manish Nag, and David M. Blei. 2013. "Exploiting Affinities Between Topic Modeling and the Sociological Perspective on Culture: Application to Newspaper Coverage of U.S. Government Arts Funding." *Poetics* 41:570–606.

Dosi, Giovanni. 1982. "Technological Paradigms and Technological Trajectories: A Suggested Interpretation of the Determinants and Directions of Technical Change." *Research Policy* 11:147–162.

Douglas, Mary. 2008 [1966]. *Purity and Danger*. Cambridge, Mass.: Harvard University Press.

Dovidio, John, Nancy Evans, and Richard Tyler. 1986. "Racial Stereotypes: The Contents of their Cognitive Representations." *Journal of Experimental and Social Psychology* 22:22–37.

Dovidio, John, Kerry Kawakami, Craig Johnson, Brenda Johnson, and Adaiah Howard. 1997. "On the Nature of Prejudice: Automatic and Controlled Processes." *Journal of Experimental Social Psychology* 33:510–540.

Dry, Matthew J. and Gert Storms. 2010. "Features of Graded Category Structure: Generalizing the Family Resemblence and Polymorphous Concept Models." *Acta Psychologica* 133:244–255.

Dubuisson, Marie-Pierre and Anil K. Jain. 1994. "A Modified Hausdorff Distance for Object Matching." In *Proceedings of the 12th International Conference on Pattern Recognition*, volume 1, pp. 566–568. IEEE Comput. Soc. Press.

Durand, Rodolphe and Lionel Paolella. 2012. "Category Stretching: Reorienting Research on Categories in Strategy, Entrepreneurship, and Organization Theory." *Journal of Management Studies* 50:1100–1123.

Durkheim, Émile and Marcel Mauss. 1969 [1903]. *Primitive Classification*. London: Routledge.

Feldman, Naomi H. and Thomas L. Griffiths. 2007. "A Rational Account of the Perceptual Magnet Effect." In *Proceedings of the 29th Annual Conference of the Cognitive Science Society*, pp. 258–262.

Feldman, Naomi H., Thomas L. Griffiths, and James L. Morgan. 2009. "The Influence of Categories on Perception: Explaining the Perceptual Magnet Effect as Optimal Statistical Inference." *Psychological Review* 116:752–782.

Fiedler, Klaus. 2012. "Meta-Cognitive Myopia and the Dilemmas of Inductive Statistical Inference." *Psychology of Learning and Motivation* 57: 1–55.

Fiske, Susan T. and Shelley E. Taylor. 2017. *Social Cognition: From Brains to Culture*. Thousand Oaks, CA: Sage, second edition.

Fleming, Lee. 2001. "Recombinant Uncertainty in Technological Search." *Management Science* 47:117–132.

Fleming, Lee and Olav Sorenson. 2004. "Science as a Map in Technological Search." *Strategic Management Journal* 25:909–928.

Galinsky, Adam, Paul Martoran, and Gillian Ku. 2003. "To Control or Not to Control Stereotypes." In *Social Judgements: Implicit and Explicit Processes*, edited by Joseph Forgas, Kipling Williams, and William von Hippel, chapter 17. Cambridge: Cambridge University Press.

Gärdenfors, Peter. 2004. *Conceptual Spaces: The Geometry of Thought*. Cambridge, Mass.: MIT Press.

Gärdenfors, Peter. 2014. *The Geometry of Meaning: Semantics Based on Conceptual Spaces*. Cambridge Mass.: MIT Press.

Geertz, Clifford. 1983. *Local Knowledge*. New York: Basic Books.

Goffman, Erving. 1959. *The Presentation of Self in Everyday Life*. Garden City, N.Y.: Anchor Doubleday.

Goffman, Erving. 1963. *Stigma: Notes on the Management of Spoiled Identity*. Englewood Cliffs, N.J.: Prentice Hall.

Goldberg, Amir, Michael T. Hannan, and Balázs Kovács. 2016. "What Does It Mean to Span Cultural Boundaries? Variety and Atypicality in Cultural Consumption." *American Sociological Review* 81:215–241.

Goldstone, Robert L., Yvonne Lippa, and Richard M. Shiffrin. 2001. "Altering Object Representations Through Category Learning." *Cognition* 78:27–43.

Goode, William J. 1978. *The Celebration of Heroes: Prestige as a Control System*. Berkeley and Los Angeles: University of California Press.

Goodman, Nelson. 1972. "Seven Strictures on Similarity." In *Problems and Projects*, pp. 437–447. Indianapolis, Ind.: Bobbs–Merril.

Griffiths, Oren, Brett K. Hayes, and Ben R. Newell. 2012. "Feature-based Versus Category-based Induction with Uncertain Categories." *Journal of Experimental Psychology: Learning, Memory, and Cognition* 38:576–595.

Griffiths, Thomas L. 2004. *Causes, Coincidences, and Theories*. Ph.D. thesis, Stanford University.

Griffiths, Thomas L., Falk Lieder, and Noah D. Goodman. 2015. "Rational Use of Cognitive Resources: Levels of Analysis Between Computational and Algorithmic." *Topics in Cognitive Science* 7:217–229.

Gumperz, John. 1968. "The Speech Community." In *International Encyclopaedia of the Social Sciences*, pp. 381–386. New York: Macmillan.

Hahn, Ulrike. 2014. "The Bayesian Boom: Good Thing or Bad?" *Frontiers in Psychology* 5:1–12.

Hahn, Ulrike, Nick Chater, and Lucy B. Richardson. 2003. "Similarity as Transformation." *Cognition* 87:1–32.

Hahn, Ulrike, James Close, and Markus Graf. 2009. "Transformation Direction Influences Shape-Similarity Judgments." *Psychological Science* 20:447–454.

Hampton, James A. 1979. "Polymorphous Concepts in Semantic Memory." *Journal of Verbal Learning and Verbal Behavior* 18:441–461.

Hampton, James A. 1982. "A Demonstration of the Intransitivity of Natural Categories." *Cognition* 12:151–164.

Hampton, James A. 1987. "Inheritance of Attributes in Natural Concept Conjunctions." *Memory and Cognition* 15:55–71.

Hampton, James A. 1991. "The Combination of Prototype Concepts." In *The Psychology of Word Meanings*, edited by Paula J. Schwanenflugel. Hillsdale, N.J.: Earlbaum.

Hampton, James A. 1995. "Testing the Prototype Theory of Concepts." *Journal of Memory and Language* 34:686–708.

Hampton, James A. 1997. "Conceptual Combination: Conjunction and Negation of Natural Concepts." *Memory and Cognition* 25:888–909.

Hampton, James A. 2007. "Typicality, Graded Membership, and Vagueness." *Cognitive Science* 31:355–383.

Hannan, Michael T. 2005. "Ecologies of Organizations: Diversity and Identity." *Journal of Economic Perspectives* 19:51–70.

Hannan, Michael T. 2010. "Partiality of Memberships in Categories and Audiences." *Annual Review of Sociology* 36:159–181.

Hannan, Michael T. and John Freeman. 1983. "Niche Width and the Dynamics of Organizational Populations." *American Journal of Sociology* 88:1116–1145.

Hannan, Michael T. and John Freeman. 1989. *Organizational Ecology.* Cambridge, Mass.: Harvard University Press.

Hannan, Michael T., László Pólos, and Glenn R. Carroll. 2007. *Logics of Organization Theory: Audiences, Codes, and Ecologies.* Princeton: Princeton University Press.

Harnad, Stevan. 1987a. *Categorical Perception: The Groundwork of Cognition.* Cambridge: Cambridge University Press.

Harnad, Stevan. 1987b. "Introduction: Psychophysical and Cognitive Aspects of Categorical Perception: An Overview." In *Categorical Perception: The Groundwork of Cognition,* edited by Stevan Harnad, pp. 1–29. New York: Cambridge University Press.

Heaney, Michael T. and Fabio Rojas. 2014. "Hybrid Activism: Social Movement Mobilization in a Multi-Movement Environment." *American Journal of Sociology* 119:1047–1103.

Hoberg, Gerard and Gordon Phillips. 2016. "Text-Based Network Industries and Endogenous Product Differentiation." *Journal of Political Economy* 124:1423–1465.

Holmes, Janet. 2013. *An Introduction to Sociolinguistics.* London: Routledge.

Hsu, Greta. 2006. "Jacks of All Trades and Masters of None: Audiences' Reactions to Spanning Genres in Feature Film Production." *Administrative Science Quarterly* 51:420–450.

Hsu, Greta and Stine Grodal. 2015. "Category Taken-for-Grantedness as a Strategic Opportunity: The Case of Light Cigarettes, 1964 to 1993." *American Sociological Review* 80:28–62.

Hsu, Greta and Michael T. Hannan. 2005. "Identities, Genres, and Organizational Forms." *Organization Science* 16:474–490.

Hsu, Greta, Michael T. Hannan, and Özgeçan Koçak. 2009. "Multiple Category Memberships in Markets: An Integrative Theory and Two Empirical Tests." *American Sociological Review* 74:150–169.

Hsu, Greta, Michael T. Hannan, and László Pólos. 2011. "Typecasting, Legitimation, and Form Emergence: A Formal Theory." *Sociological Theory* 29:97–123.

Hsu, Greta, Giacomo Negro, and Fabrizio Perretti. 2012. "Hybrids in Hollywood: A Study of the Production Performance of Genre Spanning Films." *Industrial and Corporate Change* 21:459–487.

Jaccard, Paul. 1901. "Étude Comparative de la Distribution Florale dans une Portion des Alpes et des Jura." *Bulletin de la Société Vaudoise des Sciences Naturelles* 37:547–579.

Jepperson, Ronald L. 1991. "Institutions, Institutional Effects, and Institutionalism." In *The New Institutionalism in Organizational Analysis*, edited by W. W. Powell and P. J. DiMaggio, pp. 143–163. Chicago: University of Chicago Press.

Kahneman, Daniel. 2011. *Thinking Fast and Slow*. New York: Farr, Strauss, and Giroux.

Kawakami, Kerry, John Dovidio, Jasper Moll, Sander Hermsen, and Abby Russin. 2000. "Just Say No (to Stereotyping): Effects of Training in the Negation of Stereotypic Associations on Stereotype Activation." *Journal of Personality and Social Psychology* 78:871–886.

Kay, Paul and Willett Kempton. 1984. "What is the Sapir-Whorf Hypothesis?" *American Anthropologist* 86:65–79.

Keller, Joshua and Jeffrey Loewenstein. 2011. "The Cultural Category of Cooperation: A Cultural Consensus Model Analysis for China and the United States." *Organization Science* 22:299–319.

Kenny, Charles. 2016. "Developing? Nay! Shun!" *Slate*.

Konovalova, Elizaveta and Gaël Le Mens. 2016. "Predictions with Uncertain Categorization: A Rational Model." In *Proceedings of the 38th Annual Conference of the Cognitive Science Society*, edited by J. Trueswell, A. Papafragou, and D. Grodner, D. and Mirman, pp. 722–727. Austin, TX.

Konovalova, Elizaveta and Gaël Le Mens. 2018. "Feature Inference with Uncertain Categorization: Re-assessing Anderson's Rational Model." *Psychonomic Bulletin & Review* 25:1666–1681.

Kovács, Balázs, Gianluca Carnabuci, and Filippo Carlo Wezel. 2017. "Patent Class Contrast and the Impact of Technological Innovations."

Kovács, Balázs, Glenn R. Carroll, and David W. Lehman. 2014. "Value and Categories in Socially Constructed Authenticity: Empirical Tests from Restaurant Reviews." *Organization Science* 25:458–478.

Kovács, Balázs and Michael T. Hannan. 2010. "The Consequences of Category Spanning Depend on Contrast." *Research in the Sociology of Organizations* 31:175–201.

Kovács, Balázs and Michael T. Hannan. 2015. "Conceptual Spaces and the Consequences of Category Spanning." *Sociological Science* 2:252–286.

Kuhl, Patricia K. 1991. "Human Adults and Human Infants Show a "Perceptual Magnet Effect" for the Prototypes of Speech Categories, Monkeys Do Not." *Perception & Psychophysics* 50:93–107.

Lakatos, Imre. 1976. *Proofs and Refutations: The Logic of Mathematical Discovery*. Cambridge: Cambridge University Press.

Lamont, Michèle. 1992. *Money, Morals, and Manners. The Culture of the French and the American Upper-Middle Class.* Chicago: University of Chicago Press.

Lamont, Michèle and Virág Molnár. 2002. "The Study of Boundaries in the Social Sciences." *Annual Review of Sociology* 28:167–195.

Landau, Barbara and Elizabeth Shipley. 2001. "Labeling Patterns and Object Naming." *Developmental Science* 4:109–118.

Lara, Frankie, Amanda Hahn, Na-Yung Yu, and Takashi Yamauchi. 2012. "Arbitrary Category Labels Can Change Similarity Judgments of Human Faces." In *Proceedings of the 34th Annual Conference of the Cognitive Science Society*, pp. 1179–1184.

Le Mens, Gaël, Michael T. Hannan, Anjali Bhatt, Solène Delecourt, and V. Govind Manian. 2016. "Use of Multiple Labels to Describe an Object: A Bayesian Model and Three Experiments." Organizational Ecology Conference, Catania, Sicily.

Le Mens, Gaël, Michael T. Hannan, and László Pólos. 2014. "Organizational Obsolescence, Drifting Tastes, and Age-Dependence in Organizational Life Chances." *Organization Science* 26:550–570.

Leahey, Erin. 2007. "Not by Productivity Alone: How Visibility and Specialization Contribute to Academic Earnings." *American Sociological Review* 72:533–561.

Lerner, Jennifer S. and Dacher Keltner. 2000. "Beyond Valence: Toward a Model of Emotion-Specific Influences on Judgement and Choice." *Cognition & Emotion* 14:473–493.

Leung, Ming and Amanda J. Sharkey. 2014. "Out of Sight, Out of Mind: Evidence of Perceptual Factors in the Multiple-Category Discount." *Organization Science* 25:171–184.

Liberman, Alvin M., Katherine Safford, Howard S. Hoffman, and Belver C. Griffith. 1957. "The Discrimination of Speech Sounds Within and Across Phoneme Boundaries." *Journal of Experimental Psychology* 54:358–368.

Lizardo, Omar. 2017. "Improving Cultural Analysis: Considering Personal Culture in its Declarative and Nondeclarative Modes." *American Sociological Review* 82:88–115.

Lupyan, Gary. 2008a. "The Conceptual Grouping Effect: Categories Matter (and Named Categories Matter More)." *Cognition* 108:566–577.

Lupyan, Gary. 2008b. "From Chair to "Chair": A Representational Shift Account of Object Labeling Effects on Memory." *Journal of Experimental Psychology: General* 137:348–369.

Lupyan, Gary. 2012. "What Do Words Do? Toward a Theory of Language-Augmented Thought." *Psychology of Learning and Motivation* 57:255–297.

Marr, David. 1982. *Vision: A Computational Investigation into the Human Representation and Processing of Visual Information*. San Francisco: Freeman.

Marr, David and Tomoso Poggio. 1977. "From Understanding Computation to Understanding Neural Circuitry." *Neurosciences Research Program Bulletin* 15:470–488.

McKendrick, David G. and Glenn R. Carroll. 2001. "On the Genesis of Organizational Forms: Evidence from the Market for Disk Drive Arrays." *Organization Science* 12:661–683.

McKendrick, David G. and Michael T. Hannan. 2014. "Oppositional Identities and Resource Partitioning: Distillery Ownership in Scotch Whisky, 1826–2009." *Organization Science* 25:1272–1286.

McKendrick, David G., Jonathan Jaffee, Glenn R. Carroll, and Olga M. Khessina. 2003. "In the Bud? Disk Array Producers as a (Possibly) Emergent Organizational Form." *Administrative Science Quarterly* 48: 60–93.

Medin, Douglas L. and Lance J. Rips. 2005. "Concepts and Categories: Memory, Meaning, and Metaphysics." In *The Cambridge Handbook of Thinking and Reasoning*, edited by K. J. Holyoak and R. G. Morrison, pp. 37–72. Cambridge: Cambridge University Press.

Medin, Douglas L. and Marguerite M. Schaffer. 1978. "Context Theory and Classification Learning." *Psychological Review* 85:207–238.

Medin, Douglas L. and Edward J. Shoben. 1988. "Context and Structure in Conceptual Combination." *Cogitive Psychology* 20:158–190.

Meyer, John W. and Brian Rowan. 1977. "Institutionalized Organizations: Formal Structure as Myth and Ceremony." *American Journal of Sociology* 83:340–363.

Mezias, John M. and Stephen J. Mezias. 2000. "Resource Partitioning, the Founding of Specialist Firms, and Innovation: The American Feature Film Industry, 1912–1929." *Organization Science* 11:306–322.

Murphy, Gregory L. 2002. *The Big Book of Concepts*. Cambridge: MIT Press.

Murphy, Gregory L. 2016. "Is There an Exemplar Theory of Concepts?" *Psychomonic Bulletin and Review* 23:1035–1042.

Murphy, Gregory L., Stephanie Y. Chen, and Brian H. Ross. 2012a. "Reasoning with Uncertain Categories." *Thinking & Reasoning* 18:81–117.

Murphy, Gregory L., James A. Hampton, and Goran S. Milovanovic. 2012b. "Semantic Memory Redux: An Experimental Test of Hierarchical Category Representation." *Journal of Memory and Language* 67: 521–539.

Murphy, Gregory L. and Brian H. Ross. 1994. "Predictions from Uncertain Categorizations." *Cognitive Psychology* 27:148–193.

Negro, Giacomo, Michael T. Hannan, and Magali Fassiotto. 2015. "Category Signaling and Reputation." *Organization Science* 26:584–600.

Negro, Giacomo, Michael T. Hannan, and Hayagreeva Rao. 2010. "Categorical Contrast and Audience Appeal: Niche Width and Critical Success in Winemaking." *Industrial and Corporate Change* 19: 1397–1425.

Negro, Giacomo, Michael T. Hannan, and Hayagreeva Rao. 2011. "Category Reinterpretation and Defection: Modernism and Tradition in Italian Winemaking." *Organization Science* 22:1449–1463.

Negro, Giacomo and Ming D. Leung. 2013. "'Actual' and Perceptual Effects of Category Spanning." *Organization Science* 24:684–696.

Nelson, Richard R and Sidney G. Winter. 1982. *An Evolutionary Theory of Economic Change*. Cambridge: Harvard University Press.

Nerkar, Atul. 2003. "Old is Gold? The Value of Temporal Exploration in the Creation of New Knowledge." *Management Science* 49:211–229.

Nosofsky, Robert M. 1988. "Exemplar-Based Accounts of Relations Between Classification, Recognition, and Typicality." *Journal of Experimental Psychology: Learning, Memory, and Cognition* 14:700–708.

Oldmeadow, Julian and Susan Fiske. 2010. "Social Cognition and Social Perception." *Group Processes and Intergroup Relations* 13:425–444.

Olzak, Susan. 2016. "The Effect of Category Spanning on the Lethality and Longevity of Terrorist Organizations." *Social Forces* 95:559–584.

Osherson, Daniel N. and Edward E. Smith. 1981. "On the Adequacy of Prototype Theory as a Theory of Concepts." *Cognition* 9:35–58.

Patterson, Orlando. 2014. "Making Sense of Culture." *Annual Review of Sociology* 40:1–30.

Pennebaker, James W., Ryan L. Boyd, Kayla Jordan, and Kate Blackburn. 2015. "The Development and Psychometric Properties of LIWC2015." Technical report, University of Texas, Austin.

Phillips, Damon J. and Ezra W. Zuckerman. 2001. "Middle-status Conformity: Theoretical Refinement and Empirical Demonstration in Two Markets." *American Journal of Sociology* 107:379–429.

Piazzai, Michele. 2018. *The Cognitive Infrastructure of Markets*. Ph.D. thesis, Delft University of Technology.

Pollock, Neil and Robin Williams. 2009. "The Sociology of a Market Analysis Tool: How Industry Analysts Sort Vendors and Organize Markets." *Information and Organization* 19:129–151.

Pólos, László, Michael T. Hannan, and Glenn R. Carroll. 2002. "Foundations of a Theory of Social Forms." *Industrial and Corporate Change* 11:85–115.

Polós, László, Michael T. Hannan, and Greta Hsu. 2010. "Modalities in Sociological Arguments." *Journal of Mathematical Sociology* 34:201–238.

Pontikes, Elizabeth G. 2008. *Fitting In or Starting New? An Analysis of Invention, Constraint, and the Emergence of New Categories in the Software Industry.* Ph.D. thesis, Stanford University.

Pontikes, Elizabeth G. 2012. "Two Sides of the Same Coin: How Ambiguous Classification Affects Multiple Audience Evaluations." *Administrative Science Quarterly* 57:81–118.

Pontikes, Elizabeth G. and William P. Barnett. 2015. "The Persistence of Lenient Market Categories." *Administrative Science Quarterly* 26: 1414–1431.

Pontikes, Elizabeth G. and William P. Barnett. 2017. "The Non-consensus Entrepreneur: Organizational Responses to Vita Events." *Administrative Science Quarterly* 62:140–178.

Pontikes, Elizabeth G. and Michael T. Hannan. 2014. "An Ecology of Social Categories." *Sociological Science* 1:311–343.

Pontikes, Elizabeth G. and Ruben Kim. 2017. "Strategic Categorization." *Research in the Sociology of Organizations* 51:71–111.

Quillian, M. Ross. 1966. "Semantic Memory." Scientific Report 2, Advanced Projects Research Agency.

Read, Jesse, Bernhard Pfahringer, Geoff Holmes, and Eibe Frank. 2011. "Classifier Chains for Multi-label Classifications." *Machine Learning Journal* 85:333–359.

Reber, Rolf, Norbert Schwarz, and Piotr Winkielman. 2004. "Processing Fluency and Aesthetic Pleasure: Is Beauty in the Perceiver's Processing Experience." *Personality and Social Psychology Review* 8:364–382.

Rips, Lance J., Edward J. Shoben, and Edward E. Smith. 1973. "Semantic Distance and the Verification of Semantic Relations." *Journal of Verbal Learning and Verbal Behavior* 12:1–20.

Roberts, Peter W., Giacomo Negro, and Anand Swaminathan. 2013. "Balancing the Skill Sets of Founders: Implications for the Quality of Organizational Outputs." *Strategic Organization* 11:35–55.

Romanelli, Elaine. 1991. "The Evolution of New Organizational Forms." *Annual Review of Sociology* 17:79–103.

Rosch, Eleanor H. 1973. "On the Internal Structure of Perceptual and Semantic Categories." In *Cognitive Development and the Acquisition of Language*, edited by T. E. Moore, pp. 111–144. New York: Academic Press.

Rosch, Eleanor H. 1975. "Cognitive Representations of Semantic Categories." *Journal of Experimental Psychology: General* 104:192–233.

Rosch, Eleanor H. and Carolyn B. Mervis. 1975. "Family Resemblances: Studies in the Internal Structure of Categories." *Cognitive Psychology* 7:573–605.

Rosenkopf, Lori and Atul Nerkar. 2001. "Beyond Local Search: Boundary-spanning, Exploration, and Impact in the Optical Disk Industry." *Strategic Management Journal* 22:287–306.

Ruef, Martin. 1999. "Social Ontology and the Dynamics of Organizational Forms: Creating Market Actors in the Healthcare Field, 1966–1994." *Social Forces* 77:1403–1432.

Ruef, Martin. 2000. "The Emergence of Organizational Forms: A Community Ecology Approach." *American Journal of Sociology* 106:658–714.

Ruef, Martin and Kelly Patterson. 2009. "Credit and Classification: Defining Industry Boundaries in 19th Century America." *Administrative Science Quarterly* 54:486–520.

Rumelhart, David E. 1980. "Schemata: The Building Blocks of Cognition." In *Theoretical Issues in Reading Comprehension*, edited by R. J. Spiro, pp. 33–58. Hillsdale N.J.: Lawrence Erlbaum Associates.

Samu, Margaret. 2004. "Impressionism: Art and Modernity." In *Heilbrun Timeline of Art History*. New York: The Metropolitan Museum of Art.

Sanborn, Adam N., Thomas L. Griffiths, and Richard M. Shiffrin. 2010. "Uncovering Mental Representations with Markov Chain Monte Carlo." *Cognitive Psychology* 60:63–106.

Savage, Leonard Jimmie. 1972. *The Foundations of Statistics*. Wiley, 2nd edition.

Schumpeter, Joseph. 1934. *Capitalism, Socialism, and Democracy*. New York: Harper & Row.

Selznick, Philip. 1957. *Leadership in Administration: A Sociological Interpretation*. Berkeley and Los Angeles: University of California Press.

Shannon, Claude E. 1948. "A Mathematical Theory of Communication." *Bell System Technical Journal* 27:379–423 and 623–658.

Sharkey, Amanda J. 2014. "Categories and Organizational Status: The Role of Industry Status in the Response to Organizational Deviance." *American Journal of Sociology* 119:1380–1433.

Shepard, Roger N. 1987. "Toward a Universal Law of Generalization for Psychological Science." *Science* 237:1317–1323.

Smith, Adam. 1776. *An Inquiry into the Nature and Causes of the Wealth of Nations,* volume 1. London: Strahan and Cadell.

Smith, Edward Bishop. 2011. "Identities as Lenses: How Organizational Identity Affects Audiences' Evaluation of Organizational Performance." *Administrative Science Quarterly* 56:61–94.

Smith, Edward E., Lance J. Rips, and Edward J. Shoben. 1974. "Semantic Memory and Psychological Semantics." In *The Psychology of Learning and Motivation,* edited by G. H. Bower, volume 8, pp. 1–45. New York: Academic Press.

Snow, David A., E. Burke Rochford, Steven K. Worden, and Robert D. Benford. 1986. "Frame Alignment Processes, Micromobilization, and Movement Participation." *American Sociological Review* 51: 464–481.

Strauss, Claudia and Naomi Quinn. 1997. *A Cognitive Theory of Cultural Meaning.* Cambridge: Cambridge University Press.

Suchman, Mark C. 1995. "Managing Legitimacy: Strategic and Institutional Approaches." *Academy of Management Review* 20:571–610.

Swidler, Ann. 1986. "Culture in Action: Symbols and Strategies." *American Sociological Review* 51:273–286.

Swidler, Ann. 2001. *Talk of Love. How Culture Matters.* Chicago: University of Chicago Press.

Tajfel, Henri and John Turner. 1986. *Psychology of Intergroup Relations.* Chicago: Nelson Hall.

Tarski, Alfred. 1956. *Logics, Semantics, Metamathematics.* Oxford: Oxford University Press.

Tenenbaum, Joshua B. and Thomas L. Griffiths. 2002. "Generalization, Similarity, and Bayesian Inference." *Behavioral and Brain Sciences* 24:629–640.

Treiman, Donald J. 1977. *Occupational Prestige in Comparative Perspective.* New York: Academic Press.

Tsoumakis, Grigorios and Ioannis Katakis. 2007. "Multi-label Classification: An Overview." *International Journal of Data Warehousing & Data Mining* 3:1–13.

Tversky, Amos. 1977. "Features of Similarity." *Psychological Review* 84: 327–352.

Tversky, Amos and Daniel Kahneman. 1974. "Judgment under Uncertainty: Heuristics and Biases." *Science* 185:1124–1131.

Tversky, Amos and Daniel Kahneman. 1983. "Extensional Versus Intuitive Reasoning: The Conjunction Fallacy in Probability Judgment." *Psychological Review* 90:293–315.

Vaisey, Stephen. 2009. "Motivation and Justification: A Dual-Process Model of Culture in Action." *American Journal of Sociology* 114:1675–1715.

Verheyen, Steven, James A. Hampton, and Gert Storms. 2010. "A Probabilistic Threshold Model: Analyzing Semantic Categorization Data With the Rasch Model." *Acta Psychologica* 135:216–225.

Vogel, Tobias, Evan W. Carr, Tyler Davis, and Piotr Winkielman. 2017. "Category Structure Determines the Relative Attractiveness of Global Versus Local Averages." *Journal of Experimental Psychology: Learning, Memory, and Cognition* in press.

Widdows, Dominic. 2004. *Geometry and Meaning*. Stanford, Calif.: CSLI Publications.

Winawer, Jonathan, Nathan Witthoft, Michael C. Frank, Lisa Wu, Alex R. Wade, and Lera Boroditsky. 2007. "Russian Blues Reveal Effects of Language on Color Discrimination." *Proceedings of the National Academy of Sciences* 104:7780–7785.

Winkielman, Piotr, Jamin Halberstadt, Tedra Fazendeiro, and Steve Catty. 2006. "Prototypes Are Attractive Because They Are Easy on the Mind." *Psychological Science* 17:799–806.

Winkielman, Piotr, Norbert Schwarz, Tedra A. Faziendeiro, and Rolf Berber. 2003. "The Hedonic Marking of Processing Fluency: Implications for Evaluative Judgment." In *The Psychology of Evaluation: Afffective Processes in Cognition and Emotion*, edited by J. Musch and K. C. Klauer, pp. 195–223. Mahwah, N.J.: Erlbaum.

Wittgenstein, Ludwig. 1953. *Philosophical Investigations*. New York: Macmillan.

Wood, Wendy. 2000. "Attitude Change: Persuasion and Social Influence." *Annual Review of Psychology* 51:539–570.

Wuthnow, Robert and Marsha Witten. 1987. "New Directions in the Study of Culture." *Annual Review of Sociology* 14:49–67.

Xu, Jing, Mike Dowman, and Thomas L. Griffiths. 2013. "Cultural Transmission Results in Convergence Towards Colour Term Universals." *Proceedings of the Royal Society B* 280.

Yu, Na-Yung, Yamauchi Takashi, and Jay Schumacher. 2008. "Rediscovering Symbols: The Role of Category Labels in Similarity Judgment." *Journal of Cognitive Science* 9:89–109.

Zhou, Xueguang. 2005. "The Institutional Logic of Occupational Prestige Ranking: Reconceptualization and Reanalyses." *American Journal of Sociology* 111:90–140.

Zuckerman, Ezra W. 1999. "The Categorical Imperative: Securities Analysts and the Legitimacy Discount." *American Journal of Sociology* 104: 1398–1438.

Zuckerman, Ezra W. 2000. "Focusing the Corporate Product: Securities Analysts and De-Diversification." *Administrative Science Quarterly* 45:591–619.

Index